BUTTERFLY SPREAD

Advanced Techniques with Python
for Profitable Options Trading

Hayden Van Der Post

Reactive Publishing

CONTENTS

CHAPTER 1: INTRODUCTION TO OPTIONS TRADING

Options are powerful financial instruments that provide traders and investors with unique opportunities to hedge risk, speculate on price movements, and leverage their positions. At their core, options are contracts that grant the holder the right, but not the obligation, to buy or sell an underlying asset at a predetermined price within a specified time frame. Understanding the mechanics of options is fundamental to mastering the butterfly spread strategy and other sophisticated trading techniques.

Types of Options: Call and Put

Understanding the types of options is fundamental to mastering the butterfly spread strategy and options trading as a whole. Options are versatile financial instruments that come in two primary forms: call options and put options. Each type serves distinct purposes, offers unique advantages, and carries specific risks. Mastery of these basic building blocks is essential for leveraging options to their fullest potential.

Call Options

A call option is a contract that gives the holder the right, but not the obligation, to purchase an underlying asset at a predetermined price, known as the strike price, within a specified time frame. Investors typically purchase call options when they anticipate an increase in the price of the underlying asset.

Key Characteristics of Call Options:

1. Right to Buy: The holder can buy the asset at the strike price, irrespective of the market price, before the option expires.

2. Strike Price: The price at which the holder can purchase the underlying asset.

3. Expiration Date: The deadline by which the option must be exercised.

4. Premium: The cost of purchasing the option, paid upfront to the seller.

Example: Suppose you buy a call option for Tesla Inc. (TSLwith a strike price of $700, expiring in three months, for a premium of $15. If TSLA's stock price rises to $750 before expiration, you can exercise your option to buy TSLA at $700, earning a profit of $35 per share (after subtracting the premium).

Call options can be used for various strategies, including:

- Speculation: Traders can use call options to bet on the price increase of an asset, potentially earning substantial returns with smaller initial investments.

- Hedging: Investors can protect their portfolios against rising prices by purchasing call options on assets they wish to buy in the future.

Put Options

Conversely, a put option is a contract that grants the holder the right, but not the obligation, to sell an underlying asset at a predetermined strike price within a specified time frame. Investors typically buy put options when they expect a decline in the price of the underlying asset.

Key Characteristics of Put Options:

1. Right to Sell: The holder can sell the asset at the strike price, regardless of the market price, before the option expires.

2. Strike Price: The price at which the holder can sell the underlying asset.

3. Expiration Date: The deadline by which the option must be exercised.

4. Premium: The cost to buy the option, paid upfront to the seller.

Example: Assume you purchase a put option for Apple Inc. (AAPL) with a strike price of $150, expiring in two months, for a premium of $5. If AAPL's stock price falls to $140 before expiration, you can exercise your option to sell AAPL at $150, making a profit of $5 per share (after subtracting the premium).

Put options can be utilized in several ways:

- Speculation: Traders use put options to bet on the decline of an asset's price.
- Hedging: Investors can safeguard their portfolios from potential losses by buying put options on assets they own.

Real-world Applications

Options are not just theoretical constructs; they have practical applications in various financial contexts. Understanding how to implement these strategies effectively is crucial for successful trading.

1. Hedging: A portfolio manager might use put options to protect against a potential decline in a stock's value. For instance, if a manager holds a substantial position in a stock, purchasing a put option can limit the downside risk while allowing for upside potential.

2. Speculation: Consider a trader who is confident that a particular stock will experience significant price movement. Buying call or put options can provide leveraged exposure to the anticipated change. However, this approach requires precise market predictions and a thorough understanding of the factors influencing option prices.

3. Income Generation: Writing (selling) options can generate income for investors. For example, writing covered calls

involves selling call options against shares held in a portfolio. This strategy generates additional income but caps the potential upside if the stock price rises significantly.

European vs. American Options

Options can be classified into two main categories based on their exercise style: European and American options.

- European Options: These options can only be exercised at the expiration date, making them less flexible. They are often used in indices and certain types of derivatives.

- American Options: These options can be exercised at any time before the expiration date, providing greater flexibility to the holder. Most stock options traded in the United States are American options.

Key Characteristics of Options

Options possess several defining characteristics that set them apart from other financial instruments:

1. Leverage: Options enable traders to control a larger position in the underlying asset with a relatively small investment. This leverage can magnify gains, but it also increases the potential for losses.

2. Flexibility: Options can be employed for various strategies, including hedging, speculation, and income generation. Their versatility makes them suitable for different market conditions and trader objectives.

3. Risk Management: Options offer a means to hedge

against adverse price movements in the underlying asset. By purchasing options, traders can limit their downside risk while maintaining upside potential.

4. Complexity: Unlike straightforward buying and selling of stocks, options involve multiple factors, such as time decay, volatility, and the greeks (Delta, Gamma, Theta, Vega). Mastering these elements is crucial for effective options trading.

Understanding the different types of options—call and put—is a fundamental stepping stone to mastering more advanced strategies like the butterfly spread. Each type of option offers unique opportunities and risks, and their strategic use can significantly enhance a trader's ability to manage risk and capitalize on market movements. This foundational knowledge will serve as the bedrock for delving deeper into the nuanced strategies and Python implementations that this book will explore.

Appreciating the intricacies of call and put options, you are better equipped to navigate the complexities of options trading and leverage these powerful instruments to achieve your financial goals.

Key Terminologies in Options Trading

Underlying Asset

The underlying asset is the financial instrument upon which an options contract is based. This could be a stock, bond, commodity, index, or currency. The performance of the underlying asset directly affects the value of the options contract. For example, if you hold a call option on Apple Inc. (AAPL) stock, the value of your option will fluctuate based on

AAPL's stock price movements.

Strike Price (Exercise Price)

The strike price is the predetermined price at which the holder of an options contract can buy (call option) or sell (put option) the underlying asset. This price is established at the time the contract is written and remains constant throughout the life of the option. The strike price is a critical factor in determining the intrinsic value of the option.

Expiration Date

The expiration date is the deadline by which the option must be exercised. After this date, the option becomes void and worthless. Options can have various expiration dates, ranging from a few days to several years. The time remaining until expiration is a significant factor in the option's pricing, as it influences the time value component.

Premium

The premium is the price paid by the buyer to the seller for acquiring the option. It represents the cost of the option and is determined by various factors, including the underlying asset's price, strike price, time to expiration, volatility, and interest rates. The premium comprises two components: intrinsic value and extrinsic value.

Intrinsic Value

Intrinsic value is the difference between the underlying asset's current price and the option's strike price, but only if it is favorable to the option holder. For a call option, intrinsic value is calculated as the underlying asset's price minus the strike price. For a put option, it is the strike price minus the underlying asset's price. If the result is negative or zero, the intrinsic value is considered to be zero.

Example: If you hold a call option with a strike price of $50 and the underlying stock is trading at $60, the intrinsic value is $10.

Extrinsic Value (Time Value)

Extrinsic value, or time value, is the portion of the option's premium that exceeds its intrinsic value. It accounts for the potential of the option to gain additional intrinsic value before expiration. Several factors influence extrinsic value, including the time remaining until expiration and the volatility of the underlying asset.

The Greeks

The Greeks are a set of metrics used to measure the sensitivity of an option's price to various factors. Understanding the Greeks is vital for managing options positions effectively. The primary Greeks include:

1. Delta: Measures the sensitivity of the option's price to changes in the price of the underlying asset. A delta of 0.5 indicates that the option's price will change by $0.50 for every $1 change in the underlying asset's price.

2. Gamma: Measures the rate of change of delta with respect to changes in the underlying asset's price. Gamma is highest when the option is at-the-money.

3. Theta: Measures the sensitivity of the option's price to the passage of time, also known as time decay. Options lose value as they approach expiration, and theta quantifies this decay.

4. Vega: Measures the sensitivity of the option's price to changes in the volatility of the underlying asset. Higher volatility increases the option's price.

5. Rho: Measures the sensitivity of the option's price to changes in interest rates. Rho is more significant for longer-term options.

At-the-Money (ATM), In-the-Money (ITM), Out-of-the-Money (OTM)

These terms describe the relationship between the option's strike price and the underlying asset's current price:

- At-the-Money (ATM): The strike price is approximately equal to the underlying asset's current price.
- In-the-Money (ITM): For a call option, the strike price is below the underlying asset's current price. For a put option, the strike price is above the underlying asset's current price.
- Out-of-the-Money (OTM): For a call option, the strike price is above the underlying asset's current price. For a put option, the strike price is below the underlying asset's current price.

Implied Volatility (IV)

Implied volatility represents the market's forecast of the underlying asset's volatility over the life of the option. It is derived from the option's market price and reflects the consensus expectations of future price fluctuations. Higher implied volatility leads to higher option premiums, as the potential for large price movements increases.

Bid-Ask Spread

The bid-ask spread is the difference between the highest price a buyer is willing to pay (bid) and the lowest price a seller is willing to accept (ask) for an options contract. A narrow bid-ask spread indicates a liquid market with high trading activity, while a wide spread suggests lower liquidity and potentially higher trading costs.

Open Interest

Open interest is the total number of outstanding options contracts for a particular strike price and expiration date. High open interest indicates active trading and liquidity, making it easier to enter and exit positions without significantly impacting the option's price. Monitoring open interest can provide insights into market sentiment and potential price movements.

Volatility Skew

Volatility skew refers to the pattern of implied volatility across different strike prices for the same expiration date. It illustrates how volatility varies for options that are in-the-money, at-the-money, and out-of-the-money. Understanding volatility skew helps traders identify potential mispricings and opportunities within the options market.

Exercise and Assignment

Exercise refers to the process by which the holder of an option invokes their right to buy (call) or sell (put) the underlying asset at the strike price. Assignment occurs when the seller (writer) of the option is obligated to fulfill the terms of the contract. In American-style options, exercise can occur at any time before expiration, whereas European-style options can only be exercised at expiration.

Margin Requirements

Margin requirements refer to the minimum amount of capital that must be maintained in a trading account to cover potential losses from options positions. These requirements vary based on the type of option, its underlying asset, and the trader's overall portfolio. Understanding margin requirements is crucial for managing risk and ensuring sufficient liquidity to meet obligations.

These key terminologies form the bedrock of options trading knowledge. By mastering these concepts, you will be better equipped to understand and execute complex strategies like the butterfly spread. The language of options trading can be intricate, but with these terms in your arsenal, you will navigate the world of options with greater ease and precision. As we progress through the book, these terminologies will recur, deepening your understanding and enhancing your trading acumen.

The Anatomy of an Option Quote

An option quote typically includes several key pieces of information: the underlying asset, the type of option (call or put), the expiration date, the strike price, the bid price, the ask price, and the last traded price. Each of these elements conveys crucial details that help traders make informed decisions.

1. Underlying Asset

The underlying asset is the financial instrument on which the option is based. This could be a stock, an index, a commodity, or another security. The performance of the underlying asset directly impacts the value of the option. For instance, options on Apple Inc. (AAPL) stock will react to changes in AAPL's stock price.

2. Option Type (Call or Put)

Options come in two varieties: calls and puts. A call option gives the holder the right, but not the obligation, to buy the underlying asset at the strike price before or at the expiration date. Conversely, a put option gives the holder the right to sell the underlying asset at the strike price within the same timeframe.

3. Expiration Date

The expiration date is the last day on which the option can be exercised. Options have varied expiration cycles, including weekly, monthly, and quarterly. The expiration date significantly impacts the premium, as the value of an option diminishes as it approaches expiration, a phenomenon known as time decay.

4. Strike Price (Exercise Price)

The strike price is the predetermined price at which the holder can buy (call option) or sell (put option) the underlying asset. The relationship between the strike price and the current market price of the underlying asset determines whether the option is in-the-money (ITM), at-the-money (ATM), or out-of-the-money (OTM).

5. Bid and Ask Prices

The bid price is the highest price a buyer is willing to pay for the option, while the ask price is the lowest price a seller is willing to accept. The difference between these two prices is known as the bid-ask spread, and it indicates the option's liquidity. A narrow bid-ask spread suggests high liquidity, whereas a wide spread indicates low liquidity.

6. Last Traded Price

The last traded price is the most recent price at which the option was bought or sold. This price can provide a sense of the option's current market value but should be evaluated alongside the bid and ask prices for a more comprehensive understanding.

Reading an Option Chain

An option chain is a list of all available option contracts for a particular underlying asset, organized by expiration dates and strike prices. Here's how to interpret it:

1. Organized Layout

Option chains are typically organized with calls on the left and puts on the right, or vice versa, depending on the platform. The expiration dates are listed at the top, and the strike prices run down the middle.

2. Key Data Points

For each option, the chain will display the bid and ask prices, last traded price, volume, and open interest. Volume indicates the number of contracts traded during the current session, while open interest represents the total number of outstanding contracts.

3. Selecting an Option

When selecting an option to trade, consider factors such as the bid-ask spread, volume, and open interest. High volume and open interest generally indicate a more active and liquid market, reducing the potential for significant price movement when entering or exiting positions.

Practical Example

Let's walk through an example to illustrate how to interpret an option quote. Suppose you are considering trading options on Tesla Inc. (TSLA). Here's a sample option quote:

- Underlying Asset: TSLA
- Option Type: Call
- Expiration Date: March 18, 2023
- Strike Price: $700
- Bid Price: $45.00
- Ask Price: $46.50
- Last Traded Price: $45.75
- Volume: 1,200
- Open Interest: 3,500

From this quote, you can infer that the TSLA call option with a $700 strike price expiring on March 18, 2023, has a bid price of $45.00 and an ask price of $46.50. The last trade occurred at $45.75, with a trading volume of 1,200 contracts and an open interest of 3,500 contracts. The narrow bid-ask spread indicates relatively high liquidity, making it easier to enter or exit the position without significant price slippage.

Factors Influencing Option Quotes

Several factors influence the bid and ask prices of an option, contributing to its overall premium:

1. Intrinsic Value

This is the difference between the underlying asset's current price and the option's strike price. For in-the-money options, the intrinsic value is positive; for out-of-the-money options, it is zero.

2. Extrinsic Value

Also known as time value, extrinsic value accounts for the potential of the option to gain intrinsic value before expiration. It is influenced by the time remaining until expiration and the volatility of the underlying asset.

3. Volatility

Implied volatility reflects the market's expectation of the underlying asset's future volatility. Higher implied volatility leads to higher option premiums because the potential for significant price movements increases.

4. Interest Rates

Changes in interest rates can affect the cost of carrying an option position, thus impacting option premiums. For instance, an increase in interest rates can lead to higher call option premiums.

5. Dividends

Expected dividends from the underlying asset can also influence option prices, particularly for call options. Dividends reduce the underlying asset's price, which can lower the value of call options.

Interpreting and Utilizing Option Quotes

Understanding option quotes is crucial for effective trading strategies. Here's how to utilize this information:

1. Liquidity Assessment

A tight bid-ask spread and high volume indicate good liquidity, reducing the cost of entering and exiting options positions.

2. Strategy Selection

Based on the strike price and expiration date, traders can select options that align with their market outlook and risk tolerance. For instance, if you anticipate a significant price movement in the underlying asset, you might choose an at-the-money or near-the-money option with a moderate expiration timeline.

3. Risk Management

By analyzing the Greeks, such as Delta and Theta, traders can manage their positions' risk and potential rewards more effectively. For example, options with a high Delta are more sensitive to price changes in the underlying asset, while those with a high Theta are more exposed to time decay.

4. Profit Potential

Comparing the bid and ask prices, along with the implied

volatility, helps traders estimate the potential profit from an option position. High implied volatility suggests greater price movement potential, which can be advantageous for certain strategies.

Mastering the intricacies of option quotes is an essential step in becoming a proficient options trader. By understanding each component of an option quote, interpreting an option chain, and recognizing the factors that influence option prices, you can make more informed trading decisions. Equipped with this knowledge, you are better positioned to navigate the sophisticated world of options trading, leveraging quotes to your strategic advantage. As we progress further into the book, this foundational understanding will serve as a vital tool in dissecting and implementing advanced trading strategies, including the butterfly spread.

5. Basic Concepts: Intrinsic Value and Extrinsic Value

Intrinsic Value: The Core Worth

Intrinsic value represents the inherent worth of an option— essentially, the profit that could be realized if the option were exercised at the current moment. It is calculated by comparing the underlying asset's current market price with the option's strike price.

1. Calculation of Intrinsic Value

- For call options, intrinsic value is determined by the formula:

\[

\text{Intrinsic Value (Call)} = \max(0, \text{Current Price of Underlying Asset} - \text{Strike Price})

\]

- For put options, the formula is:

\[

\text{Intrinsic Value (Put)} = \max(0, \text{Strike Price} - \text{Current Price of Underlying Asset})

\]

If the result is negative, the intrinsic value is considered zero, as an option with no potential for profit if exercised is essentially worthless in this regard.

2. In-The-Money (ITM), At-The-Money (ATM), and Out-Of-The-Money (OTM)

- In-The-Money (ITM): A call option is ITM if the underlying asset's price is above the strike price, and a put option is ITM if the underlying asset's price is below the strike price. ITM options have positive intrinsic value.

- At-The-Money (ATM): An option is ATM when the underlying asset's price is equal to the strike price. For ATM options, the intrinsic value is zero.

- Out-Of-The-Money (OTM): A call option is OTM if the underlying asset's price is below the strike price, and a put option is OTM if the underlying asset's price is above the strike price. OTM options also have zero intrinsic value.

Extrinsic Value: The Time and Potential

Extrinsic value, also known as time value, reflects the

difference between an option's premium and its intrinsic value. It encompasses various factors, including time remaining until expiration, volatility, and interest rates, which contribute to the option's potential to gain in value before it expires.

1. Calculation of Extrinsic Value

- Extrinsic value is derived using the formula:

$$\text{Extrinsic Value} = \text{Option Premium} - \text{Intrinsic Value}$$

2. Factors Affecting Extrinsic Value

- Time to Expiration: The longer the time until expiration, the higher the extrinsic value, as there is more time for the underlying asset's price to move in a favorable direction.

- Implied Volatility: Higher implied volatility increases extrinsic value since there is a greater likelihood of significant price movements.

- Interest Rates and Dividends: Changes in interest rates and expected dividends from the underlying asset can also affect extrinsic value, although this impact is generally more subtle compared to time and volatility.

3. Decay of Extrinsic Value (Theta)

- As an option approaches its expiration date, its extrinsic value diminishes, a process known as time decay. Theta measures the rate of this decay, and its impact accelerates as expiration nears. For this reason, options with shorter durations experience more rapid loss of extrinsic value.

Practical Implications for Traders

Grasping the concepts of intrinsic and extrinsic value is vital for devising and implementing effective trading strategies. Here's how traders can leverage this understanding:

1. Evaluating Option Prices

- By breaking down the premium into intrinsic and extrinsic components, traders can better assess whether an option is fairly priced. Overpricing or underpricing can present trading opportunities.

2. Strategic Selection of Options

- For traders seeking quick profits from market movements, ITM options with higher intrinsic value might be preferable due to their immediate profitability. Conversely, OTM options with higher extrinsic value might appeal to those banking on significant price moves.

3. Time Value Considerations

- Traders need to consider the impact of time decay on their positions. Holding options closer to expiration requires careful planning to mitigate the rapid loss of extrinsic value.

4. Volatility Plays

- Understanding how implied volatility affects extrinsic value allows traders to exploit periods of high volatility by purchasing options expected to benefit from pronounced price movements.

Examples

To illustrate these concepts, let's consider a real-world example involving a trader analyzing options on Microsoft Corp. (MSFT).

- Current Stock Price: $300

- Strike Price (Call Option): $290

- Option Premium: $15

1. Intrinsic Value

\[

\text{Intrinsic Value (Call)} = \max(0, 300 - 290) = \$10

\]

2. Extrinsic Value

\[

\text{Extrinsic Value} = 15 - 10 = \$5

\]

In this case, the call option is ITM with an intrinsic value of $10 and an extrinsic value of $5. The premium reflects the immediate profit potential of exercising the option, plus the additional value derived from the time remaining until expiration and the expected volatility.

Advanced Considerations

For more seasoned traders, understanding the interplay between intrinsic and extrinsic value can pave the way for advanced strategies such as spreads, straddles, and multi-leg options trades. These strategies often involve balancing intrinsic gains with extrinsic losses or vice versa to tailor risk-reward profiles to specific market conditions.

1. Butterfly Spread Strategy

- The butterfly spread, for example, capitalizes on the relationship between different strike prices and their intrinsic/extrinsic values to create a position with limited risk and defined profit potential. By constructing a spread that benefits from minimal price movement near the strike price, traders can exploit time decay to their advantage.

2. Implied Volatility Skew

- The skew in implied volatility across different strike prices allows traders to structure positions that benefit from changes in volatility expectations. Understanding how extrinsic value fluctuates with volatility is key to executing these strategies effectively.

The concepts of intrinsic and extrinsic value form the bedrock of options pricing and trading strategies. By dissecting an option's premium into these two components, traders gain insightful perspectives on the potential profitability and risks associated with their positions. This foundational understanding equips traders to navigate the complexities of the options market, making more informed decisions that align with their trading objectives. As we delve deeper into advanced strategies like the butterfly spread, the interplay between intrinsic and extrinsic value will remain a critical consideration, guiding the construction and management of sophisticated trading positions.

6. Moneyness: ITM, ATM, OTM

In the world of options trading, understanding the concept of "moneyness" is pivotal. Moneyness describes the intrinsic value of an option in its current state, categorizing it as In-The-Money (ITM), At-The-Money (ATM), or Out-Of-The-Money (OTM). Grasping these distinctions allows traders to make more informed decisions, gauge the potential profitability of their options, and formulate strategies that align with their market expectations.

In-The-Money (ITM): Potential Profit

An option is considered In-The-Money (ITM) when exercising it would result in a positive cash flow. This means that for call options, the current price of the underlying asset is above the strike price, while for put options, the underlying asset's price is below the strike price.

1. Call Options ITM

   - A call option is ITM if the underlying asset's price exceeds the strike price. For example, if the strike price is $50 and the asset's market price is $60, the call option is $10 ITM.

2. Put Options ITM

   - A put option is ITM if the underlying asset's price is below the strike price. For instance, with a strike price of $50 and the asset's market price at $40, the put option is $10 ITM.

3. Implications

   - ITM options inherently possess intrinsic value and are thus more likely to be exercised. They tend to be more expensive due to this built-in value and the reduced risk of expiring worthless.

At-The-Money (ATM): Equilibrium

An option is At-The-Money (ATM) when the price of the underlying asset is exactly equal to the option's strike price. In this scenario, the option has no intrinsic value because exercising it would not result in any profit.

1. Call and Put Options ATM

   - For both call and put options, ATM status means the strike price equals the market price of the underlying asset. For example, if the strike price is $50 and the market price is also $50, both call and put options are considered ATM.

2. Implications

   - ATM options are heavily influenced by extrinsic value, especially the time value and volatility. They are often chosen for strategies that anticipate significant movements in the underlying asset's price.

Out-Of-The-Money (OTM): Potential Loss

An option is Out-Of-The-Money (OTM) when exercising it would result in a loss. This means that for call options, the current price of the underlying asset is below the strike price, and for put options, the underlying asset's price is above the strike price.

1. Call Options OTM

   - A call option is OTM if the underlying asset's price is under the strike price. For instance, with a strike price of $50 and the asset's market price at $40, the call option is OTM by $10.

2. Put Options OTM

- A put option is OTM if the underlying asset's price exceeds the strike price. For example, with a strike price of $50 and the asset's market price at $60, the put option is $10 OTM.

3. Implications

- OTM options lack intrinsic value and are generally cheaper than ITM options. They are attractive for speculative strategies due to their lower cost and the potential for significant leverage if the underlying asset's price moves favorably.

Practical Applications

Understanding moneyness is crucial for devising effective trading strategies. Here's how traders can leverage this concept:

1. Selection of Options Based on Market Outlook

- Bullish Sentiment: Traders might prefer ITM call options for a conservative approach or OTM call options for higher potential gains but increased risk.

- Bearish Sentiment: Traders may choose ITM put options for more certain gains or OTM put options for higher potential leverage.

2. Strategic Plays

- Spreads: Utilizing combinations of ITM, ATM, and OTM options can help create balanced strategies like bull call spreads or bear put spreads.

- Straddles and Strangles: These strategies involve ATM options (straddles) or a combination of OTM call and put options (strangles) to profit from significant price swings.

3. Risk Management

 - Hedging: ITM options are often used to hedge existing positions due to their intrinsic value and higher cost, providing a safety net against adverse price movements.

 - Speculation: OTM options are favored for speculative plays due to their lower upfront costs and potential for higher percentage returns, though they come with a higher risk of expiring worthless.

Case Study: Analyzing Moneyness in Microsoft Corp. Options

Let's consider a practical example involving Microsoft Corp. (MSFT) to illustrate how moneyness affects option selection and strategy formulation.

- Current Stock Price: $300
- Strike Prices for Options:
   - ITM Call Option Strike Price: $290
   - ATM Call Option Strike Price: $300
   - OTM Call Option Strike Price: $310

Intrinsic Value Calculations:
- ITM Call Option:
   \[
   \text{Intrinsic Value} = \max(0, 300 - 290) = \$10
   \]
- ATM Call Option:
   \[

\text{Intrinsic Value} = \max(0, 300 - 300) = \$0

\]

- OTM Call Option:

\[

\text{Intrinsic Value} = \max(0, 300 - 310) = \$0

\]

Extrinsic Value Understanding:

- ITM Call Option: Higher premium due to intrinsic value.

- ATM Call Option: Premium primarily driven by extrinsic factors like time and volatility.

- OTM Call Option: Lower premium, driven solely by extrinsic value.

Strategic Decisions:

- Conservative Approach: Opting for the ITM call option to ensure some profit due to intrinsic value.

- Speculative Approach: Choosing the OTM call option for lower cost and higher potential, albeit with elevated risk.

Advanced Considerations and Adjustments

For experienced traders, moneyness provides a foundation for advanced strategies underpinned by nuanced adjustments and hedging mechanisms.

1. Dynamic Adjustments

   - Traders can dynamically adjust their positions based on shifts in moneyness. For instance, moving from OTM to ATM options as the underlying price approaches the strike can help capitalize on increasing intrinsic value.

2. Implied Volatility Skew

- Understanding the volatility skew across different strikes allows traders to identify mispriced options, creating opportunities to exploit discrepancies in extrinsic value.

Moneyness—whether an option is ITM, ATM, or OTM—plays a crucial role in determining its value, cost, and potential profitability. By comprehensively understanding these states, traders can make strategic decisions that align with their market outlook and risk tolerance. Leveraging moneyness helps traders not only in selecting appropriate options but also in constructing sophisticated strategies that can navigate the dynamic terrain of options trading. As we continue to explore further strategies like the butterfly spread, the insights gained from understanding moneyness will be instrumental in crafting precise and effective trading plans.

7. Advantages and Risks of Options

Options trading, a cornerstone of modern finance, presents a myriad of opportunities for traders to capitalize on market movements. However, it also carries inherent risks that must be judiciously managed. Understanding both the advantages and risks associated with options trading is essential for any trader aiming to harness its full potential while safeguarding their investment portfolio.

Advantages of Options Trading

1. Limited Risk and Leverage

- One of the most compelling advantages of options is their ability to provide substantial leverage with limited risk. Purchasing an option often requires a smaller capital outlay compared to buying the underlying asset outright. For instance, a trader can control 100 shares of a stock through a single options contract, potentially multiplying gains from favorable price movements. Crucially, while potential profits can be significant, the maximum loss is limited to the premium paid for the option.

2. Versatility in Strategy

- Options offer unparalleled versatility, allowing traders to construct a wide array of strategies tailored to different market conditions. From simple calls and puts to complex spreads like the butterfly spread, traders can design strategies to profit from bullish, bearish, or even neutral market outlooks. This flexibility enables traders to adapt quickly to changing market environments.

3. Income Generation

- Selling options, particularly through strategies like covered calls or cash-secured puts, provides a means of generating income. By writing covered calls, a trader can earn premiums from buyers willing to pay for the right to purchase the underlying asset at a specified price. This approach leverages existing holdings to enhance returns, making it an attractive strategy for income-focused investors.

4. Hedging and Risk Management

- Options are powerful tools for hedging and risk management. Investors can use put options to protect against potential declines in the value of their holdings, effectively setting a floor price. This form of insurance is particularly valuable in volatile markets, providing peace of mind and stability to an investment portfolio.

5. Access to Non-Correlated Assets

- Options allow traders to gain exposure to a diverse range of underlying assets, including stocks, indices, commodities, and currencies. This broad access enables the creation of diversified portfolios that can mitigate overall risk by including non-correlated assets, enhancing portfolio resilience against market fluctuations.

6. Price Discovery and Liquidity

- The options market is a significant component of the broader financial ecosystem, contributing to price discovery and market efficiency. High liquidity in options trading ensures that orders can be executed swiftly and at competitive prices, minimizing slippage and transaction costs.

7. Strategic Flexibility and Adjustments

- Options trading allows for dynamic adjustments to positions. Traders can modify their strategies in response to market movements, adjusting strike prices, expiration dates, or transitioning from one strategy to another. This adaptability is crucial for managing risk and capitalizing on emerging opportunities.

Risks of Options Trading

1. Complexity and Learning Curve

- Options trading is inherently more complex than trading stocks or other financial instruments. Understanding the interplay of factors affecting options prices—such as volatility, time decay, and interest rates—requires a steep learning curve. Novice traders may find this complexity daunting, leading to potential missteps and financial losses.

2. Time Decay (Theta)

- One of the unique aspects of options is time decay, represented by the Greek letter Theta. As the expiration date approaches, the time value of an option diminishes. This decay can erode the value of an option, particularly for out-of-the-money options, posing a significant risk to holders who must contend with the relentless march of time.

3. Volatility Risk

- While volatility can present opportunities, it also introduces considerable risk. Sudden and unexpected spikes in volatility can lead to substantial losses, particularly for sellers of options. Moreover, implied volatility changes can affect the price of options, making it challenging to anticipate market behavior accurately.

4. Market Risk

- Like all financial instruments, options are subject to market risk. Adverse movements in the underlying asset can lead to significant losses. For instance, a sharp decline in a stock's price can render call options worthless, while a sudden rally can decimate the value of put options. Traders must remain vigilant and responsive to market conditions to mitigate these risks.

5. Liquidity Risk

- Although high liquidity is a hallmark of major options markets, certain contracts on less liquid assets may suffer from wide bid-ask spreads and low trading volumes. This liquidity risk can result in higher transaction costs and difficulties in entering or exiting positions at favorable prices.

6. Execution Risk

- The intricate nature of options trading can sometimes lead to execution risk. Delays or errors in order execution, whether due to technological glitches or human error, can result in suboptimal trade outcomes. Ensuring precise execution is crucial for maintaining the integrity of trading strategies.

7. Regulatory and Operational Risks

- Options trading is subject to regulatory oversight, which can impact market dynamics. Changes in regulations or tax laws can alter the profitability and feasibility of certain strategies. Additionally, operational risks, such as system outages or data breaches, can disrupt trading activities and compromise financial security.

8. Psychological Factors

- The psychological challenges of options trading cannot be understated. The allure of high leverage and potential profits can lead to overconfidence and excessive risk-taking. Conversely, the fear of losses may result in premature exits or missed opportunities. Developing a disciplined and objective approach is essential for long-term success.

Practical Considerations for Risk Management

To navigate the advantages and risks of options trading effectively, implementing robust risk management practices is paramount. Here are some practical considerations:

1. Education and Continuous Learning

- Investing in education and staying informed about market developments is crucial. Resources such as courses, webinars, and trading simulators can equip traders with the knowledge and skills necessary to make informed decisions.

2. Diversification

- Diversifying options positions across different underlying assets, strike prices, and expiration dates can reduce exposure to any single source of risk. This strategy helps mitigate potential losses and enhances overall portfolio stability.

3. Position Sizing and Leverage Control

- Employing prudent position sizing and leverage control is essential to prevent catastrophic losses. Traders should allocate a reasonable portion of their capital to each trade, avoiding excessive exposure to any single position.

4. Risk Mitigation Strategies

- Incorporating risk mitigation strategies, such as stop-loss orders and protective puts, can limit potential losses. These tools provide a safety net, ensuring that adverse market movements do not result in disproportionate financial damage.

5. Regular Monitoring and Adjustments

- Continuous monitoring of positions and market conditions allows for timely adjustments. Traders should be prepared to adapt their strategies in response to evolving market dynamics, ensuring that their approach remains aligned with their risk tolerance and objectives.

The advantages and risks of options trading form two sides of the same coin. By leveraging the unique benefits of options—such as limited risk, versatility, and strategic flexibility—traders can unlock significant opportunities for profit and portfolio enhancement. However, the inherent complexities and risks necessitate a diligent and informed approach. Through education, strategic planning, and robust risk management practices, traders can navigate the intricate terrain of options trading, harnessing its potential while safeguarding their investments. As we proceed in this book, the insights gained from understanding the advantages and risks of options trading will serve as a foundation for developing sophisticated strategies, including the butterfly spread, that align with your trading goals and risk tolerance.

8. Market Participants in Options Trading

In the bustling world of financial markets, options trading stands out as a dynamic and multifaceted arena where a myriad of participants converge, each with their unique roles, strategies, and objectives. Understanding the various market participants is crucial for gaining a holistic view of the options market, as their interactions shape market dynamics, liquidity, and pricing.

Retail Traders

Retail traders, often individual investors, form a significant portion of the options market. These participants range from novices exploring the basics of options trading to seasoned traders employing sophisticated strategies. Retail traders are drawn to options for various reasons, including the potential for high returns, the ability to hedge other investments, and the flexibility to tailor strategies to different market conditions. While retail traders typically operate on a smaller scale compared to institutional investors, their collective actions can influence market trends and liquidity.

Objectives and Strategies:

- Retail traders often seek to capitalize on short-term price movements or hedge their existing portfolios.

- Common strategies include buying calls and puts, covered calls, and vertical spreads.

Challenges:

- Retail traders may face challenges such as limited access to information, higher transaction costs, and the steep learning curve associated with options trading.

Institutional Investors

Institutional investors, such as hedge funds, mutual funds, pension funds, and insurance companies, wield significant influence in the options market. These entities manage large pools of capital and often employ complex and diverse strategies to achieve their investment goals. Institutional investors contribute to market liquidity and play a pivotal role in price discovery.

Objectives and Strategies:

- Hedging large portfolios against adverse market movements.

- Enhancing returns through income-generating strategies like covered calls and cash-secured puts.

- Implementing sophisticated strategies such as volatility arbitrage and synthetic positions.

Advantages:

- Access to advanced analytical tools, research, and market data.

- The ability to execute large trades with lower transaction costs due to economies of scale.

Market Makers

Market makers are essential participants in the options market, providing liquidity by continuously quoting buy and sell prices for options contracts. They facilitate the smooth functioning of the market by ensuring that there is always a counterparty available for trades, thereby reducing bid-ask spreads and enhancing market efficiency.

Role and Responsibilities:

- Market makers profit from the bid-ask spread, managing their risk through hedging strategies.

- They employ sophisticated algorithms and high-frequency trading systems to maintain competitive pricing and manage large volumes of trades.

Challenges:

- Market makers must navigate the risks associated with holding large inventories of options contracts, including volatility risk and the potential for rapid market movements.

Proprietary Trading Firms

Proprietary trading firms, or "prop shops," trade options using the firm's own capital rather than client funds. These firms often employ highly skilled traders and quantitative analysts who develop and execute advanced trading strategies.

Objectives and Strategies:

- Maximizing returns through arbitrage, market making, and algorithmic trading.

- Exploiting short-term price inefficiencies and statistical patterns in options pricing.

Advantages:

- Access to cutting-edge technology and high-speed trading platforms.

- The ability to deploy substantial capital quickly to capitalize on market opportunities.

Brokers and Clearing Houses

Brokers act as intermediaries between traders and the options market, facilitating the execution of trades. They provide trading platforms, market data, and research tools to their clients, which include retail traders, institutional investors, and proprietary trading firms.

Role and Responsibilities:

- Brokers earn commissions and fees for their services, and they are regulated to ensure fair and transparent practices.

- Clearing houses, on the other hand, are responsible for the settlement and clearing of options trades, ensuring that both parties fulfill their contractual obligations.

Importance:

- Clearing houses mitigate counterparty risk by acting as the central counterparty for all trades, guaranteeing the performance of each contract.

Regulatory Bodies

Regulatory bodies, such as the Securities and Exchange Commission (SEC) in the United States, oversee the options market to ensure its integrity, transparency, and fair operation. They establish and enforce rules and regulations that govern trading practices, market conduct, and the behavior of market participants.

Role and Responsibilities:

- Protecting investors and maintaining fair and orderly markets.

- Monitoring trading activities to detect and prevent fraudulent or manipulative practices.

Impact on Market Participants:

- Regulatory bodies' actions and policies can significantly influence market dynamics, affecting how market participants trade and manage their risks.

High-Frequency Traders (HFTs)

High-frequency traders (HFTs) use sophisticated algorithms and high-speed trading systems to execute a large number of trades in fractions of a second. HFTs contribute to market liquidity and efficiency but also introduce new challenges and risks.

Objectives and Strategies:

- Exploiting short-term price discrepancies and market inefficiencies.

- Engaging in market-making activities to benefit from bid-ask spreads.

Advantages:

- The ability to react to market information almost instantaneously, providing a competitive edge in price discovery.

Challenges:

- The potential to exacerbate market volatility during periods of rapid price movements.

- Regulatory scrutiny due to concerns about market manipulation and systemic risk.

Arbitrageurs

Arbitrageurs seek to profit from price differences in the options market. They exploit discrepancies between the prices of related financial instruments, such as options and their underlying assets, to generate risk-free profits.

Objectives and Strategies:

- Engaging in strategies such as index arbitrage, statistical arbitrage, and volatility arbitrage.

- Ensuring that prices align across different markets and instruments, contributing to market efficiency.

Importance:

- Arbitrage activities help to correct mispricings and maintain the integrity of the options market.

Understanding the diverse landscape of market participants in options trading provides valuable insight into the forces that shape market behavior and dynamics. Each participant, from retail traders to institutional investors, market makers, proprietary trading firms, brokers, regulatory bodies, high-frequency traders, and arbitrageurs, plays a unique and vital role. Their interactions create a complex and dynamic ecosystem, driving liquidity, price discovery, and market efficiency. As we delve deeper into the nuances of options trading in this book, keeping in mind the perspectives and strategies of these various participants will enhance your ability to navigate the market effectively and develop well-informed trading strategies.

1.10i) Regulatory Environment for Options Trading

Regulatory Bodies

In the United States, the primary regulatory bodies overseeing options trading include the Securities and Exchange Commission (SEC), the Financial Industry Regulatory

Authority (FINRA), and the Commodity Futures Trading Commission (CFTC). Each of these entities plays a specific role in maintaining market stability and enforcing compliance.

Securities and Exchange Commission (SEC)

As the primary regulatory authority for securities markets in the U.S., the SEC oversees the activities of exchanges, brokers, and traders. The SEC's mandate includes:

- Ensuring fair and efficient markets

- Protecting investors from fraudulent practices

- Overseeing the disclosure of material information by publicly traded companies

The SEC enforces the Securities Act of 1933 and the Securities Exchange Act of 1934, which form the backbone of U.S. securities regulation. These laws mandate the registration of securities and the requirement for companies to provide significant financial information, thus enhancing transparency.

Financial Industry Regulatory Authority (FINRA)

FINRA, a self-regulatory organization, supervises brokerage firms and exchange markets. Its responsibilities encompass:

- Licensing and regulating brokerage firms and their employees

- Enforcing rules to maintain market integrity and investor protection

- Educating investors to promote informed decision-making

FINRA conducts regular audits of brokerage firms and imposes penalties for violations, ensuring that firms adhere to the highest standards of conduct.

Commodity Futures Trading Commission (CFTC)

The CFTC primarily regulates the trading of commodity futures and options in the U.S. While its focus is on futures markets, its jurisdiction extends to options on futures, ensuring these markets operate transparently and free of manipulation.

Key Regulations

The regulatory framework for options trading includes several critical regulations designed to promote fair practices and protect market participants. Some of the key regulations include:

Options Clearing Corporation (OCC) Rules

The OCC, a central clearinghouse for options trading, ensures the performance of options contracts. It mitigates counterparty risk by guaranteeing the settlement of trades. The OCC's rules require members to maintain adequate capital and adhere to stringent risk management practices.

Regulation T

Regulation T, enforced by the Federal Reserve, governs the extension of credit by brokers for the purchase of securities. This regulation sets initial margin requirements, ensuring traders do not over-leverage their positions, which could lead to systemic risk.

Pattern Day Trader (PDT) Rule

The PDT rule, enforced by FINRA, restricts day trading activities for accounts with less than $25,000 in equity. This rule aims to protect novice traders from the inherent risks of frequent trading, promoting a more stable market environment.

Disclosure Requirements

Options trading firms must provide comprehensive risk disclosures to their clients. This includes the Options Disclosure Document (ODD), which outlines the characteristics and risks of standardized options. The ODD ensures that traders are fully aware of the potential risks before engaging in options trading.

International Regulations

Options trading is a global activity, governed by a myriad of regulations across different jurisdictions. Key international regulatory bodies include the European Securities and Markets Authority (ESMA), the Financial Conduct Authority (FCin the UK, and the Australian Securities and Investments Commission (ASIC).

European Securities and Markets Authority (ESMA)

ESMA harmonizes financial market regulations across EU member states. It oversees the implementation of the Markets in Financial Instruments Directive (MiFID II), which enhances transparency and investor protection in the European markets.

Financial Conduct Authority (FCA)

The FCA regulates financial markets in the UK, ensuring market integrity and consumer protection. It enforces stringent rules on market conduct, ensuring fair and transparent trading practices.

Australian Securities and Investments Commission (ASIC)

ASIC regulates Australia's financial markets, focusing on maintaining market integrity and protecting investors. It supervises the conduct of financial service providers and enforces compliance with financial regulations.

Compliance and Enforcement

Regulatory compliance is paramount in options trading. Firms must implement robust compliance programs to adhere to the myriad of regulations. This includes regular audits, employee training, and the establishment of internal controls to detect and prevent violations.

Regulators actively monitor market activities and investigate potential infractions. Penalties for non-compliance can be severe, including fines, suspension of trading privileges, and criminal charges. Therefore, maintaining rigorous compliance practices is essential for any entity involved in options trading.

Navigating the regulatory environment of options trading

requires a thorough understanding of the rules and regulations enforced by various regulatory bodies. Compliance with these regulations not only ensures the integrity of the markets but also protects investors from fraud and systemic risk. By adhering to these standards, market participants can contribute to a transparent, fair, and efficient trading environment.

1.11j) Options Trading Platforms and Tools

Trading Platforms

Interactive Brokers (IBKR)

Interactive Brokers is renowned for its diverse range of financial products and advanced trading technology. It offers a comprehensive suite of tools for options traders including:

- Trader Workstation (TWS): A robust trading platform that supports a wide array of financial instruments and options strategies. TWS provides real-time market data, advanced charting tools, and sophisticated order types.

- Probability Lab: This tool allows traders to analyze and model the probability of different market outcomes, facilitating more informed decision-making.

- OptionTrader: Dedicated to options trading, this interface simplifies the process of creating and managing complex options strategies. It offers visual representations of P&L, greeks, and risk/reward profiles.

Thinkorswim by TD Ameritrade

Thinkorswim is a highly acclaimed trading platform known for its user-friendly interface and powerful analytical tools. It caters to both novice and experienced options traders with features such as:

- Strategy Roller: This tool automates the process of rolling options positions, enabling traders to systematically manage their strategies.

- Analyze Tab: Provides detailed analysis of potential trades, including risk graphs, probability of profit, and scenario analysis.

- Paper Trading: Allows users to practice trading strategies in a simulated environment, reducing the risk of financial loss while learning.

E*TRADE

E*TRADE offers an intuitive platform that is particularly attractive to retail traders. Its features include:

- OptionsHouse: A platform designed specifically for options trading, offering real-time data, customizable option chains, and advanced order capabilities.

- StrategySEEK: An innovative tool that assists traders in identifying options strategies based on their market outlook and risk tolerance.

- Live Action Scanner: Continuously scans the market for potential trading opportunities, alerting traders to unusual activity or significant price movements.

TradeStation

TradeStation is well-regarded for its powerful trading tools and extensive customization options. It provides options traders with:

- OptionStation Pro: An advanced tool for analyzing and executing complex options strategies. It includes features such as strategy builder, probability analysis, and detailed P&L visuals.

- RadarScreen: A real-time market scanning tool that helps traders identify opportunities based on specific criteria.

- EasyLanguage: TradeStation's proprietary coding language that allows traders to create custom indicators, strategies, and automated trading systems.

Analytical Tools

OptionVue

OptionVue is a comprehensive options analysis software that offers sophisticated modeling and analytics. Key features include:

- Volatility Analysis: Provides detailed insights into historical and implied volatility, helping traders assess the potential for price movements.

- Trade Modeling: Allows for simulation of various trading scenarios, aiding in the evaluation of potential outcomes and risk management.

- Portfolio Management: Offers tools for tracking and managing options portfolios, including risk metrics and performance analysis.

LiveVol

LiveVol is a powerful analytics platform designed for options traders seeking an edge in volatility analysis. Its offerings include:

- Volatility Surface: Visualizes the implied volatility across different strike prices and expiration dates, aiding in the identification of trading opportunities.

- Order Flow Analytics: Tracks and analyzes the flow of large options orders, providing insights into market sentiment and potential price movements.

- Historical Data: Offers extensive historical options data, allowing traders to backtest strategies and study market behavior over time.

Bloomberg Terminal

The Bloomberg Terminal is a staple in the financial industry, providing comprehensive data and analytics for a wide range of assets including options. Features beneficial to options traders include:

- Options Monitor: Displays real-time data on options prices, implied volatility, and greeks.

- Strategy Builder: Enables the construction and analysis of complex options strategies, with detailed risk/reward profiles.

- News and Research: Provides access to the latest market news, research reports, and economic data, keeping traders informed and ready to act.

Risk Management Tools

OptionNet Explorer

OptionNet Explorer is a specialized software for options traders focused on risk management and strategy optimization. It offers:

- Backtesting: Facilitates the backtesting of options strategies using historical data, helping traders refine their approaches.

- Real-Time Tracking: Monitors live positions, providing real-time updates on P&L, greeks, and risk metrics.

- Trade Journal: Allows traders to document their trades, analyze performance, and identify areas for improvement.

ORATS (Options Research & Technology Services)

ORATS provides advanced options analytics and risk management tools tailored for institutional traders. Features include:

- Volatility Forecasting: Uses proprietary models to forecast future volatility, aiding in the assessment of potential trading opportunities.

- Position Analysis: Offers detailed analysis of current positions, including risk assessments and scenario analysis.

- API Integration: Allows for seamless integration with other trading platforms and systems, enhancing operational efficiency.

Execution Tools

AlgoTrader

AlgoTrader is an institutional-grade algorithmic trading platform that supports automated options trading. Key features include:

- Automated Strategy Execution: Facilitates the automated execution of options strategies based on predefined criteria.

- Real-Time Data Integration: Integrates with real-time market data feeds, ensuring timely and accurate execution of trades.

- Custom Algorithm Development: Allows traders to develop and deploy custom trading algorithms tailored to their specific strategies.

QuantConnect

QuantConnect is a cloud-based platform that provides tools for developing, backtesting, and executing algorithmic trading strategies. Benefits for options traders include:

- Options Algorithm Framework: A dedicated framework for building and testing options trading algorithms.

- Data Library: Access to extensive historical options data for backtesting and strategy development.

- Community and Collaboration: A vibrant community of developers and traders, providing opportunities for collaboration and knowledge sharing.

The landscape of options trading platforms and tools is continually evolving, driven by advancements in technology and the increasing sophistication of market participants. By leveraging these platforms and tools, traders can enhance their analytical capabilities, execute trades with precision, and effectively manage risk. Understanding the features and benefits of these resources is essential for anyone looking to succeed in the dynamic world of options trading.

CHAPTER 2: BASICS OF BUTTERFLY SPREAD STRATEGY

I n options trading, spread strategies occupy a pivotal role, offering traders a means to manage risk, limit losses, and enhance returns. Spread strategies involve the simultaneous purchase and sale of different options contracts, typically with varying strike prices or expiration dates. By understanding the nuances of these strategies, traders can craft sophisticated positions tailored to specific market conditions and investment goals.

The Essence of Spread Strategies

At their core, spread strategies involve creating a position that balances the benefits and risks of different options. The key is to establish this balance in a way that aligns with the trader's market outlook, whether bullish, bearish, or neutral. The spread effectively caps potential losses while also limiting the potential gains, providing a structured approach to trading options.

Types of Spread Strategies

1. Vertical Spreads

Vertical spreads, also known as money spreads, involve buying and selling options of the same type (calls or puts) with the same expiration date but different strike prices. They are categorized into two main types:

- Bull Call Spread: This strategy is employed when a trader expects a moderate rise in the underlying asset's price. It involves buying a call option at a lower strike price and selling another call option at a higher strike price. The goal is to benefit from the price increase while limiting the cost of the position.

- Bear Put Spread: Conversely, a bear put spread is used when a trader anticipates a decline in the asset's price. It entails buying a put option at a higher strike price and selling another put option at a lower strike price, thus capitalizing on the downward movement.

2. Horizontal Spreads

Horizontal spreads, also known as calendar spreads, involve buying and selling options of the same type and strike price but with different expiration dates. These spreads are used to exploit the differences in time decay between the options.

- Long Calendar Spread: This strategy involves buying a longer-term option and selling a shorter-term option, typically when the trader expects the underlying asset to remain relatively stable in the short term but anticipates a significant move before the longer-term option expires.

- Short Calendar Spread: In this approach, a trader might sell a longer-term option and buy a shorter-term option to capture premium from the rapid decay of the shorter-term option, usually predicted under high volatility conditions.

3. Diagonal Spreads

Diagonal spreads are akin to a hybrid of vertical and horizontal spreads. They involve buying and selling options of the same type but with different strike prices and expiration dates.

- Long Diagonal Spread: Often used when a trader has a longer-term outlook on the underlying asset but wants to benefit from more immediate movements. This strategy might involve buying a long-term call option and selling a short-term call option with a higher strike price.

- Short Diagonal Spread: Employed when a trader expects short-term stability but long-term volatility. It could involve selling a long-term call option while simultaneously buying a short-term call option with a higher strike price.

4. Butterfly Spreads

The butterfly spread, a more advanced strategy, combines elements of both vertical and horizontal spreads. It involves buying and selling multiple options to create a position that profits from low volatility in the underlying asset.

- Long Butterfly Spread: This strategy typically entails buying one call (or put) at a lower strike price, selling two calls (or puts) at a middle strike price, and buying one call (or put) at a higher strike price. The goal is to profit from the underlying asset's price remaining near the middle strike price at expiration.

- Short Butterfly Spread: Conversely, a short butterfly spread involves selling one call (or put) at a lower strike price, buying two calls (or puts) at a middle strike price, and selling one call (or put) at a higher strike price. This strategy profits from higher volatility, where the underlying asset's price moves significantly away from the middle strike price.

Key Considerations

When employing spread strategies, traders must consider several factors to optimize their positions:

- Market Outlook: The chosen strategy should align with the trader's expectations of the underlying asset's future price movement and volatility.

- Risk Tolerance: Spread strategies inherently involve limited risk and reward. Traders must assess their risk tolerance and select spreads that provide an acceptable balance between potential gains and losses.

- Transaction Costs: Multiple options contracts in spread strategies can lead to higher transaction costs. These costs must be factored into the overall strategy to ensure it remains profitable.

- Liquidity: High liquidity in the options market is crucial for executing spread strategies efficiently. Illiquid markets can result in unfavorable bid-ask spreads and difficulty in entering or exiting positions.

varies across different spread strategies. Understanding how time affects the value of each leg of the spread is essential for effective management.

Practical Implementation

To illustrate the practical application of spread strategies, let us consider a step-by-step example of constructing a bull call spread:

1. Market Analysis: Suppose a trader expects the price of XYZ stock to rise from its current price of $50 to around $55 within the next month.

2. Option Selection: The trader decides to buy a call option with a $50 strike price (near-the-money) expiring in one month and simultaneously sell a call option with a $55 strike price (out-of-the-money) expiring in the same month.

3. Cost Calculation: The premium for the $50 call option is $3, and the premium for the $55 call option is $1. The net cost of the spread is $2 ($3 paid for the long call minus $1 received for the short call).

4. Potential Outcomes:

- If XYZ stock rises to $55 or higher, the trader's profit is capped at $3 ($5 difference in strike prices minus $2 net cost).

- If XYZ stock remains at $50, the trader loses the initial $2 paid for the spread.

- If XYZ stock falls below $50, the loss remains $2.

By constructing this bull call spread, the trader has defined their risk and reward, aligning the strategy with their bullish outlook while managing potential losses.

Spread strategies in options trading offer a versatile toolkit for managing risk and capitalizing on market movements. By understanding the various types of spreads—vertical, horizontal, diagonal, and butterfly—traders can tailor their positions to specific market conditions and investment objectives. The careful consideration of market outlook, risk tolerance, transaction costs, liquidity, and time decay is essential for optimizing these strategies. With the right approach and tools, spread strategies can significantly enhance a trader's ability to navigate the complexities of options trading and achieve their financial goals.

Introduction to Butterfly Spread

The butterfly spread, an advanced options trading strategy, embodies an intricate yet methodical approach to navigating market fluctuations. Rooted in the principles of spread strategies, it offers a balanced structure that enables traders to capitalize on low-volatility environments while maintaining well-defined risk and reward parameters.

The Structure and Mechanics of Butterfly Spread

A butterfly spread, whether crafted with calls or puts, involves a combination of buying and selling options at varying strike prices but with the same expiration date. Typically, a standard butterfly spread comprises three strike prices:

1. Lower Strike Price (A): This involves buying one option.

2. Middle Strike Price (B): Here, two options are sold.

3. Higher Strike Price (C): Finally, buying one more option.

The relationship between these strike prices is usually symmetrical, with the middle strike price equidistant from the lower and higher strike prices. This symmetry is crucial as it defines the 'wings' and 'body' of the butterfly, hence the name.

The payoff structure of a butterfly spread resembles a tent, with the maximum profit achievable when the underlying asset's price rests at the middle strike price at expiration. The potential profit and loss are capped, offering a trader a clear risk-reward profile.

Constructing a Long Butterfly Spread with Calls

To comprehend the practical application, let's illustrate the construction of a long butterfly spread using call options:

1. Market Context: Assume the stock of ABC Corp is currently trading at $100. A trader anticipates the stock will remain close to this price at expiration but does not foresee significant volatility.

2. Strike Prices Selection: The trader decides to create a butterfly spread with the following strike prices:

   - Buy one call option at a strike price of $95.

   - Sell two call options at a strike price of $100.

   - Buy one call option at a strike price of $105.

3. Premium Calculation: The premiums for these options are:

   - $10 for the $95 call.

   - $5 for the $100 calls (each).

- $2 for the $105 call.

- Total debit = $10 + ($5 x 2) - $2 = $8.

4. Potential Outcomes:

- Maximum Profit: Achieved if ABC Corp is trading at $100 at expiration. The maximum profit is calculated as the difference between the middle strike and the lower strike minus the net debit: ($100 - $95) - $8 = $5.

- Break-even Points: The break-even points are calculated as the lower strike plus the net debit and the higher strike minus the net debit: $95 + $8 = $103 and $105 - $8 = $97.

- Maximum Loss: The maximum loss occurs if the stock is either below $95 or above $105 at expiration, leading to a total loss equal to the net debit paid: $8.

Variations of Butterfly Spreads

While the most common butterfly spread is the long butterfly spread, traders can employ several variations to suit different market views and risk tolerances:

1. Short Butterfly Spread: This strategy is the inverse of the long butterfly spread. It involves selling one lower strike option, buying two middle strike options, and selling one higher strike option. The short butterfly spread benefits from significant movement in either direction, making it suitable for high-volatility forecasts.

2. Iron Butterfly Spread: This variant combines both calls and puts to create a position with a similar payoff structure to the regular butterfly spread but limits the margin requirement. It involves selling a call and a put at the middle strike price while buying a call at a higher strike and a put at a lower strike price.

Strategic Considerations

When constructing and implementing butterfly spreads, traders must account for several critical factors:

1. Volatility Forecast: Since butterfly spreads thrive in low-volatility environments, accurate volatility estimation is paramount. Tools like implied volatility indices and historical volatility measures provide valuable insights.

2. Time Decay: The passage of time has a significant impact on the butterfly spread's value. Understanding Theta, or time decay, is crucial for managing positions, particularly as expiration approaches.

3. Liquidity: High liquidity in the options market ensures tighter bid-ask spreads and easier trade execution, which is essential for the multiple legs involved in a butterfly spread.

4. Transaction Costs: Given the multiple options contracts involved, transaction costs can erode potential profits. A comprehensive cost-benefit analysis is necessary to ensure profitability.

Practical Python Implementation

Transitioning from theory to practice, Python provides a robust framework for constructing, analyzing, and optimizing butterfly spreads. Here's a walkthrough of implementing a basic long butterfly spread with calls in Python:

1. Setting Up the Environment:

```python
import numpy as np
```

```python
import matplotlib.pyplot as plt

# Define strike prices
strikes = [95, 100, 105]

# Define premiums
premiums = [10, 5, 2]
```

2. Calculating Payoff at Expiration:

```python
def butterfly_spread_payoff(stock_price, lower_strike, middle_strike, higher_strike, lower_premium, middle_premium, higher_premium):
    lower_leg = np.maximum(stock_price - lower_strike, 0) - lower_premium
    middle_leg = -2 * (np.maximum(stock_price - middle_strike, 0)) + (2 * middle_premium)
    higher_leg = np.maximum(stock_price - higher_strike, 0) - higher_premium
    return lower_leg + middle_leg + higher_leg

# Stock prices at expiration
stock_prices = np.linspace(90, 110, 100)

# Payoff calculation
payoffs = [butterfly_spread_payoff(price, 95, 100, 105, 10, 5, 2) for price in stock_prices]

# Plotting the payoff diagram
```

```python
plt.plot(stock_prices, payoffs, label="Butterfly Spread
Payoff")
plt.axhline(0, color='black', linestyle='--')
plt.axvline(95, color='grey', linestyle='--')
plt.axvline(100, color='grey', linestyle='--')
plt.axvline(105, color='grey', linestyle='--')
plt.xlabel('Stock Price at Expiration')
plt.ylabel('Payoff')
plt.title('Butterfly Spread Payoff Diagram')
plt.legend()
plt.show()
```

This code snippet sets up the basic structure for calculating and visualizing the payoff of a butterfly spread. By adjusting the strike prices and premiums, traders can simulate different scenarios and optimize their strategies accordingly.

The butterfly spread strategy serves as an elegant yet powerful tool in the options trader's arsenal. By leveraging its structured approach, traders can effectively navigate market conditions characterized by low volatility while maintaining a clear risk-reward profile. With the aid of Python, the practical implementation of butterfly spreads becomes more accessible, enabling traders to analyze, optimize, and execute their strategies with precision. As we continue our journey through the myriad facets of options trading, the butterfly spread exemplifies the blend of art and science that defines sophisticated trading methodologies.

Constructing Butterfly Spread: Components

The butterfly spread strategy is an advanced options trading technique that requires a meticulous approach to its construction. By blending a combination of options at different strike prices, this strategy offers a balanced risk-reward profile. Understanding its components is essential for effective implementation, and we'll delve into the intricate details to provide a comprehensive guide.

The Core Components of a Butterfly Spread

A butterfly spread, whether executed with call or put options, involves three distinct strike prices and a net debit or credit at initiation. Let's break down these components in greater detail:

1. Lower Strike Price (A): This option is bought, forming the initial leg of the spread.

2. Middle Strike Price (B): Two options are sold at this strike price, creating the body of the butterfly.

3. Higher Strike Price (C): Another option is bought at a higher strike price, forming the final leg or wing of the butterfly.

The symmetry in the distance between the middle strike price and the lower and higher strike prices is crucial. This symmetrical structure defines the potential payoff and risk associated with the butterfly spread.

Constructing a Long Butterfly Spread with Calls

To illustrate the construction process, let's walk through the steps of creating a long butterfly spread using call options:

1. Selecting the Underlying Asset: Assume XYZ stock is trading at $100, and a trader expects it to stay near this price by expiration.

2. Choosing Strike Prices: The trader selects the following strike prices:

   - Lower Strike Price (A): $95

   - Middle Strike Price (B): $100

   - Higher Strike Price (C): $105

3. Option Premiums: The premiums for these options are as follows:

   - $95 strike call: $10

   - $100 strike calls: $5 each

   - $105 strike call: $2

The total cost incurred (net debit) for setting up the spread can be calculated as:

$$ \text{Net Debit} = \$10 + (2 \times \$5) - \$2 = \$8 $$

4. Potential Payoff at Expiration:

   - Maximum Profit: The maximum profit occurs if XYZ stock is exactly at the middle strike price ($100) at expiration. The profit is calculated as:

$$ (\text{Middle Strike Price} - \text{Lower Strike Price}) - \text{Net Debit} = (100 - 95) - 8 = \$5 $$

   - Break-even Points: The break-even points are where the net payoff is zero and can be calculated as:

$$ \text{Lower Break-even} = \text{Lower Strike Price} + \text{Net Debit} = 95 + 8 = \$103 $$

$$\text{Higher Break-even} = \text{Higher Strike Price} - \text{Net Debit} = 105 - 8 = \$97$$

- Maximum Loss: The maximum loss occurs if the stock price is below $95 or above $105 at expiration, leading to a total loss equal to the net debit paid, which is $8.

Variations and Adjustments

While the standard long butterfly spread is common, there are variations that cater to different market conditions and trader preferences:

1. Short Butterfly Spread: This strategy involves selling one lower strike option, buying two middle strike options, and selling one higher strike option. It benefits from significant movement in either direction, suitable for environments with expected high volatility.

2. Iron Butterfly Spread: This variant combines both calls and puts to limit margin requirements. It involves selling a call and a put at the middle strike price, while buying a call at a higher strike and a put at a lower strike price, resembling the payoff structure of a regular butterfly spread.

Practical Considerations

Before executing a butterfly spread, several practical aspects must be considered to ensure effectiveness and profitability:

1. Volatility: Accurate forecasts of market volatility are critical. Butterfly spreads work best in low-volatility environments. Tools such as implied volatility indices and historical volatility measures can aid in making informed decisions.

2. Time Decay (Theta): The impact of time decay is

significant in butterfly spreads. As expiration approaches, the value of the options changes, impacting the overall strategy. Understanding Theta helps manage positions effectively.

3. Liquidity: High liquidity is essential for the multiple legs involved in a butterfly spread. It ensures tighter bid-ask spreads and easier trade execution.

4. Transaction Costs: Multiple options contracts result in higher transaction costs, which can erode potential profits. It's crucial to perform a cost-benefit analysis to ensure the strategy remains profitable.

Python Implementation

To transition from theory to practice, Python provides a powerful framework for constructing and analyzing butterfly spreads. Here's a step-by-step guide to implementing a basic long butterfly spread using Python:

1. Setting Up the Environment:
```python
import numpy as np
import matplotlib.pyplot as plt

# Define strike prices and premiums
strikes = [95, 100, 105]
premiums = [10, 5, 2]

# Define the stock price range at expiration
stock_prices = np.linspace(90, 110, 100)
```

2. Calculating Payoff at Expiration:

```python
def butterfly_spread_payoff(stock_price, lower_strike, middle_strike, higher_strike, lower_premium, middle_premium, higher_premium):
    lower_leg = np.maximum(stock_price - lower_strike, 0) - lower_premium
    middle_leg = -2 * (np.maximum(stock_price - middle_strike, 0)) + (2 * middle_premium)
    higher_leg = np.maximum(stock_price - higher_strike, 0) - higher_premium
    return lower_leg + middle_leg + higher_leg


# Calculate the payoffs for the stock price range at expiration
payoffs = [butterfly_spread_payoff(price, 95, 100, 105, 10, 5, 2) for price in stock_prices]
```

3. Visualizing the Payoff:

```python
# Plotting the payoff diagram
plt.plot(stock_prices, payoffs, label="Butterfly Spread Payoff")
plt.axhline(0, color='black', linestyle='--')
plt.axvline(95, color='grey', linestyle='--')
plt.axvline(100, color='grey', linestyle='--')
plt.axvline(105, color='grey', linestyle='--')
plt.xlabel('Stock Price at Expiration')
```

```
plt.ylabel('Payoff')
plt.title('Butterfly Spread Payoff Diagram')
plt.legend()
plt.show()
```
```

This code sets the basic structure for calculating and visualizing the payoff of a butterfly spread. By adjusting the strike prices and premiums, traders can simulate different scenarios and optimize their strategies accordingly.

Constructing a butterfly spread requires a nuanced understanding of its components and the interplay between strike prices, premiums, and market conditions. With a clear grasp of these elements, traders can effectively harness the butterfly spread strategy to navigate low-volatility environments with a defined risk-reward profile. Leveraging Python for practical implementation further empowers traders to analyze, optimize, and execute their strategies with precision and sophistication.

Long vs. Short Butterfly Spread

The butterfly spread is a sophisticated options trading strategy, renowned for its balance of risk and reward. It can be configured in two primary forms: the long butterfly spread and the short butterfly spread. Each variation serves distinct market conditions and trader expectations. Understanding the nuances between these spreads is crucial for employing them effectively within a trading strategy.

Long Butterfly Spread
```

The long butterfly spread is typically used in low volatility environments, where the trader anticipates minimal price movement in the underlying asset. This strategy involves a combination of buying and selling call or put options at three different strike prices, forming a net debit position.

Components:

1. Buy One Lower Strike Option (A): This forms the first leg of the spread.

2. Sell Two Middle Strike Options (B): These options create the body of the butterfly, at a strike price closest to the current price of the underlying asset.

3. Buy One Higher Strike Option (C): This forms the final leg of the spread.

Example:

Imagine a trader is bullish on the stock XYZ, currently trading at \$100, but expects it to not move significantly by expiration. The trader constructs a long butterfly spread using call options with the following strike prices and premiums:

- Buy 1 call at the \$95 strike for \$10.

- Sell 2 calls at the \$100 strike for \$5 each.

- Buy 1 call at the \$105 strike for \$2.

The net debit (initial cost) for this spread is calculated as:

$$ \text{Net Debit} = \$10 + 2 \times (-\$5) + \$2 = \$2 $$

Profit and Loss Characteristics:

- Maximum Profit: Occurs if the stock price is exactly at the middle strike price ($100) at expiration. The profit is:

$$\text{Max Profit} = (\text{Middle Strike Price} - \text{Lower Strike Price}) - \text{Net Debit} = (100 - 95) - 2 = \$3$$

- Break-even Points: The points where the net payoff is zero:

$$\text{Lower Break-even} = \text{Lower Strike Price} + \text{Net Debit} = 95 + 2 = \$97$$

$$\text{Higher Break-even} = \text{Higher Strike Price} - \text{Net Debit} = 105 - 2 = \$103$$

- Maximum Loss: The loss is limited to the net debit paid, which is $2, occurring if the stock price is below $95 or above $105 at expiration.

The long butterfly spread offers a favorable risk-reward ratio, limited risk, and potential for moderate gains, making it a popular choice for traders in stable market conditions.

Short Butterfly Spread

Conversely, the short butterfly spread is a strategy designed for high volatility markets, where substantial price movement is anticipated. This approach results in a net credit position, achieved by selling options at the extremities and buying options at the middle strike price.

Components:

1. Sell One Lower Strike Option (A): Initiates the first leg of the spread.

2. Buy Two Middle Strike Options (B): These options form the body of the butterfly.

3. Sell One Higher Strike Option (C): Completes the final leg of the spread.

Example:

Consider a trader expects significant volatility in the price of XYZ stock, currently trading at $100. The trader constructs a short butterfly spread with the following strike prices and premiums:

- Sell 1 call at the $95 strike for $10.

- Buy 2 calls at the $100 strike for $5 each.

- Sell 1 call at the $105 strike for $2.

The net credit (initial premium received) for this spread is:
$$ \text{Net Credit} = \$10 - 2 \times \$5 + \$2 = \$2 $$

Profit and Loss Characteristics:

- Maximum Profit: This is realized if the stock price is either below the lower strike price ($95) or above the higher strike price ($105) at expiration. The profit is equal to the net credit received:
$$ \text{Max Profit} = \$2 $$

- Break-even Points: These are defined by the points at which the net payoff is zero:
$$ \text{Lower Break-even} = \text{Lower Strike Price} + \text{Net Credit} = 95 + 2 = \$97 $$

$$ \text{Higher Break-even} = \text{Higher Strike Price} - \text{Net Credit} = 105 - 2 = \$103 $$

- Maximum Loss: The maximum loss occurs if the stock price is exactly at the middle strike price ($100) at expiration. The loss calculation is:
$$ \text{Max Loss} = (\text{Middle Strike Price} - \text{Lower Strike Price}) - \text{Net Credit} = (100 - 95) - 2 = \$3 $$

The short butterfly spread, while offering a limited profit, provides traders with the ability to benefit from significant price movements in either direction. It's suited for volatile markets where substantial shifts in the underlying asset's price are expected.

Practical Considerations

When choosing between a long and short butterfly spread, several practical factors should be taken into account:

1. Market Volatility: Assess the expected volatility in the market. The long butterfly spread is ideal for low volatility, while the short butterfly spread thrives in high volatility conditions.

2. Transaction Costs: Both strategies involve multiple options contracts, resulting in higher transaction fees. Evaluate these costs to ensure they don't erode potential profits.

3. Liquidity: High liquidity in the options market is essential for executing the multiple legs of these spreads efficiently. Ensure there is sufficient trading volume and tight bid-ask spreads for the chosen options.

4. Time Decay (Theta): Time decay affects the premiums of the options involved. Understanding its impact on your spread can help manage positions more effectively.

Python Implementation

To provide a tangible example, let's implement both long and short butterfly spreads using Python. This will help in visualizing the payoff diagrams and understanding their characteristics.

Long Butterfly Spread Implementation:

```python
import numpy as np
import matplotlib.pyplot as plt

# Define strike prices and premiums for long butterfly spread
long_strikes = [95, 100, 105]
long_premiums = [10, 5, 2]

# Define stock price range at expiration
stock_prices = np.linspace(90, 110, 100)

def long_butterfly_payoff(stock_price, strikes, premiums):
    lower_leg = np.maximum(stock_price - strikes[0], 0) - premiums[0]
    middle_leg = -2 * np.maximum(stock_price - strikes[1], 0) + 2 * premiums[1]
    higher_leg = np.maximum(stock_price - strikes[2], 0) - premiums[2]
    return lower_leg + middle_leg + higher_leg

# Calculate the payoffs
long_payoffs = [long_butterfly_payoff(price, long_strikes, long_premiums) for price in stock_prices]

# Plot the payoff diagram
plt.plot(stock_prices, long_payoffs, label="Long Butterfly Spread Payoff")
```

```python
plt.axhline(0, color='black', linestyle='--')
plt.axvline(95, color='grey', linestyle='--')
plt.axvline(100, color='grey', linestyle='--')
plt.axvline(105, color='grey', linestyle='--')
plt.xlabel('Stock Price at Expiration')
plt.ylabel('Payoff')
plt.title('Long Butterfly Spread Payoff Diagram')
plt.legend()
plt.show()
```

Short Butterfly Spread Implementation:

```python
# Define strike prices and premiums for short butterfly spread
short_strikes = [95, 100, 105]
short_premiums = [10, 5, 2]

def short_butterfly_payoff(stock_price, strikes, premiums):
    lower_leg = -np.maximum(stock_price - strikes[0], 0) + premiums[0]
    middle_leg = 2 * np.maximum(stock_price - strikes[1], 0) - 2 * premiums[1]
    higher_leg = -np.maximum(stock_price - strikes[2], 0) + premiums[2]
    return lower_leg + middle_leg + higher_leg

# Calculate the payoffs
short_payoffs = [short_butterfly_payoff(price, short_strikes,
```

short_premiums) for price in stock_prices]

```
# Plot the payoff diagram
plt.plot(stock_prices, short_payoffs, label="Short Butterfly Spread Payoff")
plt.axhline(0, color='black', linestyle='--')
plt.axvline(95, color='grey', linestyle='--')
plt.axvline(100, color='grey', linestyle='--')
plt.axvline(105, color='grey', linestyle='--')
plt.xlabel('Stock Price at Expiration')
plt.ylabel('Payoff')
plt.title('Short Butterfly Spread Payoff Diagram')
plt.legend()
plt.show()
```

These scripts provide a visual representation of the payoffs for both long and short butterfly spreads, helping traders understand their potential outcomes and make informed decisions.

The choice between a long and short butterfly spread hinges on the trader's market outlook and volatility expectations. Each strategy offers a unique risk-reward profile suited to specific market conditions. By mastering the construction and application of these spreads, traders can enhance their trading arsenals, leveraging sophisticated strategies to navigate both stable and volatile market environments effectively. The integration of Python further empowers traders by providing tools to simulate, analyze, and optimize these strategies with precision and confidence.

Strike Prices Selection

Understanding Strike Price Selection

The butterfly spread strategy involves three different strike prices: the lower strike, the middle strike, and the higher strike. The middle strike price is usually set at or near the current price of the underlying asset, while the lower and higher strike prices are equidistant from the middle strike. This symmetrical arrangement forms the characteristic "wings" of the butterfly spread.

Components of Strike Price Selection:

1. Lower Strike Price (A): The first leg of the spread, usually set below the current price.

2. Middle Strike Price (B): The central component, typically close to the current price.

3. Higher Strike Price (C): The final leg of the spread, set above the current price.

Factors Influencing Strike Price Selection

Effectively selecting strike prices involves considering several key factors:

1. Market Outlook: Assessing the expected direction and volatility of the underlying asset is crucial. For a long butterfly spread, where minimal price movement is anticipated, the middle strike should closely align with the current price. For a short butterfly spread, where significant movement is

expected, strike prices may be set further apart.

2. Volatility: The implied volatility of the underlying asset determines the premium of the options. In high volatility environments, wider spreads might be preferable to capture larger price movements. Conversely, in low volatility environments, narrower spreads may suffice.

3. Time to Expiration: The time remaining until the options expire affects the selection of strike prices. Longer durations allow for greater price movement, necessitating a different strike price configuration compared to shorter durations.

4. Risk Tolerance: A trader's risk appetite plays a pivotal role. More conservative traders may prefer closer strike prices to limit potential losses, while aggressive traders might opt for wider spreads to maximize potential gains.

5. Market Conditions: Real-time market dynamics, including liquidity and transaction costs, can influence strike price selection. Ensure the selected strike prices have sufficient trading volume and tight bid-ask spreads to facilitate efficient execution.

Practical Techniques for Strike Price Selection

To provide practical insights, let's explore some techniques for selecting strike prices using real-world scenarios.

Example 1: Long Butterfly Spread in a Low Volatility Market

Suppose XYZ stock is currently trading at $100, and the market is exhibiting low volatility. A trader anticipates that the stock price will remain relatively stable until the options' expiration. The trader constructs a long butterfly spread using call options with the following strike prices:

- Lower Strike Price (A): $95

- Middle Strike Price (B): $100

- Higher Strike Price (C): $105

The trader buys one call option at the $95 strike, sells two call options at the $100 strike, and buys one call option at the $105 strike. This setup ensures that the trader benefits if the stock price remains near $100 at expiration.

Example 2: Short Butterfly Spread in a High Volatility Market

Consider a different scenario where XYZ stock is still trading at $100, but the market is experiencing high volatility. The trader expects significant price movement in either direction and constructs a short butterfly spread using put options:

- Lower Strike Price (A): $90

- Middle Strike Price (B): $100

- Higher Strike Price (C): $110

In this case, the trader sells one put option at the $90 strike, buys two put options at the $100 strike, and sells one put option at the $110 strike. The wider spread accommodates the anticipated price fluctuations, allowing the trader to profit from substantial movements in the underlying asset.

Python Implementation for Strike Price Analysis

To facilitate strike price selection, let's implement a Python script that helps analyze potential strike prices based on historical volatility and current market conditions. This script will use historical price data to calculate implied volatility and suggest optimal strike prices for a butterfly spread.

```python
import numpy as np
import pandas as pd
import yfinance as yf
from scipy.stats import norm

# Function to calculate implied volatility
def calculate_implied_volatility(stock_prices, strike_price, option_price, time_to_expiry, risk_free_rate, option_type='call'):
    def black_scholes_price(volatility):
        d1 = (np.log(stock_prices / strike_price) + (risk_free_rate + 0.5 * volatility 2) * time_to_expiry) / (volatility * np.sqrt(time_to_expiry))
        d2 = d1 - volatility * np.sqrt(time_to_expiry)
        if option_type == 'call':
            return (stock_prices * norm.cdf(d1) - strike_price * np.exp(-risk_free_rate * time_to_expiry) * norm.cdf(d2)) - option_price
        else:
            return (strike_price * np.exp(-risk_free_rate * time_to_expiry) * norm.cdf(-d2) - stock_prices * norm.cdf(-d1)) - option_price

    implied_volatility = np.arange(0.01, 2, 0.001)
    prices = [black_scholes_price(iv) for iv in implied_volatility]
```

```python
    return implied_volatility[np.argmin(np.abs(prices))]

# Load historical stock data
ticker = 'XYZ'
data        =        yf.download(ticker,        start='2022-01-01',
end='2023-01-01')
stock_prices = data['Close']

# Calculate historical volatility
log_returns = np.log(stock_prices / stock_prices.shift(1))
historical_volatility = log_returns.std() * np.sqrt(252)

# Define current market parameters
current_stock_price = stock_prices[-1]
option_price = 5  # Example option price
time_to_expiry = 30 / 365  # 30 days to expiration
risk_free_rate = 0.01  # 1% risk-free rate

# Suggest optimal strike prices for a butterfly spread
middle_strike = current_stock_price
lower_strike = middle_strike - 5
higher_strike = middle_strike + 5

implied_volatility                                                   =
calculate_implied_volatility(current_stock_price,
middle_strike, option_price, time_to_expiry, risk_free_rate)
print(f"Optimal Strike Prices: Lower: {lower_strike}, Middle: {middle_strike}, Higher: {higher_strike}")
print(f"Implied Volatility: {implied_volatility:.2f}")
```

` ` `

This script calculates the implied volatility based on historical price data and suggests optimal strike prices for constructing a butterfly spread. Traders can adjust parameters such as time to expiration and risk-free rate to reflect current market conditions accurately.

Selecting appropriate strike prices is a critical step in constructing a butterfly spread. By considering market outlook, volatility, time to expiration, risk tolerance, and market conditions, traders can make informed decisions to optimize their strategies. Practical techniques and Python implementations further empower traders to analyze and select the most suitable strike prices effectively. With these insights and tools, you are well-equipped to navigate the complexities of strike price selection and enhance your options trading strategy.

Profit and Loss Characteristics

The Basic Structure of Profit and Loss in Butterfly Spreads

A butterfly spread is constructed using three different strike prices. The typical setup involves buying one option at the lower strike price, selling two options at the middle strike price, and buying one option at the higher strike price. This results in a net debit or credit depending on whether it is a long or short butterfly spread.

The P&L characteristics of a butterfly spread are inherently linked to the relationship between the strike prices and the underlying asset's price at expiration. Let's break down the components:

1. Long Butterfly Spread:

- Initial Cost (Premium Paid): The net debit paid to enter the position.

- Maximum Profit: Achieved when the underlying asset's price is at the middle strike price at expiration.

- Maximum Loss: Limited to the initial cost of the spread.

- Breakeven Points: Two points where the underlying asset's price equals the strike prices adjusted for the net debit.

2. Short Butterfly Spread:

- Initial Credit (Premium Received): The net credit received from entering the position.

- Maximum Profit: Limited to the initial credit received.

- Maximum Loss: Occurs when the underlying asset's price is at the middle strike price at expiration.

- Breakeven Points: Two points where the underlying asset's price equals the strike prices adjusted for the net credit.

Calculating P&L for Butterfly Spreads

To understand the P&L characteristics, we must consider the payoff at expiration. Let's examine the long butterfly spread first.

Long Butterfly Spread – Payoff Calculation:

- At Expiration:

- If the underlying price is below the lower strike: All options expire worthless.

- If the underlying price is between the lower strike and middle strike: The lower strike option has intrinsic value.

- If the underlying price is at the middle strike: Maximum profit is realized.

- If the underlying price is between the middle strike and higher strike: The higher strike option has intrinsic value.

- If the underlying price is above the higher strike: All options except the higher strike option expire worthless.

The payoff formula for a long butterfly spread can be summarized as follows:
$$ \text{Payoff} = \max(0, S - K\_1) - 2 \times \max(0, S - K\_2) + \max(0, S - K\_3) - \text{Initial Cost} $$

Where:
- $ S $ is the underlying asset's price at expiration.
- $ K_1 $, $ K_2 $, $ K_3 $ are the lower, middle, and higher strike prices, respectively.

Example Calculation:

Consider XYZ stock currently trading at $100. A trader constructs a long butterfly spread with the following strike prices:

- Lower Strike Price (K1): $95

- Middle Strike Price (K2): $100

- Higher Strike Price (K3): $105

- Initial Cost: $2 (net debit)

Let's calculate the payoff for different scenarios:

1. Underlying price at $90 (below lower strike):

   - Payoff: $\max(0, 90 - 95) - 2 \times \max(0, 90 - 100) + \max(0, 90 - 105) - 2 = 0 - 0 + 0 - 2 = -2$

2. Underlying price at $97 (between lower and middle strike):

   - Payoff: $\max(0, 97 - 95) - 2 \times \max(0, 97 - 100) + \max(0, 97 - 105) - 2 = 2 - 0 + 0 - 2 = 0$

3. Underlying price at $100 (middle strike):

   - Payoff: $\max(0, 100 - 95) - 2 \times \max(0, 100 - 100) + \max(0, 100 - 105) - 2 = 5 - 0 + 0 - 2 = 3$ (maximum profit)

4. Underlying price at $103 (between middle and higher strike):

   - Payoff: $\max(0, 103 - 95) - 2 \times \max(0, 103 - 100) + \max(0, 103 - 105) - 2 = 8 - 6 + 0 - 2 = 0$

5. Underlying price at $110 (above higher strike):

   - Payoff: $\max(0, 110 - 95) - 2 \times \max(0, 110 - 100) + \max(0, 110 - 105) - 2 = 15 - 20 + 5 - 2 = -2$

Short Butterfly Spread – Payoff Calculation:

The payoff structure for a short butterfly spread is essentially the inverse of the long butterfly spread. In a short butterfly spread, maximum profit occurs when the underlying asset's price is outside the wings (below the lower strike or above the higher strike), and maximum loss occurs at the middle strike.

The payoff formula for a short butterfly spread can be summarized as:

$$ \text{Payoff} = -\left(\max(0, S - K_1) - 2 \times \max(0, S - K_2) + \max(0, S - K_3)\right) + \text{Initial Credit} $$

Visualizing P&L with Python

To illustrate the P&L characteristics of a butterfly spread, we will use Python to plot the payoff diagrams.

```python
import numpy as np
import matplotlib.pyplot as plt

# Define strike prices and initial cost
K1 = 95
K2 = 100
K3 = 105
initial_cost = 2

# Define the range of underlying prices at expiration
S = np.linspace(80, 120, 100)

# Calculate payoffs
payoff_long = np.maximum(0, S - K1) - 2 * np.maximum(0, S - K2) + np.maximum(0, S - K3) - initial_cost
payoff_short = -payoff_long + initial_cost

# Plotting the payoffs
plt.figure(figsize=(10, 6))
plt.plot(S, payoff_long, label='Long Butterfly Spread')
```

```python
plt.plot(S, payoff_short, label='Short Butterfly Spread')
plt.axhline(0, color='black', linestyle='--')
plt.axvline(K1, color='red', linestyle='--', label='Lower Strike Price (K1)')
plt.axvline(K2, color='green', linestyle='--', label='Middle Strike Price (K2)')
plt.axvline(K3, color='blue', linestyle='--', label='Higher Strike Price (K3)')
plt.xlabel('Underlying Asset Price at Expiration ($)')
plt.ylabel('Profit and Loss ($)')
plt.title('Profit and Loss Characteristics of Butterfly Spreads')
plt.legend()
plt.grid(True)
plt.show()
```

This script generates a clear visual representation of the P&L characteristics for both long and short butterfly spreads, helping traders understand the potential outcomes at various underlying prices.

Risk-Reward Ratio

Defining Risk-Reward Ratio in Butterfly Spreads

The risk-reward ratio is a fundamental concept in trading, quantifying the potential return of a trade relative to its risk. For butterfly spreads, this ratio is particularly beneficial because it encapsulates the strategy's nature—limited risk and limited reward.

Formula:

$$\text{Risk-Reward Ratio} = \frac{\text{Potential Profit}}{\text{Potential Loss}}$$

In a butterfly spread, the maximum risk is the initial cost of establishing the spread, while the maximum reward is the difference between the middle strike price and one of the wing strike prices, minus the net premium paid.

Constructing a Butterfly Spread to Analyze Risk-Reward

Consider an example where a trader constructs a long call butterfly spread on a stock currently trading at $100. The trader buys one call option with a strike price of $95, sells two call options with a strike price of $100, and buys one call option with a strike price of $105. Suppose the cost to enter this trade is $2 per share.

Maximum Potential Loss:

The maximum loss is the net premium paid for the spread, which in this case is $2 per share.

Maximum Potential Profit:

The maximum profit occurs if the stock price at expiration is equal to the middle strike price of $100. At that point, the profit is calculated as follows:

$$\text{Max Profit} = (100 - 95) - 2 = 3 \text{ per share}$$

Risk-Reward Ratio Calculation:

$$\text{Risk-Reward Ratio} = \frac{3}{2} = 1.5$$

This ratio indicates that for every dollar risked, the potential reward is $1.50.

Visualizing Profit and Loss

To further elucidate, let's visualize the payoff diagram for our butterfly spread. Using Python and `matplotlib`, we can plot this to gain a clear understanding of potential outcomes.

Python Code Example:

```python
import numpy as np
import matplotlib.pyplot as plt

# Stock price range
stock_prices = np.linspace(80, 120, 100)

# Strike prices
K1 = 95
K2 = 100
K3 = 105

# Premium paid for butterfly spread
premium = 2

# Payoff calculations
```

```
payoff = np.where(stock_prices <= K1, -premium,
          np.where(stock_prices <= K2, stock_prices - K1 -
premium,
            np.where(stock_prices    <=    K3,    K3    -
stock_prices - premium,
              -premium)))

# Plotting the payoff diagram
plt.plot(stock_prices, payoff, label='Butterfly Spread Payoff')
plt.axhline(0, color='black', linestyle='--')
plt.axvline(K1, color='red', linestyle='--', label='Strike Price 95')
plt.axvline(K2, color='green', linestyle='--', label='Strike Price
100')
plt.axvline(K3, color='blue', linestyle='--', label='Strike Price
105')
plt.xlabel('Stock Price at Expiration')
plt.ylabel('Profit/Loss')
plt.title('Butterfly Spread Payoff Diagram')
plt.legend()
plt.grid(True)
plt.show()
` ` `
```

This plot clarifies the profit and loss scenarios across different stock prices at expiration. The peak of the graph at the middle strike price ($100) shows the maximum profit, while the flat portions at the extremities demonstrate the limited risk.

Practical Considerations

While the risk-reward ratio provides a snapshot of potential outcomes, practical trading requires additional considerations:

1. Market Conditions: Understanding market volatility and direction is crucial. Butterfly spreads are often best employed in low-volatility environments where significant price movement is not expected.

2. Transaction Costs: Commissions and fees can impact the net profitability. Always account for these costs when calculating the risk-reward ratio.

3. Adjustment Strategies: Be prepared to adjust the spread if the market moves unfavorably. Adjustments can help mitigate losses or lock in profits, affecting the initial risk-reward assessment.

Case Study: Real-World Application

In a real-world scenario, suppose a trader anticipates that a tech company's stock, currently trading at $150, will remain stable around this price through the next earnings report. The trader sets up a long call butterfly spread with strikes at $145, $150, and $155, costing $1.50 per share.

Calculations:

- Maximum Loss: $1.50 (cost of the spread)
- Maximum Profit: $(150 - 145) - 1.50 = $3.50

Risk-Reward Ratio:

$$\text{Risk-Reward Ratio} = \frac{3.50}{1.50} \approx 2.33$$

This more favorable ratio suggests a greater potential reward relative to the risk, making it an attractive setup under the given market conditions.

Mastering the risk-reward ratio in butterfly spreads is a cornerstone of effective options trading. By comprehensively analyzing potential profits and losses, traders can make informed decisions, aligning their strategies with market conditions and personal risk tolerance. The balance of risk and reward, combined with practical application through Python, empowers traders to navigate the complex yet rewarding landscape of butterfly spreads with confidence and precision.

When to Use Butterfly Spread

Ideal Market Conditions for Butterfly Spreads

1. Low Volatility Environment: Butterfly spreads are most effective in markets where low volatility is expected. This strategy profits when the underlying asset's price remains close to the middle strike price. In such environments, significant price movements are unlikely, making the limited risk and reward structure of the butterfly spread advantageous.

2. Range-Bound Markets: When you anticipate that the underlying asset will trade within a specific range, butterfly spreads can be particularly effective. For example, if a stock has strong support and resistance levels, constructing a butterfly

spread with the middle strike price near the expected trading range capitalizes on this stability.

3. Earnings Announcements: Butterfly spreads can be strategically used around earnings announcements when you predict that the stock price will not swing dramatically after the report. This tactic allows you to benefit from the potential reduction in implied volatility post-announcement.

Analyzing Market Scenarios

Consider a scenario where a trader expects the stock of XYZ Corporation, currently trading at $50, to remain stable over the next month due to a combination of strong market support and low volatility. The trader might set up a butterfly spread with the following strike prices:

- Buy one call at $45

- Sell two calls at $50

- Buy one call at $55

Assume the cost to enter this trade is $1 per share.

Profit and Loss Analysis

Maximum Potential Loss:

The maximum loss for this butterfly spread is the net premium paid, which is $1 per share.

Maximum Potential Profit:

The maximum profit occurs if the stock price at expiration is exactly $50. The profit calculation is as follows:

$$\text{Max Profit} = (50 - 45) - 1 = 4 \text{ per share}$$

Risk-Reward Ratio:

$$\text{Risk-Reward Ratio} = \frac{4}{1} = 4$$

This ratio indicates that for every dollar risked, the potential reward is $4, making it a highly attractive setup in this context.

Real-World Example: Using Butterfly Spread in a Low Volatility Market

Let's take a practical example from the technology sector. Suppose Apple Inc. (AAPL) is trading at $150, and upcoming earnings are expected to be neutral, with analysts forecasting minimal price movement. A trader anticipates that AAPL will trade within a narrow range around $150 and sets up a long call butterfly spread:

- Buy one call at $145
- Sell two calls at $150
- Buy one call at $155

The cost to enter this trade is $2 per share.

If AAPL's stock price closes at $150 at expiration, the trader's profit calculation is:

$$\text{Max Profit} = (150 - 145) - 2 = 3 \text{ per share}$$

The trader's maximum loss remains the initial cost of $2 per share.

Utilising Python for Strategy Validation

To validate the potential outcomes of this butterfly spread, we can use Python to simulate various market scenarios and visualize the results.

Python Code Example:

```python
import numpy as np
import matplotlib.pyplot as plt

# Define stock price range
stock_prices = np.linspace(130, 170, 100)

# Define strike prices
K1 = 145
K2 = 150
K3 = 155

# Premium paid for the butterfly spread
premium = 2

# Calculate payoff
payoff = np.where(stock_prices <= K1, -premium,
            np.where(stock_prices <= K2, stock_prices - K1 -
```

premium,

np.where(stock_prices <= K3, K3 - stock_prices - premium,

-premium)))

```
# Plot the payoff diagram
plt.plot(stock_prices, payoff, label='Butterfly Spread Payoff')
plt.axhline(0, color='black', linestyle='--')
plt.axvline(K1, color='red', linestyle='--', label='Strike Price 145')
plt.axvline(K2, color='green', linestyle='--', label='Strike Price 150')
plt.axvline(K3, color='blue', linestyle='--', label='Strike Price 155')
plt.xlabel('Stock Price at Expiration')
plt.ylabel('Profit/Loss')
plt.title('Butterfly Spread Payoff Diagram for AAPL')
plt.legend()
plt.grid(True)
plt.show()
```
`` `

This payoff diagram provides a visual representation of potential profit and loss scenarios across a range of stock prices at expiration. The peak at $150 illustrates the maximum profit point, while the flat sections indicate the limited risk.

Key Considerations

1. Market Sentiment: Assessing market sentiment and anticipating low volatility are crucial. Butterfly spreads are not suited for highly volatile markets where large price swings could lead to significant losses.

2. Strike Price Selection: Choosing appropriate strike prices is essential. The middle strike price should be close to the expected stock price at expiration, while the wing strikes should be equidistant from the middle strike.

3. Time Decay (Theta): Butterfly spreads benefit from time decay, as the options approach expiration. However, ensure that the time frame aligns with your market predictions to maximize profitability.

4. Transaction Costs: Factor in transaction costs, as butterfly spreads involve multiple options. These costs can impact the net profitability of the trade.

Case Study: Short-Term Stability in a Financial Stock

Consider a scenario involving a financial stock, ABC Bank, currently trading at $100. The bank is poised to release its quarterly earnings, with analysts predicting minimal impact on the stock price due to stable financial performance. A trader anticipates that ABC Bank's stock will remain around $100 and sets up a butterfly spread with the following strikes:

- Buy one call at $95

- Sell two calls at $100

- Buy one call at $105

The cost to enter the trade is $1.50 per share.

Profit Calculation:

If ABC Bank's stock price closes at $100 at expiration, the trader's profit calculation is:

$$\text{Max Profit} = (100 - 95) - 1.50 = 3.50 \text{ per share}$$

Risk-Reward Ratio:

$$\text{Risk-Reward Ratio} = \frac{3.50}{1.50} \approx 2.33$$

This favorable ratio underscores the potential for substantial reward relative to the risk, making it a compelling strategy for this scenario.

Determining when to use a butterfly spread requires a keen understanding of market conditions, volatility expectations, and strategic planning. This strategy is best employed in stable, low-volatility environments where significant price movements are not anticipated. By leveraging Python for validation and meticulous planning, traders can optimize the use of butterfly spreads to achieve balanced and profitable trades, mitigating risk while maximizing potential rewards. Through careful analysis and practical application, butterfly spreads become a powerful tool in the trader's arsenal, adept at navigating the complexities of options trading with precision and confidence.

Comparing Butterfly Spread with Other Strategies

Butterfly Spread versus Vertical Spreads

Definition and Structure:

- Vertical Spread: A vertical spread involves buying and selling options of the same type (either calls or puts) with different strike prices but the same expiration date. Common types include bull call spreads and bear put spreads.

- Butterfly Spread: This strategy constructs a position by purchasing one option at the lower strike price, selling two options at the middle strike price, and buying one option at the higher strike price, all with the same expiration date.

Risk and Reward:

- Vertical Spread: Typically, a vertical spread limits both the maximum profit and maximum loss, offering a favorable risk-reward ratio in trending markets. For instance, in a bull call spread, the maximum loss is limited to the net premium paid, while the maximum profit is the difference between the strike prices minus the net premium.

- Butterfly Spread: The butterfly spread also limits both potential profit and loss. However, it is most effective in stable, low-volatility environments where the underlying asset's price remains close to the middle strike at expiration.

Example Comparison:

Consider XYZ stock, trading at $50.

- Bull Call Spread: Buy a $50 call for $3 and sell a $55 call for $1. The net premium paid is $2.

- Butterfly Spread: Buy a $45 call for $5, sell two $50 calls for $3 each, and buy a $55 call for $1. The net premium paid is $1.

Payoff Analysis:

- Bull Call Spread:
  - Maximum Profit: $5 - $2 = $3 per share
  - Maximum Loss: $2 per share
- Butterfly Spread:
  - Maximum Profit: $5 - $1 = $4 per share
  - Maximum Loss: $1 per share

While the bull call spread offers a straightforward approach in a bullish market, the butterfly spread provides a more nuanced strategy for capturing profits in a narrow price range.

Butterfly Spread versus Iron Condor

Definition and Structure:

- Iron Condor: This strategy combines a bull put spread and a bear call spread, creating a position with four strike prices. It involves selling one put with a lower strike, buying one put with an even lower strike, selling one call with a higher strike, and buying one call with an even higher strike.

- Butterfly Spread: As previously defined, involves three strike prices with a symmetric structure around the middle strike.

Risk and Reward:

- Iron Condor: An iron condor profits in stable, low-volatility markets, much like the butterfly spread. The main difference lies in the wider range of profit, as the iron condor benefits if the underlying asset's price remains between the two middle strikes.

- Butterfly Spread: Offers a narrower profit range but potentially higher maximum profit relative to the net premium paid.

Example Comparison:

Consider AAPL, trading at $150.

- Iron Condor: Sell a $140 put for $2, buy a $135 put for $1, sell a $160 call for $2, and buy a $165 call for $1. The net premium received is $2.
- Butterfly Spread: Buy a $145 call for $5, sell two $150 calls for $3 each, and buy a $155 call for $1. The net premium paid is $1.

Payoff Analysis:

- Iron Condor:

  - Maximum Profit: Net premium received = $2 per share

  - Maximum Loss: Difference between the strikes minus the net premium = $3 per share

- Butterfly Spread:

  - Maximum Profit: Difference between strikes minus net premium = $5 - $1 = $4 per share

  - Maximum Loss: Net premium paid = $1 per share

The iron condor provides a wider profit range, catering to traders expecting minimal price movement within a broader range, while the butterfly spread targets precision around the middle strike.

Butterfly Spread versus Straddle

Definition and Structure:

- Straddle: A straddle involves buying a call and a put with the same strike price and expiration date. It is designed to profit from significant price movements in either direction.

- Butterfly Spread: Designed to profit from minimal price movement, the butterfly spread captures gains if the underlying asset remains near the middle strike price.

Risk and Reward:

- Straddle: High potential profit if the underlying asset experiences significant volatility. The maximum loss is limited to the total premium paid, which can be substantial.

- Butterfly Spread: Limited risk and reward, optimal for low-volatility environments. The maximum loss is the net premium paid, which is typically lower than that of a straddle.

Example Comparison:

Consider ABC Bank, trading at $100.

- Straddle: Buy a $100 call for $4 and a $100 put for $3. The total premium paid is $7.

- Butterfly Spread: Buy a $95 call for $3, sell two $100 calls for $2 each, and buy a $105 call for $1. The net premium paid is $1.

Payoff Analysis:

- Straddle:

  - Maximum Profit: Unlimited (if the price moves significantly in either direction)

  - Maximum Loss: Total premium paid = $7 per share

- Butterfly Spread:

 - Maximum Profit: Difference between strikes minus net premium = $5 - $1 = $4 per share

 - Maximum Loss: Net premium paid = $1 per share

Straddles are suitable for traders anticipating high volatility, whereas butterfly spreads are ideal for those expecting stability.

Utilizing Python for Comparative Analysis

To compare these strategies under various market conditions, we can use Python to simulate their payoffs and visualize the results.

Python Code Example:

```python
import numpy as np
import matplotlib.pyplot as plt

# Define stock price range
stock_prices = np.linspace(80, 120, 100)

# Define strike prices and premiums
K1, K2, K3 = 95, 100, 105
premium_straddle = 7
premium_butterfly = 1

# Calculate payoffs
```

```
payoff_straddle = np.maximum(stock_prices - 100, 0) +
np.maximum(100 - stock_prices, 0) - premium_straddle

payoff_butterfly = np.where(stock_prices <= K1, -
premium_butterfly,

                np.where(stock_prices <= K2, stock_prices -
K1 - premium_butterfly,

                    np.where(stock_prices <= K3, K3 -
stock_prices - premium_butterfly,

                        -premium_butterfly)))


# Plot the payoff diagrams

plt.plot(stock_prices, payoff_straddle, label='Straddle Payoff')

plt.plot(stock_prices, payoff_butterfly, label='Butterfly Spread
Payoff')

plt.axhline(0, color='black', linestyle='--')

plt.xlabel('Stock Price at Expiration')

plt.ylabel('Profit/Loss')

plt.title('Comparison of Straddle and Butterfly Spread Payoffs')

plt.legend()

plt.grid(True)

plt.show()
` ` `
```

The resulting plot clearly illustrates the different payoff structures, with the straddle showing high potential profits for significant price movements and the butterfly spread highlighting the peak profit around the middle strike.

Choosing the right options strategy hinges on market

conditions, volatility expectations, and individual risk tolerance. The butterfly spread stands out for its precision in stable environments, offering a unique risk-reward profile. By comparing it to vertical spreads, iron condors, and straddles, traders gain a comprehensive understanding of where and when to deploy each strategy. Using tools like Python to model and visualize these strategies enhances strategic planning, equipping traders with the insights needed for effective decision-making in the dynamic world of options trading.

Real-World Examples

Case Study 1: Earnings Season Stability

Scenario:

TechCorp, a leading technology company, is set to announce its quarterly earnings. Historically, the stock price has demonstrated minimal movement post-earnings, making it an ideal candidate for a butterfly spread strategy.

Market Conditions:

- Current stock price (S): $150

- Expected volatility: Low

- Time to expiration: 30 days

Strategy Execution:

1. Strike Price Selection:

   - Buy 1 call option at $145 for $6

   - Sell 2 call options at $150 for $3 each

   - Buy 1 call option at $155 for $1

   - Net premium paid: $6 - $6 + $1 = $1

2. Payoff Analysis:

Using Python, we visualize the potential payoff at expiration.

```python
import numpy as np
import matplotlib.pyplot as plt

# Define stock price range
stock_prices = np.linspace(140, 160, 100)

# Define strike prices and premiums
K1, K2, K3 = 145, 150, 155
premium = 1

# Calculate payoff for each strike price
payoff = np.where(stock_prices <= K1, -premium,
            np.where(stock_prices <= K2, stock_prices - K1 -
premium,
                np.where(stock_prices <= K3, K3 -
stock_prices - premium,
                    -premium)))

# Plot the payoff diagram
plt.plot(stock_prices, payoff, label='Butterfly Spread Payoff')
plt.axhline(0, color='black', linestyle='--')
plt.xlabel('Stock Price at Expiration')
plt.ylabel('Profit/Loss')
```

```
plt.title('Butterfly Spread Payoff for TechCorp')
plt.legend()
plt.grid(True)
plt.show()
```
` ` `

3. Outcome:

   - Maximum profit occurs if TechCorp's stock closes at $150, resulting in a $4 profit per share (difference between strikes minus premium).

   - Maximum loss is limited to the net premium paid, $1 per share.

Analysis:

This example highlights how a butterfly spread can capitalize on an expected period of low volatility around an earnings announcement. The strategy limits risk while offering a substantial reward if the stock price remains near the central strike price.

Case Study 2: Pre-Event Anticipation

Scenario:

Global Pharma is awaiting FDA approval for a new drug. Market sentiment predicts minimal price movement until the announcement, making it another suitable candidate for a butterfly spread.

Market Conditions:

- Current stock price (S): $100

- Expected volatility: Low until FDA announcement

- Time to expiration: 45 days

Strategy Execution:

1. Strike Price Selection:

   - Buy 1 put option at $95 for $4

   - Sell 2 put options at $100 for $2.50 each

   - Buy 1 put option at $105 for $1

   - Net premium paid: $4 - $5 + $1 = $0

2. Payoff Analysis:

   Visualizing the potential payoff at expiration using Python.

```python
# Define stock price range
stock_prices = np.linspace(90, 110, 100)

# Define strike prices and premiums
K1, K2, K3 = 95, 100, 105
premium = 0

# Calculate payoff for each strike price
payoff = np.where(stock_prices <= K1, K1 - stock_prices - premium,
            np.where(stock_prices <= K2, stock_prices - K1 - premium,
                np.where(stock_prices <= K3, K3 - stock_prices - premium,
                    -premium)))
```

```
# Plot the payoff diagram
plt.plot(stock_prices, payoff, label='Butterfly Spread Payoff')
plt.axhline(0, color='black', linestyle='--')
plt.xlabel('Stock Price at Expiration')
plt.ylabel('Profit/Loss')
plt.title('Butterfly Spread Payoff for Global Pharma')
plt.legend()
plt.grid(True)
plt.show()
```

3. Outcome:

- Maximum profit occurs if Global Pharma's stock closes at $100, yielding a $5 profit per share.

- Maximum loss is negligible, as the net premium paid is zero.

Analysis:

In scenarios where market price is anticipated to remain stable until a significant event, the butterfly spread provides a strategic option with minimal risk and potential high reward, leveraging market stability.

Case Study 3: Post-Market Correction

Scenario:

Following a significant market correction, MegaBank's stock has stabilized. The market sentiment suggests low volatility in the coming weeks, providing an opportunity for a butterfly spread.

Market Conditions:
- Current stock price (S): $200
- Expected volatility: Low post-correction
- Time to expiration: 60 days

Strategy Execution:
1. Strike Price Selection:
    - Buy 1 call option at $190 for $12
    - Sell 2 call options at $200 for $8 each
    - Buy 1 call option at $210 for $5
    - Net premium paid: $12 - $16 + $5 = $1

2. Payoff Analysis:
    Using Python for visualization.

```python
# Define stock price range
stock_prices = np.linspace(180, 220, 100)

# Define strike prices and premiums
K1, K2, K3 = 190, 200, 210
premium = 1

# Calculate payoff for each strike price
payoff = np.where(stock_prices <= K1, -premium,
            np.where(stock_prices <= K2, stock_prices - K1 -
premium,
```

```
                np.where(stock_prices <= K3, K3 -
stock_prices - premium,

                -premium)))

# Plot the payoff diagram
plt.plot(stock_prices, payoff, label='Butterfly Spread Payoff')
plt.axhline(0, color='black', linestyle='--')
plt.xlabel('Stock Price at Expiration')
plt.ylabel('Profit/Loss')
plt.title('Butterfly Spread Payoff for MegaBank')
plt.legend()
plt.grid(True)
plt.show()
```
```

3. Outcome:

   - Maximum profit occurs if MegaBank's stock closes at $200, resulting in a $9 profit per share.

   - Maximum loss is limited to the net premium paid, $1 per share.

Analysis:

Post-market correction scenarios can be leveraged using butterfly spreads to capitalize on expected low volatility. This approach minimizes risk while targeting significant profits if the stock remains near the central strike price.

Practical Insights

Risk Management:
```

- Diversification: Employing butterfly spreads on multiple stocks or sectors can mitigate risk.

- Adjustments: Rolling strike prices or expiration dates can enhance flexibility in volatile markets.

Market Sentiment Analysis:

- News Monitoring: Staying informed on macroeconomic indicators and company-specific news can guide strike price selection and timing.

- Volatility Indicators: Utilizing tools like the VIX (Volatility Index) can help assess market conditions suitable for butterfly spreads.

Utilizing Technology:

- Python Scripts: Automating the monitoring and execution of butterfly spreads using Python can reduce human error and increase efficiency.

- Real-time Data: Integrating real-time data feeds into Python models ensures timely and accurate decision-making.

Real-world examples underscore the butterfly spread's adaptability and efficacy in various market conditions. By examining practical scenarios, you gain a profound understanding of the strategy's application, enhancing your ability to deploy it effectively. Leveraging Python for modeling and visualization further empowers you to make informed decisions, optimizing your trading strategy in the intricate world of options trading.

CHAPTER 3: THEORETICAL FOUNDATIONS OF BUTTERFLY SPREAD

U nderstanding options pricing models is fundamental to mastering the butterfly spread strategy. Two pivotal models, the Black-Scholes model and the Binomial model, serve as the backbone of modern options pricing theory. Both models provide a framework for valuing options, but each has its own unique approach and application.

The Black-Scholes Model

Developed by Fischer Black, Myron Scholes, and Robert Merton in the early 1970s, the Black-Scholes model revolutionized options pricing. It provides a closed-form solution for European-style options, which can only be exercised at expiration. The model is based on the following assumptions:

1. The underlying asset follows a geometric Brownian motion

with constant volatility and drift.

2. There are no dividends paid out during the life of the option.

3. Markets are frictionless, with no transaction costs or taxes.

4. The risk-free rate is constant and known.

5. There are no arbitrage opportunities.

The Black-Scholes formula for a European call option is given by:

$$ C = S_0 N(d_1) - X e^{-rT} N(d_2) $$

Where:

- C is the call option price
- S_0 is the current price of the underlying asset
- X is the strike price
- r is the risk-free interest rate
- T is the time to expiration
- $N(\cdot)$ is the cumulative distribution function of the standard normal distribution
- d_1 and d_2 are calculated as follows:

$$ d_1 = \frac{\ln(S_0/X) + (r + \sigma^2/2)T}{\sigma \sqrt{T}} $$

$$ d_2 = d_1 - \sigma \sqrt{T} $$

Here, σ represents the volatility of the underlying asset.

Example: Calculating a Call Option Price

Consider a stock currently priced at $100. The strike price of the call option is $105, the risk-free rate is 5%, the time to expiration is 1 year, and the volatility of the stock is 20%. Using the Black-Scholes formula, we can calculate the price of the call option:

```python
import numpy as np
from scipy.stats import norm

# Given parameters
S0 = 100  # Current stock price
X = 105   # Strike price
r = 0.05  # Risk-free rate
T = 1     # Time to expiration (1 year)
sigma = 0.20  # Volatility of the stock

# Calculate d1 and d2
d1 = (np.log(S0 / X) + (r + 0.5 * sigma2) * T) / (sigma * np.sqrt(T))
d2 = d1 - sigma * np.sqrt(T)

# Calculate the call option price
call_price = S0 * norm.cdf(d1) - X * np.exp(-r * T) * norm.cdf(d2)
print(f"The price of the European call option is: ${call_price:.2f}")
```

Running this code yields the call option price.

The Binomial Model

The Binomial model, introduced by Cox, Ross, and Rubinstein in 1979, provides a discrete-time framework for options pricing. It is particularly useful for American-style options, which can be exercised at any time before expiration. The model operates by dividing the time to expiration into n discrete intervals, creating a binomial tree of possible stock prices.

Each node in the binomial tree represents a possible price of the underlying asset at a given point in time. The model assumes that at each step, the stock price can either move up by a factor u or down by a factor d. The probability of an upward move is p, and the probability of a downward move is $1 - p$.

The up and down factors are calculated as follows:

$$u = e^{\sigma \sqrt{\Delta t}}$$
$$d = e^{-\sigma \sqrt{\Delta t}}$$

Where $\Delta t = \frac{T}{n}$ is the length of each time step.

The risk-neutral probability p is given by:

$$p = \frac{e^{r \Delta t} - d}{u - d}$$

Using the binomial tree, we can recursively calculate the option price at each node, starting from the final nodes at expiration and working backward to the present value.

Example: Calculating a Call Option Price Using the Binomial Model

Consider the same stock as in the Black-Scholes example, with the same parameters. We'll use a 3-step binomial tree to calculate the call option price.

```python
import numpy as np

# Given parameters
S0 = 100  # Current stock price
X = 105   # Strike price
r = 0.05  # Risk-free rate
T = 1     # Time to expiration (1 year)
sigma = 0.20  # Volatility of the stock
n = 3     # Number of steps

# Calculate parameters for the binomial model
dt = T / n
u = np.exp(sigma * np.sqrt(dt))
d = np.exp(-sigma * np.sqrt(dt))
p = (np.exp(r * dt) - d) / (u - d)

# Initialize asset prices at maturity
ST = np.zeros((n + 1, n + 1))
for i in range(n + 1):
    for j in range(i + 1):
```

```
    ST[i, j] = S0 * (uj) * (d(i - j))
```

```
# Initialize option values at maturity
option_values = np.maximum(ST - X, 0)
```

```
# Backward induction to calculate option price
for i in range(n - 1, -1, -1):
    for j in range(i + 1):
        option_values[i, j] = np.exp(-r * dt) * (p * option_values[i +
1, j + 1] + (1 - p) * option_values[i + 1, j])
```

```
call_price = option_values[0, 0]
print(f"The price of the European call option using the
Binomial model is: ${call_price:.2f}")
```
```

Running this code yields the call option price using the Binomial model.

Comparing the Models

While both models are powerful tools for pricing options, they have distinct differences and applications:

- Black-Scholes Model:

  - Assumes constant volatility and interest rates.

  - Provides a closed-form solution for European options.

  - Less flexible for pricing American options or options with dividends.
```

- Binomial Model:

  - Can handle varying volatility and interest rates.

  - Suitable for American options, providing discrete-time stepping for early exercise.

  - Easier to adapt for options with complex features, such as dividends.

Leveraging the strengths of both models, traders can make informed decisions when pricing options and developing strategies like the butterfly spread. Understanding these models not only enhances theoretical knowledge but also equips traders with practical tools for navigating the intricacies of options trading.

In the next section, we will delve into the Greeks—key sensitivities that measure the risk associated with options and provide deeper insights into the dynamics of options pricing and strategies.

Understanding Greeks: Delta, Gamma, Theta, Vega

The Greeks play a crucial role in options trading, providing essential insights into how various factors influence the price of an option. These sensitivities—Delta, Gamma, Theta, and Vega—serve as the foundation for managing the risk and rewards associated with options positions. Mastering the Greeks enables traders to optimize their strategies, making them vital tools in the arsenal of any options trader.

Delta (Δ)

Delta measures the sensitivity of an option's price to changes in the price of the underlying asset. It represents the rate of change of the option's value with respect to a $1 change in the underlying asset's price.

For call options, Delta ranges from 0 to 1, while for put options, Delta ranges from -1 to 0. A higher Delta indicates a greater sensitivity to price changes in the underlying asset.

$$ \Delta = \frac{\partial C}{\partial S} $$

Where:

- C is the call option price

- S is the price of the underlying asset

Example: Calculating Delta

Consider a call option with a current Delta of 0.5. If the stock price increases by $2, the option's price is expected to increase by approximately $1 (0.5 * $2).

```python
# Given parameters
stock_price = 100 # Current stock price
delta = 0.5 # Delta of the call option
price_change = 2 # Change in stock price

# Calculate the change in option price
option_price_change = delta * price_change
print(f"The change in the option price is: $
{option_price_change:.2f}")
```

` ` `

Running this code demonstrates how the option's price responds to changes in the stock price.

Gamma (Γ)

Gamma measures the rate of change of Delta with respect to changes in the underlying asset's price. It provides insight into the curvature of the option's value curve and helps traders understand how Delta will change as the underlying asset's price fluctuates.

\[\Gamma = \frac{\partial^2 C}{\partial S^2} \]

Gamma is highest for at-the-money options and decreases as the options move further in or out of the money.

Example: Understanding Gamma

Consider a call option with a Gamma of 0.1. If the stock price increases by $2, the Delta is expected to increase by 0.2 (0.1 * $2).

```python
# Given parameters
gamma = 0.1  # Gamma of the call option
price_change = 2  # Change in stock price

# Calculate the change in Delta
delta_change = gamma * price_change
```

```
print(f"The change in Delta is: {delta_change:.2f}")
```
` ` `

This example shows how Gamma affects the Delta of an option, providing a more dynamic view of the option's sensitivity to the underlying asset's price changes.

Theta (Θ)

Theta measures the sensitivity of an option's price to the passage of time. It represents the rate of decline in the option's value as time progresses, also known as time decay. Theta is typically negative for long options positions because the option's time value erodes as expiration approaches.

\[\Theta = \frac{\partial C}{\partial t} \]

Where:
- \(t \) is the time to expiration

Example: Calculating Theta

Consider a call option with a Theta of -0.05. This means the option's price is expected to decrease by $0.05 for each day that passes.

` ` `python
# Given parameters
theta = -0.05 # Theta of the call option
days_passed = 1 # Number of days that passed

Calculate the change in option price

option_price_change = theta * days_passed

print(f"The change in the option price due to time decay is: ${option_price_change:.2f}")

` ` `

This example illustrates the impact of time decay on an option's price, highlighting the importance of managing Theta in options trading.

Vega (v)

Vega measures the sensitivity of an option's price to changes in the volatility of the underlying asset. It represents the amount by which the option's price changes for a 1% change in the underlying asset's volatility.

$$\nu = \frac{\partial C}{\partial \sigma}$$

Where:

- σ is the volatility of the underlying asset

Vega is highest for at-the-money options and decreases for in-the-money and out-of-the-money options.

Example: Calculating Vega

Consider a call option with a Vega of 0.2. If the volatility of the underlying asset increases by 5%, the option's price is expected to increase by $1 (0.2 * 5).

```python
# Given parameters
vega = 0.2  # Vega of the call option
volatility_change = 5  # Change in volatility (percentage)

# Calculate the change in option price
option_price_change = vega * volatility_change
print(f"The change in the option price due to volatility change is: ${option_price_change:.2f}")
```

This example demonstrates how volatility affects an option's price through Vega, underscoring the need to account for volatility when trading options.

Practical Applications of the Greeks

Understanding the Greeks is crucial for managing the risk and optimizing the performance of options strategies, including the butterfly spread. Here are some practical applications:

1. Delta Neutral Hedging: Traders can use Delta to create a Delta-neutral portfolio, minimizing the directional risk. For instance, if a portfolio has a total Delta of 100, the trader can hedge by shorting 100 shares of the underlying asset.

2. Dynamic Adjustments with Gamma: Monitoring Gamma helps traders adjust their positions dynamically. When Gamma is high, small movements in the underlying asset's price can lead to significant changes in Delta, requiring frequent rebalancing.

3. Managing Time Decay with Theta: Theta is essential for options with approaching expiration. Traders can use Theta to manage positions by understanding the impact of time decay on their options' value, particularly for strategies like the butterfly spread that involve multiple options with different expiration times.

4. Volatility Trading with Vega: Vega plays a significant role in strategies that rely on volatility predictions. For instance, traders can design strategies to profit from expected increases or decreases in volatility, adjusting their positions based on Vega to maximize returns.

The Greeks—Delta, Gamma, Theta, and Vega—are indispensable tools for options traders. By understanding and utilizing these sensitivities, traders can better manage the risk and rewards associated with their strategies. Whether hedging against price movements, adjusting for time decay, or capitalizing on volatility changes, the Greeks provide the insights necessary for informed decision-making in the complex world of options trading. As we continue to explore advanced strategies like the butterfly spread, mastering the Greeks will serve as a cornerstone for success.

Implied Volatility and Its Impact

Implied volatility (IV) is a critical concept in options trading, reflecting the market's expectations of future volatility of the underlying asset. Unlike historical volatility, which measures past price movements, implied volatility provides a forward-looking projection, making it an essential tool for pricing options and managing risks.

Understanding Implied Volatility

Implied volatility is derived from the market price of an option rather than being directly observable. It is the volatility value that, when input into an options pricing model (such as Black-Scholes), yields the current market price of the option. Essentially, IV indicates the market's consensus on how volatile the asset will be over the option's life.

$$IV = \sigma_{implied}$$

Where:
- $\sigma_{implied}$ is the implied volatility

High implied volatility suggests that the market expects significant price movements, while low implied volatility indicates expectations of relatively stable prices.

Example: Calculating Implied Volatility

Consider a call option priced at $5 for a stock trading at $100 with 30 days to expiration. Using the Black-Scholes model, you input all variables except volatility and solve for the implied value that matches the market price.

```python
from scipy.optimize import minimize
from scipy.stats import norm
import numpy as np

# Given parameters
```

```
S = 100  # Current stock price
K = 100  # Strike price
T = 30 / 365  # Time to expiration in years
r = 0.01  # Risk-free interest rate
market_price = 5  # Market price of the option

# Black-Scholes call price formula
def black_scholes_call_price(S, K, T, r, sigma):
    d1 = (np.log(S / K) + (r + 0.5 * sigma2) * T) / (sigma * np.sqrt(T))
    d2 = d1 - sigma * np.sqrt(T)
    call_price = S * norm.cdf(d1) - K * np.exp(-r * T) * norm.cdf(d2)
    return call_price

# Objective function to minimize
def objective_function(sigma):
- market_price)2

# Find the implied volatility
result = minimize(objective_function, x0=0.2, bounds=[(0.01, 3.0)])
implied_volatility = result.x[0]
print(f"The implied volatility is: {implied_volatility:.2%}")
```

This script uses numerical methods to find the implied volatility, showcasing how traders can estimate IV using Python.

Impact of Implied Volatility on Options Pricing

Implied volatility directly influences the premium of an option. Higher IV leads to higher option premiums because the potential for significant price moves increases the likelihood of the option ending in-the-money. Conversely, lower IV results in lower premiums.

For example, consider two options with the same strike price and expiration but different implied volatilities. The option with higher IV will have a higher price, reflecting the greater expected price fluctuation of the underlying asset.

Practical Applications of Implied Volatility

Implied volatility serves as a crucial metric for several trading strategies and risk management practices:

1. Volatility Trading: Traders often speculate on changes in IV using strategies like straddles or strangles, which are designed to profit from increased volatility regardless of the direction of the price movement.

2. Volatility Skew Analysis: IV is not uniform across all strike prices and expirations, leading to the concept of the volatility skew or smile, which can provide insights into market sentiment and potential price movements.

3. Options Pricing and Strategy Selection: By understanding the current level of IV, traders can make informed decisions about which strategies to employ. For instance, in a high-IV environment, selling options (such as covered calls) might be

more attractive due to the higher premiums received.

4. Risk Management: Monitoring IV helps traders manage the risk and adjust their positions accordingly. Sudden spikes in IV can signal potential market instability, prompting risk-averse actions such as hedging.

Example: Volatility Skew Analysis

Suppose we want to analyze the volatility skew of a stock's options with different strike prices but the same expiration.

```python
import matplotlib.pyplot as plt

# Sample data for different strike prices
strike_prices = [90, 95, 100, 105, 110]
implied_vols = [0.25, 0.22, 0.20, 0.23, 0.27]  # Hypothetical IV values

plt.plot(strike_prices, implied_vols, marker='o')
plt.title('Implied Volatility Skew')
plt.xlabel('Strike Price')
plt.ylabel('Implied Volatility')
plt.grid(True)
plt.show()
```

This visualization helps traders identify the skew and make decisions based on the shape of the IV curve.

Implied Volatility in Butterfly Spreads

In the context of a butterfly spread, implied volatility plays a significant role in strategy performance. A butterfly spread, which involves buying and selling options at multiple strike prices, is sensitive to changes in IV:

- Low IV Environment: Butterfly spreads generally perform well when IV is low because the underlying asset's price is expected to remain stable, increasing the probability of the spread expiring close to the central strike price.
- High IV Environment: In high-IV conditions, butterfly spreads are less attractive due to the increased potential for significant price swings, which can move the underlying asset away from the profitable zone of the spread.

Example: Butterfly Spread in Different IV Scenarios

Consider constructing a butterfly spread with the following options:

- Buy 1 call option at strike price $100
- Sell 2 call options at strike price $105
- Buy 1 call option at strike price $110

We can simulate how changes in IV affect the profitability of this spread.

```python
# Given parameters for calculating option prices using Black-Scholes
```

```python
def calculate_option_price(S, K, T, r, sigma, option_type='call'):
    d1 = (np.log(S / K) + (r + 0.5 * sigma2) * T) / (sigma * np.sqrt(T))
    d2 = d1 - sigma * np.sqrt(T)
    if option_type == 'call':
        price = S * norm.cdf(d1) - K * np.exp(-r * T) * norm.cdf(d2)
    else:
        price = K * np.exp(-r * T) * norm.cdf(-d2) - S * norm.cdf(-d1)
    return price


# Parameters
S = 105  # Current stock price
K1 = 100  # Lower strike price
K2 = 105  # Middle strike price
K3 = 110  # Upper strike price
T = 30 / 365  # Time to expiration in years
r = 0.01  # Risk-free interest rate


# Different IV scenarios
iv_scenarios = [0.15, 0.20, 0.25]


for sigma in iv_scenarios:
    option1_price = calculate_option_price(S, K1, T, r, sigma)
    option2_price = calculate_option_price(S, K2, T, r, sigma)
    option3_price = calculate_option_price(S, K3, T, r, sigma)

    butterfly_spread_cost = option1_price - 2 * option2_price + option3_price
```

```
    print(f"IV: {sigma:.2%}  |  Butterfly Spread Cost: $
{butterfly_spread_cost:.2f}")
` ` `
```

This script demonstrates how different levels of IV impact the cost and potential profitability of a butterfly spread.

Implied volatility is a pivotal component in the world of options trading, influencing option prices, trading strategies, and risk management practices. By mastering the concept of IV and its applications, traders can gain a significant edge in the market. Whether through direct volatility trading or using IV as a guide for strategy adjustments, understanding and leveraging implied volatility is essential for achieving success in the dynamic landscape of options trading.

and Its Effects on Strategies

Time decay, commonly represented by the Greek letter Theta (Θ), is a crucial concept in options trading that significantly impacts the profitability and risk of strategies. Theta measures the rate at which an option's value declines as it approaches its expiration date, highlighting the temporal dimension of options pricing. Understanding and managing Theta is essential for developing and executing effective trading strategies.

Understanding Theta

Theta represents the extrinsic value decay of an option as

time progresses. It quantifies the erosion of an option's price due to the passage of time, holding other factors constant. Mathematically, Theta is expressed as the change in the option's price per day of time decay:

$$\Theta = \frac{\partial C}{\partial t}$$

Where:
- Θ is Theta
- C is the option price
- t is time to expiration

Theta is generally negative, indicating that options lose value as expiration nears. The decay accelerates as the option gets closer to its expiration date, particularly for at-the-money (ATM) options, which tend to have the highest Theta values.

Example: Calculating Theta

Consider a call option on a stock priced at $100 with a strike price of $100, 30 days to expiration, and an implied volatility of 20%. The risk-free rate is 1%. We can compute the Theta using the Black-Scholes model.

```python
from scipy.stats import norm
import numpy as np

# Given parameters
S = 100  # Current stock price
K = 100  # Strike price
```

```python
T = 30 / 365  # Time to expiration in years
r = 0.01  # Risk-free interest rate
sigma = 0.20  # Implied volatility

# Black-Scholes Theta formula for a call option
def black_scholes_theta(S, K, T, r, sigma):
    d1 = (np.log(S / K) + (r + 0.5 * sigma2) * T) / (sigma * np.sqrt(T))
    d2 = d1 - sigma * np.sqrt(T)
    theta = (- (S * sigma * norm.pdf(d1)) / (2 * np.sqrt(T))
            - r * K * np.exp(-r * T) * norm.cdf(d2)) / 365
    return theta

theta = black_scholes_theta(S, K, T, r, sigma)
print(f"The Theta of the call option is: {theta:.4f} per day")
```

This computation provides the daily rate of time decay for the specified option, illustrating how much value it loses each day due to the passage of time.

Impact of Theta on Different Options Strategies

Theta affects various options strategies differently, depending on their structure and objectives. Here are some common strategies and how they interact with Theta:

1. Long Options (Calls and Puts):

   - Long Call: Buying a call option exposes the trader to negative Theta, meaning the option will lose value daily. This decay is detrimental unless the underlying asset's price moves significantly in favor of the option holder.

- Long Put: Similarly, buying a put option incurs negative Theta. The option's value decreases with time, requiring a substantial downward move in the underlying asset to offset the time decay.

2. Short Options (Calls and Puts):

- Short Call: Writing a call option benefits from positive Theta. The option writer gains as time decay erodes the option's value, provided the underlying asset's price does not rise significantly.

- Short Put: Selling a put option also results in positive Theta, where the option writer profits from the diminishing value of the put as expiration approaches, assuming the underlying asset does not fall sharply.

3. Spreads:

- Vertical Spreads: These involve buying and selling options at different strike prices but the same expiration. The net Theta depends on the relative positions. For instance, in a bull call spread (buying a lower strike call and selling a higher strike call), the trader benefits from the positive Theta of the sold call reducing the overall negative Theta of the strategy.

and buying a longer-term option (with lower Theta). The strategy profits from the faster decay of the near-term option relative to the longer-term option.

4. Butterfly Spreads:

- Long Butterfly: This strategy, consisting of buying one option at a lower strike, selling two options at a middle strike, and buying one option at an upper strike, generally has a low net Theta. The central (sold) options' high Theta offsets the outer (bought) options' lower Theta. The strategy profits from low volatility and time decay when the underlying asset's price remains near the middle strike.

- Short Butterfly: Conversely, a short butterfly spread, which involves selling one lower strike option, buying two middle strike options, and selling one upper strike option, has a net positive Theta. This strategy benefits from time decay when the underlying asset's price stays away from the middle strike.

Example: Theta in a Long Butterfly Spread

Consider constructing a long butterfly spread with the following options:

- Buy 1 call option at strike price $95
- Sell 2 call options at strike price $100
- Buy 1 call option at strike price $105

We can analyze the net Theta of this spread.

```python
# Given parameters for calculating option prices using Black-Scholes
def calculate_theta(S, K, T, r, sigma, option_type='call'):
    d1 = (np.log(S / K) + (r + 0.5 * sigma2) * T) / (sigma * np.sqrt(T))
    d2 = d1 - sigma * np.sqrt(T)
    theta = (- (S * sigma * norm.pdf(d1)) / (2 * np.sqrt(T))
        - r * K * np.exp(-r * T) * norm.cdf(d2)) / 365
    return theta
```

```
# Parameters
S = 100  # Current stock price
K1 = 95  # Lower strike price
K2 = 100  # Middle strike price
K3 = 105  # Upper strike price
T = 30 / 365  # Time to expiration in years
r = 0.01  # Risk-free interest rate
sigma = 0.20  # Implied volatility

# Calculate Thetas
theta1 = calculate_theta(S, K1, T, r, sigma)
theta2 = calculate_theta(S, K2, T, r, sigma)
theta3 = calculate_theta(S, K3, T, r, sigma)

# Net Theta for the long butterfly spread
net_theta = theta1 - 2 * theta2 + theta3
print(f"The net Theta of the long butterfly spread is: {net_theta:.4f} per day")
```

This calculation demonstrates the cumulative effect of Theta on a butterfly spread, illustrating how the strategy's value decays over time.

Practical Considerations for Managing Theta

Effectively managing Theta is vital for optimizing options trading strategies. Here are some practical considerations:

1. Monitoring Time Decay: Regularly assessing Theta helps traders understand the expected daily decay and adjust their positions accordingly. Tools and software that provide real-time Theta values are invaluable for staying informed.

or volatility risk (Vegcan lead to suboptimal outcomes.

3. Timing Strategies: Implementing options strategies with a clear understanding of time decay helps in timing entries and exits. For instance, entering a long call position too early can result in significant Theta losses if the underlying asset's price does not move quickly enough.

4. Adjusting Positions: Traders can adjust their positions to manage Theta risk. For example, converting a long option to a spread can reduce net Theta and mitigate time decay losses. Dynamic adjustments based on changing market conditions and Theta values are crucial for maintaining strategy effectiveness.

5. Utilizing Theta-Positive Strategies: In certain market conditions, employing Theta-positive strategies like short spreads or iron condors can be advantageous. These strategies benefit from time decay, providing consistent income as long as the underlying asset remains within a specific price range.

Time decay, represented by Theta, is a fundamental aspect of options trading that directly impacts strategy performance. By understanding and managing Theta, traders can optimize their positions, mitigate risks, and enhance profitability. Whether through direct Theta-focused strategies or incorporating Theta management into broader trading plans, mastering time decay is essential for success in the dynamic world of options trading.

Volatility Skew

The concept of volatility skew is pivotal in the realm of options trading, offering insights into market sentiment and potential price movements. Volatility skew, also known as the volatility smile or smirk, refers to the pattern that emerges when plotting implied volatility against different strike prices of options with the same expiration date. This phenomenon can reveal underlying market expectations and is crucial for constructing strategies like the butterfly spread.

Understanding Volatility Skew

At its core, volatility skew illustrates how implied volatility varies across options with different strike prices. Implied volatility is derived from the market prices of options, reflecting the market's forecast of future volatility. Typically, this is not uniform across all strikes; instead, a skewed pattern emerges where out-of-the-money (OTM) options often exhibit higher implied volatility compared to at-the-money (ATM) options.

Types of Volatility Skew

1. Regular Skew (Smirk): In equity markets, it is common to observe a "smirk" where OTM puts (lower strike prices) have higher implied volatilities than OTM calls (higher strike prices). This pattern indicates a market bias towards downside risk, suggesting that traders are more concerned about significant drops in the asset's price than sharp increases.

2. Reverse Skew (Smile): In some markets or specific conditions, a "smile" can appear where both deep OTM puts and calls exhibit higher implied volatilities compared to ATM options. This implies increased uncertainty or potential for large moves in either direction.

Causes of Volatility Skew

Several factors contribute to the formation of volatility skew:

- Demand and Supply Imbalances: Higher demand for protective puts or speculative calls can drive up the implied volatility for those strikes.

- Market Sentiment: If investors are fearful of a market decline, they will pay more for OTM puts, increasing their implied volatility.

- Historical Volatility Patterns: Historical price movements can shape expectations and thus the implied volatilities.

- Skew Risk Premium: Traders may demand a premium to write options that expose them to left-tail risk (significant declines).

Implications of Volatility Skew for Butterfly Spread

When constructing a butterfly spread, understanding and leveraging volatility skew becomes essential:

1. Strike Price Selection: The choice of strike prices in a butterfly spread can influence the strategy's profitability. For example, in a market with a regular skew, selecting strikes that capitalize on higher implied volatility for OTM puts can enhance potential returns.

2. Premiums and Payouts: Volatility skew affects the option premiums paid and received. Higher implied volatility for certain strikes results in higher premiums, impacting the net cost or credit of the spread.

3. Risk Management: By analyzing the skew, traders can better anticipate market movements and adjust their strategies accordingly. For instance, a pronounced skew might indicate a higher likelihood of sharp price drops, prompting adjustments to protect against downside risk.

Practical Example with Python

To bring theory into practice, let's explore how to analyze and visualize volatility skew using Python. We'll use libraries like `pandas`, `numpy`, and `matplotlib` to fetch data and plot the skew.

```python
import pandas as pd
import numpy as np
import matplotlib.pyplot as plt
import yfinance as yf

# Fetching option chain data for a specific stock (e.g., AAPL)
ticker = 'AAPL'
stock = yf.Ticker(ticker)
expiration = stock.options[0]
options_chain = stock.option_chain(expiration)

# Extracting strike prices and implied volatilities for calls and puts
```

```
calls = options_chain.calls
puts = options_chain.puts

# Plotting the volatility skew
plt.figure(figsize=(10, 6))
plt.plot(calls['strike'], calls['impliedVolatility'], label='Calls', marker='o')
plt.plot(puts['strike'], puts['impliedVolatility'], label='Puts', marker='x')
plt.xlabel('Strike Price')
plt.ylabel('Implied Volatility')
plt.title(f'Volatility Skew for {ticker} Options (Expiry: {expiration})')
plt.legend()
plt.grid()
plt.show()
```

In this example, we first fetch the options chain for Apple (AAPL) using Yahoo Finance. We then extract the strike prices and their corresponding implied volatilities for both calls and puts. Finally, we plot these values to visualize the volatility skew.

Analyzing the Skew

By examining the plotted skew, traders can gain valuable insights:

- Identify Extreme Points: Look for strikes with unusually high implied volatility. These points may indicate strong market expectations for significant moves.

- Strategic Adjustments: Adjust the butterfly spread's strikes to take advantage of the skew. For instance, if OTM puts have high implied volatility, consider positioning the wings of the spread to capitalize on this.

- Risk Assessment: Use the skew to gauge market sentiment and potential risks. A steep skew might prompt more conservative positioning or additional hedging.

Volatility skew is more than a mere graphical representation; it encapsulates collective market sentiment and expectations. By understanding and analyzing volatility skew, traders can construct more informed and potentially profitable strategies. The butterfly spread, with its inherent flexibility, can be fine-tuned to leverage these insights, making it a powerful tool in the trader's arsenal. Through careful study and practical application, the nuances of volatility skew can be harnessed to enhance trading outcomes, merging the art and science of options trading into a cohesive and dynamic practice.

Theoretical Payoff Diagrams

Theoretical payoff diagrams serve as crucial tools for visualizing and understanding the potential outcomes of various strategies. These diagrams graphically represent the profit and loss (P&L) of an options position at expiration, based on different underlying asset prices. For the butterfly spread strategy, payoff diagrams provide a clear depiction of its risk-reward profile, illustrating the potential gains and losses under varying market conditions.

The Anatomy of a Payoff Diagram

A payoff diagram typically plots the underlying asset's price on the horizontal axis and the strategy's profit or loss on the vertical axis. Key points on this graph include the breakeven points, maximum profit, and maximum loss. For a butterfly spread, the diagram visually demonstrates the strategy's unique characteristics—limited risk, capped maximum profit, and the specific price range within which the strategy is most effective.

Constructing Payoff Diagrams for Butterfly Spread

To construct a theoretical payoff diagram for a butterfly spread, follow these steps:

1. Identify Strike Prices:

- Assume three strike prices, K_1 (lower strike), K_2 (middle strike), and K_3 (higher strike).

- For a long butterfly spread, the position typically involves buying one option at K_1, selling two options at K_2, and buying one option at K_3.

2. Calculate Payoff at Expiration:

- Determine the payoff for each component option at various underlying asset prices at expiration.

- Aggregate these payoffs to obtain the net payoff for the entire butterfly spread.

3. Plot the Payoff Diagram:

- Plot the underlying asset's price on the x-axis and the net payoff on the y-axis.

- Mark key points such as the maximum profit, maximum

loss, and breakeven points.

Example Calculation

Let's illustrate this with a concrete example. Consider a long butterfly spread using call options with strike prices $K_1 = 100$, $K_2 = 110$, and $K_3 = 120$. Each option costs \$2, \$1, and \$0.5 respectively.

1. Determine Payoffs:

- At $S < 100$: All options expire worthless. Net payoff = $-2 + 1 \times 2 - 0.5 = -1.5$

- At $100 \leq S < 110$: Only the first option (K1) has intrinsic value. Net payoff = $(S - 100) - 2 + 1 \times 2 - 0.5 = S - 101.5$

- At $110 \leq S < 120$: Both K1 and K2 have intrinsic value. Net payoff = $(S - 100) - 2 + 2 \times (110 - S) \times 1 - 0.5 = 8.5 - S$

- At $S \geq 120$: All options have intrinsic value. Net payoff = $(S - 100) - 2 + 2 \times (110 - S) \times 1 + (S - 120) \times 0.5 = -1.5$

2. Plotting the Diagram:

```python
import matplotlib.pyplot as plt
import numpy as np

# Define strike prices and premiums
K1, K2, K3 = 100, 110, 120
premium_K1, premium_K2, premium_K3 = 2, 1, 0.5
```

```python
# Define ranges for stock prices
S = np.linspace(80, 140, 100)

# Calculate payoffs
payoff_K1 = np.maximum(S - K1, 0) - premium_K1
payoff_K2 = 2 * (premium_K2 - np.maximum(S - K2, 0))
payoff_K3 = np.maximum(S - K3, 0) - premium_K3

# Aggregate payoffs
net_payoff = payoff_K1 + payoff_K2 + payoff_K3

# Plot the payoff diagram
plt.figure(figsize=(10, 6))
plt.plot(S, net_payoff, label='Butterfly Spread', color='blue')
plt.axhline(0, color='black', linestyle='--')
plt.axvline(K1, color='red', linestyle='--', label='K1 (100)')
plt.axvline(K2, color='green', linestyle='--', label='K2 (110)')
plt.axvline(K3, color='purple', linestyle='--', label='K3 (120)')
plt.xlabel('Underlying Asset Price at Expiration')
plt.ylabel('Profit / Loss')
plt.title('Butterfly Spread Payoff Diagram')
plt.legend()
plt.grid(True)
plt.show()
```

In this example, we use Python to plot the payoff diagram.

The `numpy` library helps in creating the range of underlying prices, while `matplotlib` is used to visualize the net payoff.

Analyzing the Payoff Diagram

Upon examining the payoff diagram, several key insights emerge:

1. Breakeven Points:

- The breakeven points occur where the net payoff crosses the zero line. For our example, the breakeven points are approximately around 101.5 and 118.5.

2. Maximum Profit:

- The maximum profit is achieved when the underlying price is equal to the middle strike price K_2. In our example, the maximum profit of 8.5 is realized when the underlying price is 110.

3. Maximum Loss:

- The maximum loss, limited to the net premium paid, occurs when the underlying price is outside the range of K_1 and K_3. For our example, the maximum loss is 1.5.

4. Risk-Reward Profile:

- The butterfly spread's payoff diagram showcases its balanced risk-reward profile. The strategy profits from low volatility conditions, where the underlying asset price is expected to remain near the middle strike price.

Strategic Adjustments Based on Payoff Diagrams

Payoff diagrams are not static tools but dynamic instruments that guide strategic adjustments:

- Adjusting Strikes:

By shifting the strike prices based on volatility skew or market outlook, traders can tailor the butterfly spread to better align with anticipated market movements.

- Combining Strategies:

Integrating the butterfly spread with other strategies (like vertical spreads or iron condors) can enhance the overall risk-reward structure. Payoff diagrams for combined strategies offer a holistic view of potential outcomes.

- Adaptive Risk Management:

Real-time monitoring of payoff diagrams helps in making informed decisions about adjusting or closing positions in response to market changes. This proactive approach mitigates risks and maximizes returns.

Theoretical payoff diagrams are indispensable in demystifying the complexities of options trading strategies like the butterfly spread. They provide a visual representation that aids in understanding the potential profit and loss scenarios, allowing traders to make data-driven decisions. By integrating these insights with practical Python implementations, traders can refine their strategies, enhance their risk management techniques, and ultimately achieve better trading outcomes. The journey from theory to practice, illuminated by payoff diagrams, epitomizes the blend of analytical rigor and strategic acumen that defines successful options trading.

Probability of Profit in Butterfly Spread

Understanding the probability of profit is crucial for traders employing the butterfly spread strategy. This probability measures the likelihood of the underlying asset's price landing within a profitable range at expiration. By examining the probability of profit, traders can better gauge the potential success of their trades, enabling more informed decision-making.

The Concept of Probability of Profit (PoP)

At its core, the probability of profit (PoP) represents the chance that an options strategy will result in a positive payoff by expiration. For a butterfly spread, this involves the asset's price ending up within a certain range defined by the strategy's strike prices. Calculating PoP involves understanding the distribution of potential future prices for the underlying asset and integrating this with the structure of the butterfly spread.

Components Affecting PoP in Butterfly Spreads

Several factors influence the probability of profit in a butterfly spread, including:

1. Strike Price Selection:

   - The choice of strike prices (K_1, K_2, and K_3) significantly impacts PoP. More conservative spreads with closely spaced strikes tend to have higher PoP but offer lower maximum profit, while wider spreads carry higher risk but potentially greater returns.

2. Implied Volatility (IV):

- Implied volatility affects the range of price movements expected for the underlying asset. Higher IV suggests a broader range of potential outcomes, often reducing PoP for a butterfly spread centered around a specific price range.

3. Time to Expiration:

- The amount of time until the options expire plays a role in PoP. With more time, there's greater uncertainty and potential for the underlying asset to move outside the profitable range of the butterfly spread.

4. Market Conditions:

- Market trends, events, and overall sentiment can influence the underlying asset's price movements, directly affecting the probability of profit.

Calculating Probability of Profit

To calculate the probability of profit, traders often utilize statistical models and computational tools. One common approach involves using the cumulative distribution function (CDF) of the normal distribution, adjusted for the asset's volatility and the time remaining until expiration. Here are the steps to calculate PoP for a butterfly spread:

1. Determine the Expected Price Range:

- Identify the expected price range for the underlying asset based on historical volatility and market forecasts.

2. Calculate Standard Deviations:

- Calculate the standard deviation (σ) of the underlying asset's price movements. This is often derived from the asset's historical or implied volatility.

3. Define the Price Boundaries:

- Establish the upper and lower limits of the butterfly spread's profitable range. These are typically defined by the lower strike price (K_1) and the higher strike price (K_3).

4. Use the Cumulative Distribution Function (CDF):

- Apply the normal distribution CDF to approximate the probability that the underlying asset's price will fall within the defined range at expiration.

Practical Example

Let's illustrate this with a practical example. Suppose we have a butterfly spread with the following parameters:

- Lower strike price (K_1): $100

- Middle strike price (K_2): $110

- Higher strike price (K_3): $120

- Implied volatility (σ): 20%

- Time to expiration (T): 30 days

First, convert the time to expiration into years:

$$ T = \frac{30}{365} \approx 0.082 $$

Next, calculate the standard deviation of the underlying asset's price using the implied volatility:

$$ \sigma_T = \sigma \sqrt{T} = 0.20 \times \sqrt{0.082} $$

\approx 0.057 \]

Using the normal distribution, we calculate the probability that the asset's price will be between \(K_1 \) and \(K_3 \) at expiration. The cumulative distribution function (CDF) for the normal distribution is denoted as \(\Phi \).

\[\text{PoP} = \Phi\left(\frac{K_3 - S_0}{\sigma_T}\right) - \Phi\left(\frac{K_1 - S_0}{\sigma_T}\right) \]

Assuming the current price (\(S_0 \)) of the underlying asset is $110:

\[\text{PoP} = \Phi\left(\frac{120 - 110}{0.057}\right) - \Phi\left(\frac{100 - 110}{0.057}\right) \]

Using a standard normal distribution table or a computational tool to find the CDF values:

\[\text{PoP} = \Phi(175.44) - \Phi(-175.44) \]

Given that \(\Phi(175.44) \approx 1 \) and \(\Phi(-175.44) \approx 0 \):

\[\text{PoP} \approx 1 - 0 = 1 \]

Thus, in this simplified example, the PoP is approximately 100%. However, in real-world scenarios, the PoP will be less than 100% due to the complexities of market dynamics and more precise calculations.

Python Implementation

Here's how you can calculate the probability of profit using Python. We'll use the `scipy.stats` library for the normal distribution CDF.

```python
import numpy as np
from scipy.stats import norm

# Parameters
S0 = 110  # Current price
K1 = 100  # Lower strike price
K2 = 110  # Middle strike price
K3 = 120  # Higher strike price
sigma = 0.20  # Implied volatility
T = 30 / 365  # Time to expiration in years

# Calculate standard deviation
sigma_T = sigma * np.sqrt(T)

# Calculate CDF values
cdf_upper = norm.cdf((K3 - S0) / sigma_T)
cdf_lower = norm.cdf((K1 - S0) / sigma_T)

# Probability of Profit
probability_of_profit = cdf_upper - cdf_lower

print("Probability of Profit for the Butterfly Spread: {:.2f}%".format(probability_of_profit * 100))
```

` ` `

Running this code provides an estimate of the probability of profit for the butterfly spread based on the given parameters.

Interpreting PoP in Trading Decisions

The probability of profit is a critical metric in strategy selection and risk management:

1. Strategy Selection:

   - Higher PoP strategies can be more appealing for conservative traders focusing on consistent, albeit smaller, profits. Conversely, strategies with lower PoP but higher potential payouts might attract more aggressive traders.

2. Risk Management:

   - Understanding PoP helps in setting realistic expectations and managing risk. Traders can use PoP to adjust position sizes, set stop-loss orders, and determine appropriate hedge strategies.

3. Scenario Analysis:

   - By varying input parameters such as volatility, time to expiration, and strike prices, traders can perform scenario analysis to see how changes in market conditions impact the PoP.

4. Backtesting:

   - Historical backtesting of strategies with calculated PoP provides insights into their performance under different market environments, aiding in strategy refinement.

The probability of profit in butterfly spreads is a vital tool for assessing the potential success of this strategy. By integrating statistical models and computational tools, traders can quantify the likelihood of various outcomes, enabling more informed decisions. As the landscape of options trading evolves, mastering the calculation and interpretation of PoP will remain an essential skill for achieving consistent and profitable trading results. Integrating these insights with Python implementations ensures a robust, data-driven approach to options trading.

Breakeven Points Analysis

In options trading, a breakeven point is the price level at which the total cost of the positions is recovered, meaning the trader neither profits nor incurs a loss. For a butterfly spread, which involves multiple strike prices and options contracts, identifying these points can be more complex but is essential for effective strategy assessment and risk management.

Components of Breakeven Points in Butterfly Spreads

To understand breakeven points in a butterfly spread, consider the following components:

1. Strike Prices:

   - The butterfly spread comprises three strike prices: K_1 (lower strike), K_2 (middle strike), and K_3 (higher strike). These strikes define the range within which the strategy operates.

2. Net Premium Paid:

- The net premium paid for establishing the butterfly spread is critical. It's the total cost incurred by purchasing and selling the options involved in the spread.

3. Expiration Date:

- The breakeven points are determined based on the prices at expiration, where the intrinsic value of the options can be calculated accurately.

Calculating Breakeven Points

To calculate the breakeven points for a butterfly spread, follow these steps:

1. Define the Strategy Components:

- Identify the strike prices (K_1, K_2, and K_3) and the net premium paid.

2. Identify the Upper and Lower Breakeven Points:

- The butterfly spread typically has two breakeven points: one below the middle strike and one above it. These points are calculated as follows:
    - Lower Breakeven Point:
    $$
    \text{Lower Breakeven} = K_1 + \text{Net Premium Paid}
    $$
    - Upper Breakeven Point:
    $$

\text{Upper Breakeven} = K_3 - \text{Net Premium Paid}
\]

3. Consider Transaction Costs:

   - Factor in any transaction costs or fees associated with entering the butterfly spread. These costs can slightly adjust the breakeven points.

Practical Example

Let's illustrate the calculation of breakeven points with an example. Suppose we have a butterfly spread with the following parameters:

- Lower strike price (K_1): $100

- Middle strike price (K_2): $110

- Higher strike price (K_3): $120

- Net premium paid: $2

Using the formulas provided, we calculate the breakeven points:

1. Lower Breakeven Point:

   \[
   \text{Lower Breakeven} = 100 + 2 = 102
   \]

2. Upper Breakeven Point:

   \[
   \text{Upper Breakeven} = 120 - 2 = 118
   \]

Thus, for this butterfly spread, the breakeven points are $102 and $118. If the underlying asset's price at expiration is between these two points, the trader will realize a profit; otherwise, a loss will be incurred.

Python Implementation

Here's a Python script to calculate the breakeven points for a butterfly spread. This script employs basic arithmetic operations to determine the breakeven points based on the input parameters.

```python
def calculate_breakeven_points(K1, K3, net_premium_paid):
    lower_breakeven = K1 + net_premium_paid
    upper_breakeven = K3 - net_premium_paid
    return lower_breakeven, upper_breakeven

# Example parameters
K1 = 100  # Lower strike price
K3 = 120  # Higher strike price
net_premium_paid = 2  # Net premium paid

# Calculate breakeven points
lower_breakeven, upper_breakeven = calculate_breakeven_points(K1, K3, net_premium_paid)

print("Lower Breakeven Point: $
{:.2f}".format(lower_breakeven))
print("Upper Breakeven Point: $
```

```
{:.2f}".format(upper_breakeven))
` ` `
```

Running this code will output:

```
` ` `
```

Lower Breakeven Point: $102.00

Upper Breakeven Point: $118.00

```
` ` `
```

This script offers a straightforward way to compute breakeven points for any butterfly spread configuration, ensuring traders can quickly assess the critical price levels for their strategies.

Interpreting Breakeven Points in Trading Decisions

Understanding and utilizing breakeven points is vital for making informed trading decisions:

1. Risk Assessment:

   - Knowing the breakeven points allows traders to assess the risk associated with their positions. If the current market price is close to the breakeven points, the strategy might require adjustments to mitigate potential losses.

2. Profit Potential:

   - Breakeven points help traders visualize the potential profit zone. If the underlying asset's price is expected to remain within the breakeven range, the butterfly spread can be a lucrative strategy.

3. Strategic Adjustments:

- Traders can use breakeven points to decide when to enter or exit positions. For instance, if market conditions change and the underlying asset's price moves outside the breakeven range, it might be prudent to close the position or implement hedging strategies.

4. Scenario Planning:

- By calculating breakeven points under different market scenarios, traders can prepare for various outcomes. This proactive approach enhances decision-making and strategic planning.

5. Stress Testing:

- Incorporating breakeven analysis into stress testing allows traders to evaluate how extreme market movements could impact their strategies. This helps in developing robust risk management frameworks.

Breakeven points analysis is an indispensable tool in the arsenal of options traders employing butterfly spreads. By accurately calculating and interpreting these points, traders can effectively manage risk, optimize profit potential, and make informed decisions under varying market conditions. Integrating this analysis with Python implementations ensures a precise, data-driven approach, enhancing the overall effectiveness of the butterfly spread strategy. As you continue to refine your trading techniques, a deep understanding of breakeven points will serve as a cornerstone for achieving consistent and profitable outcomes in options trading.

Adjustments to Butterfly Spread

Butterfly spreads are designed to profit from low volatility environments where the underlying asset's price remains within a specific range. However, markets are inherently unpredictable. Adjustments become crucial when the following scenarios emerge:

1. Price Drifts:

   - When the underlying asset's price moves significantly away from the center strike price.

2. Volatility Changes:

   - Sudden increases or decreases in market volatility impacting the spread's risk-reward profile.

3. Time Decay (Theta):

   - As expiration approaches, the impact of time decay becomes pronounced, necessitating strategic shifts.

4. Changes in Market Sentiment:

   - News, economic data releases, or other events altering market sentiment.

Common Adjustment Techniques

To navigate these challenges, traders employ various adjustment techniques. Below are some of the most effective methods:

1. Rolling the Spread:

   - If the underlying price drifts significantly, rolling the spread involves closing the current butterfly position and opening a new one at a different strike price. For instance, if the initial spread is centered around a strike price of $110, and the asset price moves to $120, the trader might roll the spread to be centered at $120.

```python
def roll_spread(current_center, new_center, options_data):
    # Close existing positions
    close_positions(current_center, options_data)
    # Open new positions at the new center
    open_positions(new_center, options_data)

# Example usage
current_center = 110
new_center = 120
options_data = get_options_data()

roll_spread(current_center, new_center, options_data)
```

2. Adding Additional Spreads (Double Butterfly):

- When volatility increases, traders might add another butterfly spread, creating a double butterfly. This adjustment aims to widen the profitable range and reduce risk.

```python
def add_double_butterfly(center1, center2, options_data):
    # Open first butterfly centered at center1
    open_positions(center1, options_data)
```

```python
    # Open second butterfly centered at center2
    open_positions(center2, options_data)

# Example usage
center1 = 110
center2 = 130
options_data = get_options_data()

add_double_butterfly(center1, center2, options_data)
```

3. Converting to an Iron Butterfly:

- If the underlying price is expected to remain stable but the trader seeks a more conservative risk profile, converting to an iron butterfly, which uses both calls and puts, can be beneficial. This adjustment reduces margin requirements and provides a different risk-reward structure.

```python
def    convert_to_iron_butterfly(call_center,    put_center, options_data):
    # Close existing positions
    close_positions(call_center, options_data)
    # Open new iron butterfly positions
    open_iron_butterfly(call_center,              put_center, options_data)

# Example usage
call_center = 110
put_center = 110
```

```python
options_data = get_options_data()

convert_to_iron_butterfly(call_center,          put_center,
options_data)
```

4. Hedging with Vertical Spreads:

- To mitigate risk from a significant price movement, traders might hedge with vertical spreads. These involve buying and selling options at different strike prices to offset potential losses.

```python
def    hedge_with_vertical_spread(upper_leg,    lower_leg,
options_data):
    # Open vertical spread positions
    open_vertical_spread(upper_leg,              lower_leg,
options_data)

# Example usage
upper_leg = 120
lower_leg = 100
options_data = get_options_data()

hedge_with_vertical_spread(upper_leg,            lower_leg,
options_data)
```

5. Adjusting Position Size:

- Reducing or increasing the number of contracts in the

spread can control exposure. If the market becomes too volatile, reducing the position size can limit potential losses.

```python
def adjust_position_size(current_size, new_size, options_data):
    # Close existing positions
    close_positions_by_size(current_size, options_data)
    # Open new positions with adjusted size
    open_positions_by_size(new_size, options_data)

# Example usage
current_size = 10
new_size = 5
options_data = get_options_data()

adjust_position_size(current_size, new_size, options_data)
```

Practical Considerations

Adjustments should not be made arbitrarily. Consider the following when deciding on an adjustment strategy:

1. Market Conditions:

- Assess current market conditions, volatility levels, and the underlying asset's price trajectory.

2. Cost of Adjustment:

- Evaluate the transaction costs and potential slippage

associated with making adjustments.

3. Impact on Risk-Reward Profile:

   - Understand how adjustments will alter the risk-reward dynamics of the existing spread.

4. Time to Expiration:

   - Closer to expiration, adjustments might be less effective due to the accelerating impact of time decay.

5. Capital Requirements:

   - Ensure sufficient capital is available to implement adjustments without over-leveraging the account.

Python Implementation for Monitoring and Adjustments

Automating the monitoring and adjustment process can provide a systematic approach to managing trades. Below is a Python script to monitor a butterfly spread and suggest adjustments based on predefined criteria.

```python
import pandas as pd

def monitor_butterfly_spread(current_price, lower_breakeven, upper_breakeven, volatility):
    if current_price < lower_breakeven:
        return "Consider rolling the spread or hedging with a vertical spread."
    elif current_price > upper_breakeven:
        return "Consider rolling the spread or hedging with a
```

vertical spread."

```
    elif volatility > threshold_volatility:
        return "Consider adding a double butterfly or converting to an iron butterfly."
    else:
        return "No adjustment needed."

# Example parameters
current_price = 115
lower_breakeven = 102
upper_breakeven = 118
threshold_volatility = 0.3
current_volatility = 0.35

# Monitor and suggest adjustments
suggestion    =    monitor_butterfly_spread(current_price,
lower_breakeven, upper_breakeven, current_volatility)
print(suggestion)
```
` ` `

Running this code will output:
` ` `

Consider adding a double butterfly or converting to an iron butterfly.
` ` `

This script provides a foundation for more sophisticated monitoring and adjustment strategies, allowing traders to automate and streamline their decision-making process.

Adjusting butterfly spreads is an essential skill for options traders seeking to navigate unpredictable markets. By understanding and implementing various adjustment techniques, traders can enhance their ability to manage risk, optimize profitability, and adapt to changing market conditions. Integrating these adjustments with Python automations ensures a methodical and data-driven approach, empowering traders to make informed decisions and maintain a competitive edge in the world of options trading.

Case Study: Theoretical Analysis

Constructing the Butterfly Spread

To lay the groundwork, let's construct a butterfly spread with the following parameters:

- Underlying Asset: XYZ Corporation stock

- Current Stock Price: $100

- Strike Prices: $95, $100, $105

- Expiry: 30 days

- Option Type: Call

The butterfly spread involves:

1. Buying 1 call option at $95

2. Selling 2 call options at $100

3. Buying 1 call option at $105

This setup creates a position that is cost-effective and designed to capitalize on the stock price remaining near $100 at expiration.

```python
# Python function to construct a butterfly spread
def construct_butterfly_spread(stock_price, strike_prices, option_prices):
    # Buying 1 call at lower strike
    buy_lower = option_prices[strike_prices[0]]
    # Selling 2 calls at middle strike
    sell_middle = 2 * option_prices[strike_prices[1]]
    # Buying 1 call at higher strike
    buy_upper = option_prices[strike_prices[2]]

    # Net cost of the butterfly spread
    net_cost = buy_lower - sell_middle + buy_upper
    return net_cost

# Example usage
stock_price = 100
strike_prices = [95, 100, 105]
option_prices = {95: 8, 100: 5, 105: 3}

net_cost = construct_butterfly_spread(stock_price, strike_prices, option_prices)
print(f"Net cost of the butterfly spread: ${net_cost}")
```

Analyzing Profit and Loss Scenarios

The theoretical profit and loss (P&L) analysis is pivotal in understanding the butterfly spread's behavior under different market conditions. Let's examine the P&L at various stock prices at expiration.

1. If the stock price is at $95:
   - The $95 call expires at intrinsic value (worth $0)
   - The $100 calls expire worthless (worth $0)
   - The $105 call expires worthless (worth $0)
   - Net P&L: -Net cost of the spread

2. If the stock price is at $100:
   - The $95 call is worth $5
   - The $100 calls expire worthless
   - The $105 call expires worthless
   - Net P&L: $5 - Net cost of the spread

3. If the stock price is at $105:
   - The $95 call is worth $10
   - The $100 calls are worth $5 each (total $10)
   - The $105 call expires worthless
   - Net P&L: $10 - $10 - Net cost of the spread

```python
# Python function to calculate P&L at expiration
def calculate_pnl_at_expiration(stock_prices, strike_prices, net_cost):
    pnl = []
    for price in stock_prices:
        lower_call_value = max(0, price - strike_prices[0])
```

```python
    middle_call_value = max(0, price - strike_prices[1])
    upper_call_value = max(0, price - strike_prices[2])

    pnl_at_price = lower_call_value - 2 * middle_call_value +
upper_call_value - net_cost
    pnl.append(pnl_at_price)

  return pnl

# Example usage
stock_prices = [90, 95, 100, 105, 110]
net_cost = 1  # Net cost from previous calculation

pnl = calculate_pnl_at_expiration(stock_prices, strike_prices,
net_cost)
for price, profit in zip(stock_prices, pnl):
    print(f"Stock Price: ${price}, P&L: ${profit}")
```

Impact of Market Conditions

Volatility

Volatility plays a crucial role in the behavior of a butterfly spread. In periods of low volatility, the spread tends to perform better as the underlying price remains within a narrow range. Conversely, high volatility can lead to significant price movements, potentially moving the underlying price away from the center strike, thus impacting profitability.

```python
```

```python
# Python function to simulate the impact of volatility
def simulate_volatility_impact(stock_price, strike_prices,
volatilities, option_prices):
    results = {}
    for vol in volatilities:
        adjusted_prices = {k: v * vol for k, v in
option_prices.items()}
        net_cost = construct_butterfly_spread(stock_price,
strike_prices, adjusted_prices)
        pnl = calculate_pnl_at_expiration(stock_prices,
strike_prices, net_cost)
        results[vol] = pnl

    return results

# Example usage
volatilities = [0.8, 1.0, 1.2]
results = simulate_volatility_impact(stock_price,
strike_prices, volatilities, option_prices)
for vol, pnl in results.items():
    print(f"Volatility: {vol}")
    for price, profit in zip(stock_prices, pnl):
        print(f" Stock Price: ${price}, P&L: ${profit}")
```
```

# Time Decay (Theta)

As the expiration date approaches, the time value of options erodes, known as theta decay. Butterfly spreads are particularly sensitive to theta, as the strategy involves
```

multiple options with varying degrees of time decay. The impact of theta is more pronounced as the options near expiration.

```python
# Python function to simulate time decay impact
def simulate_time_decay(stock_price, strike_prices, days_to_expiration, option_prices):
    results = {}
    for days in days_to_expiration:
        decay_factor = days / 30   # Assuming 30 days to expiration
        adjusted_prices = {k: v * decay_factor for k, v in option_prices.items()}
        net_cost = construct_butterfly_spread(stock_price, strike_prices, adjusted_prices)
        pnl = calculate_pnl_at_expiration(stock_prices, strike_prices, net_cost)
        results[days] = pnl

    return results

# Example usage
days_to_expiration = [30, 15, 5]
results = simulate_time_decay(stock_price, strike_prices, days_to_expiration, option_prices)
for days, pnl in results.items():
    print(f"Days to Expiration: {days}")
    for price, profit in zip(stock_prices, pnl):
        print(f" Stock Price: ${price}, P&L: ${profit}")
```

` ` `

Theoretical Insights

This theoretical analysis underscores the importance of understanding the butterfly spread's sensitivity to various market factors. It highlights:

1. Price Sensitivity: The spread's profitability hinges on the underlying asset's movement around the center strike.
2. Volatility Impact: Low volatility favors the butterfly spread, while high volatility necessitates adjustments.
3. Time Decay: The closer to expiration, the more significant the impact of theta decay.

Leveraging Python for simulation and analysis, we can gain deeper insights into the butterfly spread's performance under different conditions, allowing for more informed decision-making.

The theoretical analysis of the butterfly spread provides a robust foundation for practical applications. Understanding the intricate dynamics of price movements, volatility, and time decay enables traders to anticipate market behavior and make strategic adjustments. By integrating these theoretical insights with Python-based simulations, traders can enhance their strategies, optimize profitability, and better navigate the complexities of options trading.

CHAPTER 4: PYTHON FOR OPTIONS TRADING

T he first step in setting up your Python environment involves selecting the appropriate tools and platforms. Python is a versatile language, and its ecosystem includes a plethora of tools that can enhance your trading activities.

1. Python Distribution: Start with the official Python distribution from [python.org](https://www.python.org/). Ensure that you download the latest stable release to take advantage of recent features and security updates.

2. Integrated Development Environment (IDE): An IDE like PyCharm, Visual Studio Code, or Jupyter Notebook is essential for writing, testing, and debugging your code. Jupyter Notebook is particularly popular for financial analysis due to its interactive nature and support for visualizations.

Installing Python

To begin, download and install the latest version of Python

from the official website:

1.   Download   Python: Visit   [python.org](https://
www.python.org/downloads/) and download the installer for
your operating system (Windows, MacOS, Linux).

2. Run the Installer: Follow the prompts to install Python.
Ensure you check the box to add Python to your system PATH,
which simplifies running Python from the command line.

3. Verify Installation: Open your terminal or command
prompt and type `python --version`. This command should
display the installed Python version, confirming a successful
installation.

```shell
# Verify Python installation
python --version
```

Setting Up a Virtual Environment

A virtual environment is a self-contained directory that
contains a Python installation for a particular version of
Python, plus a number of additional packages. It helps
in managing dependencies and avoiding conflicts between
projects.

1. Create Virtual Environment: Navigate to your project's
directory and create a virtual environment using the `venv`
module.

```shell
# Create a virtual environment
```

```
python -m venv trading_env
```
` ` `

2. Activate the Virtual Environment: Once created, activate the virtual environment.

- Windows:

` ` `shell

```
trading_env\Scripts\activate
```
` ` `

- MacOS/Linux:

` ` `shell

```
source trading_env/bin/activate
```
` ` `

3. Deactivate Virtual Environment: To deactivate the virtual environment, simply use the `deactivate` command.

` ` `shell

```
# Deactivate the virtual environment
deactivate
```
` ` `

Installing Essential Libraries

With your virtual environment activated, the next step is to install essential libraries that will be instrumental in your options trading analysis. These libraries include `pandas` for data manipulation, `numpy` for numerical operations, `matplotlib` for visualization, and `scipy` for scientific computations.

1. pandas: A powerful library for data manipulation and analysis.

```shell
pip install pandas
```

2. numpy: A fundamental package for scientific computing with Python.

```shell
pip install numpy
```

3. matplotlib: A plotting library for creating static, animated, and interactive visualizations.

```shell
pip install matplotlib
```

4. scipy: A library used for scientific and technical computing.

```shell
pip install scipy
```

5. Other Libraries: Depending on your specific needs, you may

also want to install libraries like `quantlib`, `yfinance`, and `requests` for financial data and API interactions.

```shell
pip install quantlib yfinance requests
```

Configuring Jupyter Notebook

Jupyter Notebook is an invaluable tool for interactive development and data analysis. To use Jupyter Notebook, follow these steps:

1. Install Jupyter: Install the Jupyter Notebook package.

```shell
pip install jupyter
```

2. Start Jupyter Notebook: Launch Jupyter Notebook from the terminal.

```shell
jupyter notebook
```

3. Create a New Notebook: In the Jupyter interface, create a new Python notebook and start coding.

Setting Up Version Control

Version control is crucial for managing changes to your codebase, especially in collaborative settings. Git is a widely used version control system that integrates seamlessly with platforms like GitHub.

1. Install Git: Download and install Git from [git-scm.com] (https://git-scm.com/).

2. Initialize Git Repository: Navigate to your project directory and initialize a Git repository.

```shell
git init
```

3. Commit Changes: Track and commit your changes to the repository.

```shell
git add .
git commit -m "Initial commit"
```

4. Create a Remote Repository: On GitHub, create a new repository and link it to your local repository.

```shell
git remote add origin <repository-url>
git push -u origin master
```

Setting Up IDE

Choosing the right Integrated Development Environment (IDE) can significantly enhance your productivity. PyCharm and Visual Studio Code are popular choices due to their extensive features and ease of use.

1. PyCharm: Download and install PyCharm from [jetbrains.com](https://www.jetbrains.com/pycharm/). Configure it to use your virtual environment by navigating to `Settings -> Project -> Project Interpreter` and selecting your virtual environment.

2. Visual Studio Code: Download and install VS Code from code.visualstudio.com. Install the Python extension and configure the interpreter to use your virtual environment.

Best Practices for Organizing Code

Organizing your codebase efficiently is critical for maintaining readability and ease of use. Here are some best practices:

1. Folder Structure:

- src: Contains source code files.

- data: Stores datasets and data files.

- notebooks: Jupyter Notebooks for interactive development.

- tests: Unit tests for your code.

- docs: Documentation files.

``` shell
```

```
├── src
├── data
├── notebooks
├── tests
└── docs
    ` ` `
```

2. Modular Code: Write modular code by breaking down your scripts into smaller, reusable functions and classes.

3. Documentation: Use docstrings and comments to document your code, making it easier for others (and your future self) to understand.

4. Version Control: Regularly commit your changes and push them to your remote repository to keep your codebase updated and backed up.

Setting up a Python environment is the first step towards harnessing the power of Python for options trading. By carefully selecting the right tools, installing essential libraries, and organizing your code efficiently, you lay a solid foundation for advanced trading strategies and data analysis. This environment will serve as the bedrock for the subsequent chapters, where we delve deeper into the practical applications of options trading with Python.

Installing Necessary Libraries (Pandas, Numpy, Matplotlib, etc.)

Setting Up Your Virtual Environment

Before diving into the installation of libraries, it's crucial to create and activate a virtual environment. This practice ensures that your project dependencies are isolated and manageable, avoiding conflicts with system-wide packages.

1. Create a Virtual Environment:

```shell
python -m venv trading_env
```

2. Activate the Virtual Environment:

   - Windows:

   ```shell
   trading_env\Scripts\activate
   ```

   - MacOS/Linux:

   ```shell
   source trading_env/bin/activate
   ```

Installing Pandas for Data Manipulation

`pandas` is a powerful library for data manipulation and analysis. It provides data structures like DataFrames that are ideal for handling and analyzing structured data.

1. Install Pandas:

```shell
pip install pandas
```

2. Verify Installation:

```python
import pandas as pd
print(pd.__version__)
```

Pandas simplifies tasks such as data cleaning, transformation, and aggregation. For instance, reading CSV files and performing exploratory data analysis becomes straightforward with Pandas.

```python
# Sample code to read a CSV file using Pandas
import pandas as pd

data = pd.read_csv('historical_options_data.csv')
print(data.head())
```

Installing Numpy for Numerical Computation

`numpy` is the cornerstone of numerical computing in Python, offering support for large multi-dimensional arrays and matrices, along with a collection of mathematical functions to operate on these arrays.

1. Install Numpy:

```shell
pip install numpy
```

2. Verify Installation:

```python
import numpy as np
print(np.__version__)
```

Numpy is essential for performing numerical operations required in options pricing models, risk management, and statistical analysis.

```python
# Sample code for basic Numpy operations
import numpy as np

prices = np.array([100, 105, 110, 95, 90])
returns = np.diff(prices) / prices[:-1]
print(returns)
```

```
```

Installing Matplotlib for Data Visualization

`matplotlib` is a versatile plotting library for creating static, animated, and interactive visualizations in Python. It is pivotal for visualizing financial data, option payoffs, and performance metrics.

1. Install Matplotlib:

```shell
pip install matplotlib
```

2. Verify Installation:

```python
import matplotlib.pyplot as plt
print(plt.__version__)
```

With Matplotlib, you can create a variety of plots such as line charts, bar charts, histograms, and scatter plots, which are essential for analyzing trends and patterns in financial data.

```python
# Sample code to plot a simple line chart using Matplotlib
import matplotlib.pyplot as plt
```

```
days = np.arange(5)
prices = [100, 105, 110, 95, 90]

plt.plot(days, prices, marker='o')
plt.title('Stock Prices Over Time')
plt.xlabel('Days')
plt.ylabel('Price')
plt.show()
```

Installing Scipy for Scientific Computing

`scipy` builds on Numpy and provides a large number of higher-level scientific algorithms. It includes modules for optimization, integration, interpolation, eigenvalue problems, and more.

1. Install Scipy:

```shell
pip install scipy
```

2. Verify Installation:

```python
import scipy
print(scipy.__version__)
```

Scipy's optimization module is particularly useful for calibrating models and finding optimal parameters in trading strategies.

```python
# Sample code for optimization using Scipy
from scipy.optimize import minimize

def objective_function(x):
    return x2 + 5*np.sin(x)

result = minimize(objective_function, x0=0)
print(result.x)
```

Additional Libraries for Financial Data and Analysis

Depending on your specific requirements, you may find other libraries beneficial. Some of these include:

1. Quantlib: A comprehensive library for quantitative finance, offering tools for pricing options, bonds, and other financial instruments.

```shell
pip install QuantLib-Python
```

2. Yfinance: A convenient library for fetching historical market data from Yahoo Finance.

```shell
pip install yfinance
```

3. Requests: A simple and elegant HTTP library for interacting with APIs.

```shell
pip install requests
```

Combining these libraries with Pandas, Numpy, and Matplotlib enables the creation of powerful and flexible trading models.

```python
# Sample code to fetch historical stock data using yfinance
import yfinance as yf

ticker = 'AAPL'
data = yf.download(ticker, start='2020-01-01', end='2021-01-01')
print(data.head())
```

Best Practices for Managing Dependencies

To ensure consistency and reproducibility in your projects, it's advisable to manage your dependencies carefully. Using `requirements.txt` or `pipenv` can help achieve this.

1. Creating a requirements.txt File:

```shell
pip freeze > requirements.txt
```

2. Installing from requirements.txt:

```shell
pip install -r requirements.txt
```

3. Using Pipenv for Dependency Management:

```shell
pip install pipenv
pipenv install pandas numpy matplotlib scipy yfinance requests
```

Installing and managing essential libraries is a critical step in setting up a Python environment tailored for options trading. By leveraging Pandas for data manipulation, Numpy for numerical computations, Matplotlib for visualization, and Scipy for scientific computing, you equip yourself with a powerful toolkit. These libraries form the backbone of your analytical and trading capabilities, facilitating the development of sophisticated models and strategies.

Connecting to Financial Data Sources

Understanding Data Sources

Before diving into the technical aspects, it's crucial to understand the types of data sources available:

1. Historical Data Providers: These include services like Alpha Vantage, Quandl, and Yahoo Finance, providing extensive historical data necessary for backtesting and modeling.

2. Real-time Data Feed Providers: Examples include IEX Cloud, Alpaca, and Interactive Brokers, which supply live data feeds essential for real-time trading applications.

3. Market Data Aggregators: Platforms like Bloomberg, Reuters, and Google Finance aggregate data from multiple sources, offering a comprehensive view of market conditions.

Setting Up API Connections

To fetch data programmatically, you'll often use APIs (Application Programming Interfaces). Here's a step-by-step guide to set up API connections with common data providers:

Example: Connecting to Alpha Vantage

Alpha Vantage offers a free tier for daily stock data and other financial metrics. Let's walk through how to connect and fetch data using Python.

1. Obtain an API Key: Register on the Alpha Vantage website to

get your free API key.

2. Install Necessary Libraries:

```bash
pip install pandas requests
```

3. Fetch Data with Python:

```python
import pandas as pd
import requests

# Define the API key and endpoint
api_key = 'YOUR_API_KEY'
symbol = 'AAPL'
url = f'https://www.alphavantage.co/query?function=TIME_SERIES_DAILY&symbol={symbol}&apikey={api_key}'

# Make a request to the API
response = requests.get(url)
data = response.json()

# Extract the time series data
time_series = data['Time Series (Daily)']

# Convert the data to a pandas DataFrame
df = pd.DataFrame.from_dict(time_series, orient='index')
df = df.rename(columns={'1. open': 'open', '2. high': 'high', '3. low': 'low', '4. close': 'close', '5. volume': 'volume'})
df.index = pd.to_datetime(df.index)
```

```
df = df.astype(float)

print(df.head())
```

This snippet demonstrates how to obtain and transform daily stock data into a pandas DataFrame for further analysis.

Real-time Data Integration

For real-time trading, accessing live data is indispensable. Here's how you can connect to IEX Cloud, a popular real-time data provider:

1. Register and Obtain an API Key from the IEX Cloud website.
2. Install Necessary Libraries:

```bash
pip install pandas requests
```

3. Fetch Real-time Data:

```python
import requests
import pandas as pd

# Define the API key and endpoint
api_key = 'YOUR_API_KEY'
symbol = 'AAPL'
url = f'https://cloud.iexapis.com/stable/stock/{symbol}/quote?token={api_key}'
```

```python
# Make a request to the API
response = requests.get(url)
data = response.json()

# Convert the data to a pandas DataFrame
df = pd.DataFrame([data])
print(df[['symbol', 'latestPrice', 'latestVolume']])
```

This code connects to the IEX Cloud API and fetches the latest price and volume for a specified stock symbol, providing a foundation for real-time data integration in your trading algorithms.

Advanced Data Handling and Storage

Accessing data is just the beginning. Transforming, storing, and ensuring the data's integrity are equally vital. Python provides robust tools for these tasks:

1. Data Cleaning: Leveraging pandas for handling missing values, filtering outliers, and normalizing data.

```python
# Handling missing values
df.dropna(inplace=True)

# Filtering outliers
df = df[(df['close'] > df['close'].quantile(0.05)) & (df['close'] < df['close'].quantile(0.95))]
```

```python
# Normalizing data
df['normalized_close'] = (df['close'] - df['close'].min()) / (df['close'].max() - df['close'].min())
print(df.head())
```

2. Data Storage: Using databases like SQLite or PostgreSQL for efficient storage and retrieval.

```python
import sqlite3

# Connect to SQLite database
conn = sqlite3.connect('financial_data.db')
df.to_sql('daily_prices', conn, if_exists='replace', index=True)

# Retrieve data
retrieved_df = pd.read_sql('SELECT * FROM daily_prices', conn)
print(retrieved_df.head())
```

Integrating Data into Trading Algorithms

Once the data is clean and accessible, integrating it into your trading strategies is the next step. Here's a simple example using fetched data to construct a butterfly spread strategy:

1. Define the Strategy Parameters:

```python
# Define strike prices and expiration for the butterfly spread
strikes = [100, 105, 110]
expiration = '2023-12-15'

# Fetch options data (pseudo-code, replace with actual API call)
options_data = fetch_options_data(symbol, expiration)
```

2. Construct the Butterfly Spread:

```python
def construct_butterfly_spread(options_data, strikes):
    # Extract call options for the given strikes
    call1 = options_data[(options_data['strike'] == strikes[0]) & (options_data['type'] == 'call')]
    call2 = options_data[(options_data['strike'] == strikes[1]) & (options_data['type'] == 'call')]
    call3 = options_data[(options_data['strike'] == strikes[2]) & (options_data['type'] == 'call')]

    # Construct the butterfly spread
    butterfly_spread = -call1['price'] + 2 * call2['price'] - call3['price']
    return butterfly_spread

butterfly_spread = construct_butterfly_spread(options_data, strikes)
print(f'Butterfly Spread Cost: {butterfly_spread}')
```

` ` `

Connecting to financial data sources effectively is the linchpin of executing successful trading strategies. By leveraging APIs from reliable providers and utilizing Python's extensive data manipulation capabilities, you create a strong foundation for your trading algorithms. The seamless integration of historical and real-time data not only enhances the accuracy of your models but also ensures that your strategies can adapt to market dynamics in real-time, fostering a robust and dynamic trading system.

Basic Data Manipulation with Pandas

Introduction to Pandas

`pandas` is a high-level data manipulation tool built on the `numpy` package. It is particularly well-suited for working with structured data, such as time series data and tabular data, commonly found in financial markets. The two primary data structures in `pandas` are:

1. DataFrame: A two-dimensional, size-mutable, and heterogeneous tabular data structure with labeled axes (rows and columns).

2. Series: A one-dimensional array-like structure designed for handling and manipulating single-column data.

Setting Up Pandas

Before diving into data manipulation, ensure that you have `pandas` installed in your Python environment. You can install it using `pip`:

```bash
pip install pandas
```

Loading Data

The first step in data manipulation is loading the data into a `pandas` DataFrame. This data can come from various sources, including CSV files, Excel files, SQL databases, and even directly from APIs.

```python
import pandas as pd

# Loading data from a CSV file
data = pd.read_csv('historical_options_data.csv')

# Display the first few rows of the DataFrame
print(data.head())
```

Inspecting the Data

Understanding the structure and contents of your data is vital. `pandas` provides several methods for inspecting data:

```python
# Display summary statistics for numeric columns
```

```
print(data.describe())
```

```
# Display information about the DataFrame (e.g., data types
and non-null values)
print(data.info())
```

```
# Display the first few rows (default is 5)
print(data.head())
```

```
# Display the last few rows (default is 5)
print(data.tail())
```
` ` `

Data Cleaning

Raw financial data often contains missing values, duplicates, or outliers that need to be addressed. `pandas` offers a suite of functions for cleaning and preparing your data.

Handling Missing Values

Missing data can be problematic for analysis and modeling. The following methods help to handle missing values:

` ` `python
```
# Check for missing values
print(data.isnull().sum())
```

```
# Drop rows with missing values
data_cleaned = data.dropna()
```

Fill missing values with a specified value or method (e.g., forward fill)

data_filled = data.fillna(method='ffill')
```

# Removing Duplicates

Duplicates in data can skew analysis and results. Removing them ensures the integrity of your dataset:

```python
# Remove duplicate rows
data_no_duplicates = data.drop_duplicates()
```

Filtering and Selecting Data

Filtering data is essential for focusing on relevant subsets. `pandas` allows you to filter data based on conditions:

```python
# Filter rows where the 'close' price is greater than a certain value
filtered_data = data[data['close'] > 100]

# Select specific columns
selected_data = data[['date', 'close', 'volume']]
```
```

Data Transformation

Transforming data involves modifying its structure or values to make it suitable for analysis and modeling. Common transformations include renaming columns, changing data types, and creating new columns.

Renaming Columns

Clear and consistent column names improve data readability and usability:

```python
# Rename columns
data_renamed       =       data.rename(columns={'adj_close':
'adjusted_close'})
```

Changing Data Types

Ensuring the correct data types is crucial for proper data manipulation:

```python
# Convert column to datetime
data['date'] = pd.to_datetime(data['date'])

# Convert column to numeric
data['volume'] = pd.to_numeric(data['volume'])
```

Creating New Columns

Creating new columns based on existing data can provide additional insights:

```python
# Calculate daily returns
data['daily_return'] = data['close'].pct_change()

# Calculate moving averages
data['50_day_MA'] = data['close'].rolling(window=50).mean()
```

Aggregating Data

Aggregation involves summarizing data to extract meaningful insights. This can be done using group-by operations, pivot tables, and resampling.

Group-By Operations

Grouping data by specific columns allows for aggregation and summary statistics:

```python
# Group by a column (e.g., month) and calculate the mean
monthly_data = data.groupby(data['date'].dt.month).mean()
```

Pivot Tables

Pivot tables provide a powerful way to reorganize and summarize data:

```python
# Create a pivot table to summarize data
pivot_table = data.pivot_table(index='date', columns='symbol', values='close')
```

Resampling Time Series Data

Resampling is essential for time series data to aggregate data into different time frequencies:

```python
# Resample daily data to monthly data and calculate the mean
monthly_data = data.resample('M', on='date').mean()
```

Merging and Joining Data

Combining multiple DataFrames is often necessary for comprehensive analysis. `pandas` provides several methods for merging and joining data:

```python
# Merge two DataFrames on a common column
```

```
merged_data = pd.merge(data1, data2, on='symbol')

# Join two DataFrames on their indexes
joined_data = data1.join(data2, lsuffix='_left', rsuffix='_right')
```

Visualization with Pandas

Visualizing data helps in understanding patterns and trends. While `matplotlib` is often used for complex visualizations, `pandas` offers convenient plotting capabilities for quick insights.

```python
import matplotlib.pyplot as plt

# Plot a time series
data['close'].plot(title='Closing Prices')
plt.show()

# Plot multiple columns
data[['close', '50_day_MA']].plot(title='Closing Prices and 50-day MA')
plt.show()
```

Mastering basic data manipulation with `pandas` is a critical step in developing robust options trading strategies. By efficiently loading, cleaning, transforming, and visualizing data, you lay the groundwork for more advanced analyses and algorithmic trading.

Introduction to QuantLib

Setting Up QuantLib

Before diving into the functionalities of QuantLib, you must first ensure it is installed in your Python environment. QuantLib is a C++ library wrapped for Python use, and you can install it using `pip`:

```bash
pip install QuantLib-Python
```

Once installed, you can import it in your Python scripts:

```python
import QuantLib as ql
```

Understanding QuantLib's Core Components

QuantLib's power lies in its extensive toolkit that covers a wide range of financial instruments, models, and pricing engines. Here are some of its core components:

1. Date and Calendar: Handling dates and business calendars accurately is fundamental in financial modeling.
2. Interest Rate Curves: Constructing and managing yield curves is essential for pricing and risk management.

3. Financial Instruments: QuantLib supports a broad range of financial instruments, including bonds, options, swaps, and more.

4. Pricing Engines: These are the algorithms used to calculate the price of financial instruments.

5. Stochastic Models: QuantLib provides various models to simulate the behavior of financial variables over time.

Working with Dates and Calendars

QuantLib's date and calendar functionalities are crucial for managing financial schedules, fixing dates, and maturity dates. Here's a basic example of how to work with dates and calendars in QuantLib:

```python
# Import QuantLib
import QuantLib as ql

# Create a date object
evaluation_date = ql.Date(15, 3, 2023)
ql.Settings.instance().evaluationDate = evaluation_date

# Print the evaluation date
print(f"Evaluation Date: {evaluation_date}")

# Define a calendar (e.g., United States calendar)
us_calendar = ql.UnitedStates()

# Check if a date is a business day
```

```
is_business_day                           =
us_calendar.isBusinessDay(evaluation_date)
print(f"Is business day: {is_business_day}")

# Advance the date by one month
advanced_date    =    us_calendar.advance(evaluation_date,
ql.Period(1, ql.Months))
print(f"Advanced Date: {advanced_date}")
```

Constructing Yield Curves

Yield curves are pivotal in discounting cash flows and pricing derivatives. QuantLib provides tools to construct and manipulate these curves efficiently. Here's an example of building a simple yield curve:

```python
# Import QuantLib
import QuantLib as ql

# Define the settlement date
settlement_date = ql.Date(15, 3, 2023)
ql.Settings.instance().evaluationDate = settlement_date

# Define the interest rates for the yield curve
rates = [0.01, 0.015, 0.02, 0.025, 0.03]

tenors   =   [ql.Period(1,   ql.Years),   ql.Period(2,   ql.Years),
ql.Period(3,  ql.Years),  ql.Period(5,  ql.Years),  ql.Period(10,
ql.Years)]
```

```python
# Create rate helpers
rate_helpers =
[ql.DepositRateHelper(ql.QuoteHandle(ql.SimpleQuote(rate)),
tenor, 2, ql.TARGET(), ql.ModifiedFollowing, False,
ql.Actual360()) for rate, tenor in zip(rates, tenors)]

# Build the yield curve
yield_curve = ql.PiecewiseYieldCurve(0, ql.TARGET(),
rate_helpers, ql.Actual360())

# Print the discount factor for a specific date
discount_factor = yield_curve.discount(ql.Date(15, 3, 2028))
print(f"Discount Factor: {discount_factor}")
```

Pricing Financial Instruments

QuantLib excels at pricing a wide array of financial instruments. Let's consider a simple example of pricing a European call option using the Black-Scholes model:

```python
# Import QuantLib
import QuantLib as ql

# Define the option parameters
spot_price = 100
strike_price = 105
maturity_date = ql.Date(15, 3, 2024)
```

```python
volatility = 0.2
dividend_rate = 0.01
risk_free_rate = 0.05

# Create the option payoff and exercise
payoff = ql.PlainVanillaPayoff(ql.Option.Call, strike_price)
exercise = ql.EuropeanExercise(maturity_date)

# Create the option
european_option = ql.VanillaOption(payoff, exercise)

# Define the market variables
spot_handle = ql.QuoteHandle(ql.SimpleQuote(spot_price))
flat_ts                                                    =
ql.YieldTermStructureHandle(ql.FlatForward(settlement_dat
e, risk_free_rate, ql.Actual360()))
dividend_yield                                             =
ql.YieldTermStructureHandle(ql.FlatForward(settlement_dat
e, dividend_rate, ql.Actual360()))
flat_vol_ts                                                =
ql.BlackVolTermStructureHandle(ql.BlackConstantVol(settle
ment_date, ql.NullCalendar(), volatility, ql.Actual360()))

# Set up the Black-Scholes process
bsm_process   =   ql.BlackScholesMertonProcess(spot_handle,
dividend_yield, flat_ts, flat_vol_ts)

# Price the option using the analytic European engine
european_option.setPricingEngine(ql.AnalyticEuropeanEngi
ne(bsm_process))
```

```
npv = european_option.NPV()
print(f"European Call Option NPV: {npv}")
` ` `
```

Advanced Topics in QuantLib

QuantLib's true strength is revealed in its advanced functionalities, which allow for the modeling of complex derivatives and risk management scenarios. Some of these advanced topics include:

- Monte Carlo Simulations: Used for pricing complex derivatives by simulating various paths of the underlying asset.

- Interest Rate Models: QuantLib supports a variety of interest rate models including Hull-White, Black-Karasinski, and others, which are critical for pricing interest rate derivatives.

- Credit Risk Models: Tools for modeling credit risk and pricing credit derivatives.

Visualizing Data with Matplotlib

Introduction to Matplotlib

Matplotlib is renowned for its ability to generate high-quality graphs and charts with minimal effort. Before you start using it, ensure that Matplotlib is installed in your Python environment. You can install it using `pip`:

```bash
pip install matplotlib
```

` ` `

Once installed, you can import Matplotlib in your Python scripts:

```python
import matplotlib.pyplot as plt
```

Basic Plotting with Matplotlib

Matplotlib's simplicity allows you to create basic plots with just a few lines of code. Let's begin with a simple line plot to visualize the closing prices of a stock over time.

```python
import matplotlib.pyplot as plt
import pandas as pd

# Sample data: closing prices of a stock
data = {
    'Date':    pd.date_range(start='2023-01-01',    periods=10,
freq='D'),
    'Close': [150, 152, 153, 151, 154, 156, 157, 158, 159, 160]
}

# Create a DataFrame
df = pd.DataFrame(data)

# Plotting the closing prices
```

```python
plt.figure(figsize=(10, 6))
plt.plot(df['Date'], df['Close'], marker='o')
plt.title('Stock Closing Prices Over Time')
plt.xlabel('Date')
plt.ylabel('Closing Price')
plt.grid(True)
plt.show()
```

This example demonstrates how to create a basic line plot. The `marker='o'` argument adds markers to the data points, making it easier to see individual values. The `figure` function allows you to specify the size of the plot, and `grid(True)` adds a grid for better readability.

Customizing Plots

Matplotlib offers extensive customization options to tailor your plots to specific needs. You can customize titles, labels, colors, line styles, and more. Here's an example of a more customized plot:

```python
plt.figure(figsize=(10, 6))
plt.plot(df['Date'], df['Close'], marker='o', color='b', linestyle='--', linewidth=2, markersize=8)
plt.title('Stock Closing Prices Over Time', fontsize=16)
plt.xlabel('Date', fontsize=14)
plt.ylabel('Closing Price', fontsize=14)
plt.xticks(rotation=45)
```

```python
plt.grid(True, linestyle='--', linewidth=0.5)
plt.show()
```
` ` `

In this example, we changed the line color to blue (`color='b'`), used a dashed line style (`linestyle='--'`), increased the line width (`linewidth=2`), and changed the marker size (`markersize=8`). We also rotated the x-axis labels for better readability.

Visualizing Options Data

Visualizing options data, such as payoff diagrams and volatility surfaces, can provide valuable insights for traders. Let's look at how to create a payoff diagram for a simple call option using Matplotlib:

```python
import numpy as np

# Parameters for the call option
strike_price = 100
premium = 5
stock_prices = np.arange(50, 150, 1)

# Payoff calculation
payoff = np.maximum(stock_prices - strike_price, 0) - premium

# Plotting the payoff diagram
plt.figure(figsize=(10, 6))
```

```python
plt.plot(stock_prices, payoff, label='Call Option Payoff',
color='g')
```

plt.axhline(0, color='black', linewidth=0.5)

plt.axvline(strike_price, color='r', linewidth=0.5, linestyle='--',
label='Strike Price')

plt.title('Call Option Payoff Diagram')

plt.xlabel('Stock Price at Expiration')

plt.ylabel('Profit/Loss')

plt.legend()

plt.grid(True)

plt.show()

` ` `

This example showcases how Matplotlib can be used to visualize the payoff of a call option. The strike price is highlighted with a vertical dashed red line, and the x-axis and y-axis are labelled accordingly.

Creating Subplots

Subplots are useful when you need to display multiple plots in a single figure. This is particularly helpful for comparing different metrics or visualizing related data sets. Here's an example of creating subplots:

```python
fig, axs = plt.subplots(2, 1, figsize=(10, 10))

# Plot 1: Stock closing prices
axs[0].plot(df['Date'], df['Close'], marker='o', color='b')
```

```
axs[0].set_title('Stock Closing Prices Over Time')

axs[0].set_xlabel('Date')

axs[0].set_ylabel('Closing Price')

axs[0].grid(True)


# Plot 2: Call option payoff

axs[1].plot(stock_prices, payoff, label='Call Option Payoff',
color='g')

axs[1].axhline(0, color='black', linewidth=0.5)

axs[1].axvline(strike_price,      color='r',      linewidth=0.5,
linestyle='--', label='Strike Price')

axs[1].set_title('Call Option Payoff Diagram')

axs[1].set_xlabel('Stock Price at Expiration')

axs[1].set_ylabel('Profit/Loss')

axs[1].legend()

axs[1].grid(True)


plt.tight_layout()

plt.show()
```
` ` `

By using `subplots`, we created two vertically stacked plots within a single figure. This technique is particularly useful for comparing different aspects of financial data.

Interactive Visualizations

While static plots serve many purposes, interactive plots can provide a more dynamic and engaging way to explore data. Matplotlib integrates well with libraries like `mplfinance` and `plotly` to create interactive visualizations. Here's a simple example using `mplfinance` to create an interactive candlestick chart:

```python
import mplfinance as mpf

# Create a sample DataFrame with OHLC data
ohlc_data = {
    'Date': pd.date_range(start='2023-01-01', periods=10, freq='D'),
    'Open': [150, 151, 152, 153, 154, 155, 156, 157, 158, 159],
    'High': [151, 152, 153, 154, 155, 156, 157, 158, 159, 160],
    'Low': [149, 150, 151, 152, 153, 154, 155, 156, 157, 158],
    'Close': [150, 152, 153, 151, 154, 156, 157, 158, 159, 160]
}
ohlc_df = pd.DataFrame(ohlc_data)
ohlc_df.set_index('Date', inplace=True)

# Plot the candlestick chart
mpf.plot(ohlc_df, type='candle', style='charles', title='Stock OHLC Data', ylabel='Price')
```

In this example, `mplfinance` is used to plot an interactive candlestick chart, which is commonly used to represent the open, high, low, and closing prices of a stock over a specific period.

Implementing Basic Options Pricing Models

The Black-Scholes Model

The Black-Scholes Model, introduced by Fischer Black and Myron Scholes in 1973, revolutionized the field of financial derivatives. This model provides a closed-form solution for pricing European call and put options, assuming constant volatility and interest rates.

Formula and Parameters

The Black-Scholes formula for a European call option is given by:

$$ C = S_0 N(d_1) - X e^{-rT} N(d_2) $$

Where:
- C is the call option price
- S_0 is the current stock price
- X is the strike price
- r is the risk-free interest rate
- T is the time to expiration
- $N(d)$ is the cumulative distribution function of the standard normal distribution
- d_1 and d_2 are defined as:

$$ d_1 = \frac{\ln(S_0 / X) + (r + \sigma^2 / 2)T}{\sigma \sqrt{T}} $$
$$ d_2 = d_1 - \sigma \sqrt{T} $$

Here, σ is the volatility of the stock.

Implementing Black-Scholes in Python

Let's implement the Black-Scholes model in Python. We'll start by defining a function to calculate the option price:

```python
import numpy as np
from scipy.stats import norm

def black_scholes_call(S, X, T, r, sigma):
    d1 = (np.log(S / X) + (r + 0.5 * sigma2) * T) / (sigma * np.sqrt(T))
    d2 = d1 - sigma * np.sqrt(T)
    call_price = S * norm.cdf(d1) - X * np.exp(-r * T) * norm.cdf(d2)
    return call_price

# Example usage
S = 100  # Current stock price
X = 105  # Strike price
T = 1    # Time to expiration (1 year)
r = 0.05 # Risk-free interest rate (5%)
sigma = 0.2  # Volatility (20%)

call_price = black_scholes_call(S, X, T, r, sigma)
print(f"The price of the call option is: {call_price:.2f}")
```

This function calculates the price of a call option using the Black-Scholes formula. By adjusting the parameters, you can evaluate different option scenarios.

The Binomial Option Pricing Model

The Binomial Option Pricing Model is another fundamental method for valuing options. Developed by John Cox, Stephen Ross, and Mark Rubinstein in 1979, this model uses a discrete-time framework to simulate the possible price paths of the underlying asset. It is particularly useful for pricing American options, which can be exercised at any time before expiration.

Binomial Tree Construction

The model operates by constructing a binomial tree, where each node represents a possible price of the underlying asset at a given time step. The tree evolves over time steps until expiration, factoring in upward and downward price movements and their associated probabilities.

Implementing the Binomial Model in Python

Here's how to implement the Binomial Option Pricing Model for a European call option:

```python
def binomial_call(S, X, T, r, sigma, n):
    dt = T / n
    u = np.exp(sigma * np.sqrt(dt))
    d = 1 / u
```

```python
    p = (np.exp(r * dt) - d) / (u - d)

    # Initialize asset prices at maturity
    asset_prices = np.zeros(n + 1)
    for i in range(n + 1):
        asset_prices[i] = S * (u  (n - i)) * (d  i)

    # Initialize option values at maturity
    option_values = np.maximum(0, asset_prices - X)

    # Backward induction
    for j in range(n - 1, -1, -1):
        for i in range(j + 1):
            option_values[i] = np.exp(-r * dt) * (p * option_values[i]
+ (1 - p) * option_values[i + 1])

    return option_values[0]

# Example usage
S = 100  # Current stock price
X = 105  # Strike price
T = 1   # Time to expiration (1 year)
r = 0.05 # Risk-free interest rate (5%)
sigma = 0.2  # Volatility (20%)
n = 100  # Number of time steps

call_price = binomial_call(S, X, T, r, sigma, n)
print(f"The price of the call option is: {call_price:.2f}")
```
` ` `

In this implementation, `binomial_call` constructs the binomial tree and performs backward induction to compute the call option price. The parameter `n` controls the number of time steps in the tree, with higher values providing more accurate results.

Comparing Black-Scholes and Binomial Models

While both models aim to price options, they have distinct advantages and limitations:

- Black-Scholes Model:

  - Provides a closed-form solution, making it computationally efficient.

  - Assumes constant volatility and interest rates, which may not hold in real markets.

  - Best suited for European options.

- Binomial Model:

  - More flexible, can handle varying volatility and interest rates.

  - Suitable for both European and American options.

  - Computationally intensive for large numbers of time steps.

Practical Applications and Strategy Optimization

relies on these models to assess sensitivity and risk.

By integrating these models into Python scripts, traders can automate the evaluation of different option strategies, backtest their performance, and optimize parameters for maximum profitability.

Implementing basic options pricing models like Black-Scholes and Binomial in Python equips traders with powerful tools to analyze and execute options strategies. These models lay the groundwork for more advanced techniques discussed in subsequent sections. By mastering these fundamentals, you can develop a robust framework for making well-informed trading decisions and enhancing your overall strategy toolkit. As you progress, the integration of these models with real-time data and advanced analytics will further empower your trading capabilities.

Automating Data Fetching and Cleaning

Importance of Data Automation

Manual data handling is prone to errors and delays. In contrast, automated data fetching guarantees consistency and reliability. Automated processes can continuously pull data from various sources, parse it, and store it efficiently, making it available for immediate analysis and model updates. This automation is particularly crucial in high-frequency trading where decisions are made in milliseconds.

Setting Up the Environment

Before diving into automation, ensure your Python environment is equipped with the necessary libraries. The primary libraries for data fetching and cleaning are `pandas`, `requests`, and `beautifulsoup4` for web scraping, and `yfinance` for financial data.

```bash
pip install pandas requests beautifulsoup4 yfinance
```

Fetching Data Using APIs

APIs (Application Programming Interfaces) provide a standardized way to access financial data. Yahoo Finance, Alpha Vantage, and Quandl are popular APIs for fetching market data.

Using Yahoo Finance with `yfinance`

The `yfinance` library is a powerful tool for accessing Yahoo Finance data. Here's an example of fetching historical stock data:

```python
import yfinance as yf

def fetch_stock_data(ticker, start_date, end_date):
    stock = yf.Ticker(ticker)
    hist = stock.history(start=start_date, end=end_date)
    return hist

# Example usage
ticker = "AAPL"
start_date = "2020-01-01"
end_date = "2021-01-01"
```

```python
data = fetch_stock_data(ticker, start_date, end_date)
print(data.head())
```

This script fetches historical data for Apple Inc. (`AAPL`) between the specified dates. The data includes open, high, low, close prices, volume, and dividends.

Using Alpha Vantage

Alpha Vantage provides a rich set of financial data, including stock prices, forex, and cryptocurrencies. You'll need an API key to access their services.

```python
import requests
import pandas as pd

def fetch_alpha_vantage_data(symbol, api_key, function="TIME_SERIES_DAILY"):
    url = f"https://www.alphavantage.co/query?function={function}&symbol={symbol}&apikey={api_key}&datatype=csv"
    response = requests.get(url)
    data = pd.read_csv(pd.compat.StringIO(response.text))
    return data

# Example usage
api_key = "your_api_key"
symbol = "MSFT"
```

```python
data = fetch_alpha_vantage_data(symbol, api_key)
print(data.head())
```
```

This example fetches daily time series data for Microsoft (`MSFT`). The data comes in CSV format, which is then converted to a pandas DataFrame for further manipulation.

Web Scraping for Custom Data

Sometimes, APIs may not provide all the necessary data. In such cases, web scraping becomes a valuable tool. The `requests` and `beautifulsoup4` libraries are commonly used for this purpose.

```python
import requests
from bs4 import BeautifulSoup
import pandas as pd

def fetch_custom_data(url):
    response = requests.get(url)
    soup = BeautifulSoup(response.content, 'html.parser')
    table = soup.find('table')
    rows = table.find_all('tr')

    data = []
    for row in rows:
        cols = row.find_all('td')
        cols = [ele.text.strip() for ele in cols]
```
```

```
        data.append(cols)

    df = pd.DataFrame(data)
    return df

# Example usage
url = "https://example.com/data"
data = fetch_custom_data(url)
print(data.head())
```

This script demonstrates how to scrape tabular data from a webpage. Adjust the `url` and parsing logic according to the structure of the target webpage.

Cleaning and Preprocessing Data

Once the data is fetched, it needs cleaning to ensure it is suitable for analysis. Cleaning involves handling missing values, correcting data types, and normalizing formats.

Handling Missing Values

Missing data can distort analysis and model predictions. There are several strategies for handling missing values, including imputation and removal.

```python
def clean_missing_values(df):
    # Drop rows with missing values
```

```python
df = df.dropna()

# Alternatively, fill missing values with the mean
df = df.fillna(df.mean())

return df

# Example usage
cleaned_data = clean_missing_values(data)
print(cleaned_data.head())
```

This example shows how to drop rows with missing values or fill them with the mean of the column.

Converting Data Types

Ensuring that data types are consistent and appropriate is critical for accurate analysis.

```python
def convert_data_types(df):
    df['Date'] = pd.to_datetime(df['Date'])
    df['Volume'] = df['Volume'].astype(int)
    return df

# Example usage
converted_data = convert_data_types(data)
print(converted_data.dtypes)
```

```
```

This function converts the 'Date' column to datetime format and the 'Volume' column to integers.

Normalizing Data Formats

Different data sources may have varying formats. Normalizing these formats ensures consistency.

```python
def normalize_data(df):
    df.columns = df.columns.str.lower().str.replace(' ', '_')
    return df

# Example usage
normalized_data = normalize_data(data)
print(normalized_data.head())
```

This function standardizes column names by converting them to lowercase and replacing spaces with underscores.

Automating the Entire Process

To automate the entire data fetching and cleaning process, combine the above functions into a single workflow.

```python
def automate_data_pipeline(ticker, start_date, end_date,
```

```
api_key):
    data = fetch_stock_data(ticker, start_date, end_date)
    data = clean_missing_values(data)
    data = convert_data_types(data)
    data = normalize_data(data)
    return data

# Example usage
ticker = "AAPL"
start_date = "2020-01-01"
end_date = "2021-01-01"
api_key = "your_api_key"
final_data    =    automate_data_pipeline(ticker,    start_date,
end_date, api_key)
print(final_data.head())
` ` `
```

This comprehensive function automates the process of fetching, cleaning, and normalizing data, ensuring a streamlined workflow that can be easily integrated into larger trading systems.

Automating data fetching and cleaning is a foundational step in modern options trading. By leveraging Python and its robust libraries, traders can ensure they have access to accurate, timely, and clean data essential for making informed decisions. The techniques covered here lay the groundwork for more advanced data manipulation and analysis, pivotal for developing and optimizing trading strategies. As you progress, integrating these automated workflows with real-time data and sophisticated analytics will further enhance your trading capabilities and efficiency.

Introduction to Jupyter Notebooks for Project Management

What are Jupyter Notebooks?

Jupyter Notebooks are interactive computational environments where you can combine code execution, text, mathematics, plots, and rich media. Originating from the IPython project, Jupyter supports over 40 programming languages, including Python, making it a powerful tool for data analysis and scientific computing.

Setting Up Jupyter Notebooks

Before exploring Jupyter Notebooks, ensure that you have it installed in your Python environment. You can install Jupyter via pip:

```bash
pip install jupyter
```

Once installed, you can start Jupyter Notebook by running:

```bash
jupyter notebook
```

This command will open the Jupyter interface in your default web browser, providing an intuitive and interactive platform for your projects.

Creating and Structuring a Jupyter Notebook

Creating a new notebook is straightforward. From the Jupyter home page, you can create a new notebook by selecting the "New" button and choosing "Python 3".

Organizing Your Notebook

A well-organized notebook is crucial for managing complex projects. Consider structuring your notebook as follows:

1. Title and Introduction: Begin with a descriptive title and a brief introduction to the project. Use Markdown cells for text to provide context and explain the objectives.

```markdown
# Butterfly Spread Strategy Analysis
```
This notebook explores the butterfly spread strategy in options trading, including data acquisition, model implementation, and performance analysis.
```
```

2. Setup and Imports: Include all necessary library imports and initial setups in one place.

```python
import pandas as pd
import numpy as np
```

```python
import matplotlib.pyplot as plt
import yfinance as yf
```

3. Data Acquisition: Write code cells to fetch and display the data. Clearly annotate each step with Markdown cells to explain what the code does.

```python
# Fetching historical stock data
ticker = "AAPL"
start_date = "2020-01-01"
end_date = "2021-01-01"
data = yf.download(ticker, start=start_date, end=end_date)
data.head()
```

4. Data Cleaning and Preprocessing: Include steps to clean and preprocess the data, ensuring it's ready for analysis.

```python
# Handling missing values
data.dropna(inplace=True)

# Convert date to datetime format
data.index = pd.to_datetime(data.index)
```

5. Analysis and Visualization: Perform your analysis and

visualize the results. Use clear headings and Markdown explanations for each section.

```python
# Plotting the closing prices
plt.figure(figsize=(10, 5))
plt.plot(data['Close'])
plt.title('AAPL Closing Prices')
plt.xlabel('Date')
plt.ylabel('Price')
plt.show()
```

6. Model Implementation: Implement your trading strategy or model. Document each step thoroughly.

```python
# Example: Calculating moving averages
data['MA50'] = data['Close'].rolling(window=50).mean()
data['MA200'] = data['Close'].rolling(window=200).mean()
```

7. Results and Interpretation: Summarize the findings, interpret the results, and provide conclusions.

```markdown
## Results
```

The moving average strategy shows potential signals for trading based on the crossover points of the 50-day and 200-

day moving averages.

```
` ` `
```

Advantages of Using Jupyter Notebooks

Jupyter Notebooks offer several advantages for project management in options trading:

1. Interactivity: The ability to run code in small blocks and see results immediately fosters an interactive development approach. This interactivity is invaluable when testing and refining trading strategies.

2. Documentation: Combining code with narrative text and visualizations in a single document enhances readability and reproducibility. It allows you to document your thought process and methodology comprehensively.

3. Visualization: Jupyter supports rich visualizations using libraries like `matplotlib`, `seaborn`, and `plotly`. This capability is essential for analyzing and presenting complex financial data.

4. Collaboration: Notebooks can be shared easily with collaborators via platforms like GitHub or JupyterHub. This facilitates collaborative research and development.

5. Reproducibility: By keeping code, data, and documentation in one place, Jupyter Notebooks enhance the reproducibility of your work. Others can rerun your notebook to verify results or build upon your work.

Practical Example: Butterfly Spread Strategy

Let's walk through a practical example of using Jupyter Notebooks to implement a butterfly spread strategy.

Step 1: Data Acquisition

```python
import yfinance as yf
import pandas as pd

# Fetching historical stock data
ticker = "AAPL"
start_date = "2020-01-01"
end_date = "2021-01-01"
data = yf.download(ticker, start=start_date, end=end_date)
data.head()
```

Step 2: Data Cleaning

```python
# Handling missing values
data.dropna(inplace=True)

# Convert date to datetime format
data.index = pd.to_datetime(data.index)
```

Step 3: Strategy Implementation

```python
# Define the butterfly spread strategy
def butterfly_spread(data, strike_prices):
    # Calculate the payoff for each leg of the butterfly spread
    payoffs = {}
    for strike in strike_prices:
        payoffs[strike] = data['Close'].apply(lambda x: max(x - strike, 0))

    # Combine the legs to get the butterfly spread payoff
    payoff = 0.5 * payoffs[strike_prices[0]] - payoffs[strike_prices[1]] + 0.5 * payoffs[strike_prices[2]]
    return payoff

# Example usage with sample strike prices
strike_prices = [120, 130, 140]
data['Butterfly_Spread'] = butterfly_spread(data, strike_prices)
data[['Close', 'Butterfly_Spread']].head()
```

Step 4: Visualization

```python
import matplotlib.pyplot as plt

# Plotting the butterfly spread payoff
plt.figure(figsize=(10, 5))
plt.plot(data.index, data['Butterfly_Spread'])
```

```python
plt.title('Butterfly Spread Payoff')
plt.xlabel('Date')
plt.ylabel('Payoff')
plt.show()
```

Jupyter Notebooks provide a robust framework for managing and executing complex trading projects. Their interactive and integrative nature makes them an ideal choice for documenting and refining strategies like the butterfly spread. By leveraging the power of Jupyter, traders can enhance their workflow, ensure reproducibility, and collaborate effectively, ultimately leading to more informed and strategic trading decisions. As you integrate Jupyter Notebooks into your options trading toolkit, you'll find them indispensable for both learning and professional trading environments.

Practical Examples

Example 1: Constructing a Basic Butterfly Spread

Let's start with a simple example to construct a basic butterfly spread using historical stock data. We'll use Apple Inc. (AAPL) as our underlying asset.

Step 1: Data Acquisition

First, we'll fetch the historical stock data for AAPL using the `yfinance` library.

```python
```

```
import yfinance as yf
import pandas as pd

# Fetching historical stock data
ticker = "AAPL"
start_date = "2020-01-01"
end_date = "2021-01-01"
data = yf.download(ticker, start=start_date, end=end_date)
data.head()
```

Step 2: Define Strike Prices and Expiry

Next, we set the strike prices and expiry date for our options. For simplicity, we'll assume strike prices are $120, $130, and $140, with an expiry date of one month from the start date.

```python
strike_prices = [120, 130, 140]
expiry_date = "2020-02-01"
```

Step 3: Calculate Payoff

We create a function to calculate the payoff of our butterfly spread. The butterfly spread consists of buying one in-the-money call, selling two at-the-money calls, and buying one out-of-the-money call.

```python
```

```python
import numpy as np

def butterfly_spread_payoff(S, K1, K2, K3):
    payoff = np.maximum(S - K1, 0) - 2 * np.maximum(S - K2, 0) + np.maximum(S - K3, 0)
    return payoff

# Example stock prices at expiry
stock_prices = np.linspace(100, 150, 100)
payoffs = butterfly_spread_payoff(stock_prices, strike_prices[0], strike_prices[1], strike_prices[2])
```

Step 4: Visualization

Visualizing the payoff helps in understanding the risk-reward profile of the butterfly spread.

```python
import matplotlib.pyplot as plt

plt.figure(figsize=(10, 5))
plt.plot(stock_prices, payoffs, label='Butterfly Spread Payoff')
plt.axhline(0, color='black', lw=1)
plt.title('Butterfly Spread Payoff Diagram')
plt.xlabel('Stock Price at Expiry')
plt.ylabel('Payoff')
plt.legend()
plt.show()
```

```
` ` `
```

This basic example provides a clear view of how the butterfly spread profit and loss profile looks under various stock price scenarios at expiry.

Example 2: Back-testing Butterfly Spread Strategy

Back-testing is crucial for validating the effectiveness of any trading strategy. In this example, we'll back-test a butterfly spread strategy using historical data to determine its performance.

Step 1: Data Preparation

We'll start by preparing our data, including calculating moving averages which will serve as signals for entering and exiting trades.

```python
# Calculating moving averages
data['MA50'] = data['Close'].rolling(window=50).mean()
data['MA200'] = data['Close'].rolling(window=200).mean()

# Signal: when MA50 crosses above MA200, enter a butterfly spread
data['Signal'] = np.where(data['MA50'] > data['MA200'], 1, 0)
` ` `
```

Step 2: Strategy Implementation

We implement the butterfly spread based on the generated signals.

```python
def implement_strategy(data, strike_prices):
    data['Butterfly_Spread'] = np.nan
    for i in range(len(data)):
        if data['Signal'].iloc[i] == 1:
            data['Butterfly_Spread'].iloc[i]                          =
butterfly_spread_payoff(data['Close'].iloc[i],    strike_prices[0],
strike_prices[1], strike_prices[2])
    return data

data = implement_strategy(data, strike_prices)
```

Step 3: Performance Analysis

Analyzing the performance involves calculating the strategy's profit and loss over time.

```python
# Calculating cumulative return
data['Cumulative_Return']                                           =
data['Butterfly_Spread'].cumsum()

# Plotting cumulative returns
plt.figure(figsize=(10, 5))
plt.plot(data.index,                      data['Cumulative_Return'],
```

```
label='Cumulative Return')
plt.title('Butterfly Spread Strategy Cumulative Return')
plt.xlabel('Date')
plt.ylabel('Cumulative Return')
plt.legend()
plt.show()
```

This back-test example demonstrates how the butterfly spread strategy performs over a given period, providing insights into its profitability and risks.

Example 3: Incorporating Greeks Analysis

is essential for managing an options portfolio. In this example, we'll incorporate Greeks into our analysis to explore their impact on the butterfly spread.

Step 1: Calculate Greeks

We use a library like `QuantLib` to calculate the Greeks for our options.

```python
from QuantLib import *

# Setting up the environment
calendar = UnitedStates()
day_count = Actual365Fixed()
spot_price = SimpleQuote(130)
```

```python
volatility = BlackConstantVol(0, calendar, 0.2, day_count)
risk_free_rate = YieldTermStructureHandle(FlatForward(0, calendar, 0.01, day_count))

# Options setup
expiry = Date(1, 2, 2020)
call_option = EuropeanOption(PlainVanillaPayoff(Option.Call, 130), EuropeanExercise(expiry))
call_option.setPricingEngine(AnalyticEuropeanEngine(BlackScholesMertonProcess(spot_price, risk_free_rate, volatility)))

# Calculating Greeks
delta = call_option.delta()
gamma = call_option.gamma()
theta = call_option.theta()
vega = call_option.vega()

print(f"Delta: {delta}, Gamma: {gamma}, Theta: {theta}, Vega: {vega}")
```

Step 2: Integrate Greeks into Strategy

We integrate the calculated Greeks into our trading strategy to manage risks more effectively.

```python
# Adjusting strategy based on Greeks
def adjust_strategy_based_on_greeks(data, delta, gamma, theta, vega):
```

```python
    data['Adjusted_Strategy'] = np.nan
    for i in range(len(data)):
        if data['Signal'].iloc[i] == 1:
            greek_adjustment = delta * data['Close'].iloc[i] +
gamma * (data['Close'].iloc[i] 2) + theta + vega
            data['Adjusted_Strategy'].iloc[i]                        =
butterfly_spread_payoff(data['Close'].iloc[i]                         +
greek_adjustment,      strike_prices[0],      strike_prices[1],
strike_prices[2])
    return data

data = adjust_strategy_based_on_greeks(data, delta, gamma,
theta, vega)
```

Step 3: Analyze the Impact

We analyze how the inclusion of Greeks affects the strategy's performance.

```python
# Plotting adjusted strategy performance
data['Adjusted_Cumulative_Return']                              =
data['Adjusted_Strategy'].cumsum()

plt.figure(figsize=(10, 5))
plt.plot(data.index,      data['Adjusted_Cumulative_Return'],
label='Adjusted Cumulative Return')
plt.title('Adjusted Butterfly Spread Strategy Cumulative
Return')
```

```
plt.xlabel('Date')
plt.ylabel('Cumulative Return')
plt.legend()
plt.show()
```
```

This example underscores the importance of Greeks analysis in refining and optimizing options trading strategies, offering a nuanced approach to managing risks and enhancing returns.

These practical examples illustrate the application of theoretical concepts in real-world scenarios. By leveraging Python and its powerful libraries, we can construct, back-test, and optimize butterfly spread strategies, providing a robust framework for successful options trading. As you delve into these examples, remember to adapt and experiment with the parameters to discover what works best for your trading style and objectives. The hands-on experience gained here lays a solid foundation for more advanced explorations in options trading.
```

CHAPTER 5: CODING THE BUTTERFLY SPREAD STRATEGY IN PYTHON

T o start coding the butterfly spread strategy in Python, a meticulous planning phase is essential. This phase will lay down the groundwork, setting up a robust framework that ensures our project is both scalable and easy to maintain. The butterfly spread strategy, with its intricate mechanics and precision-oriented execution, demands a structured approach to coding.

Identifying Goals and Requirements

The first step in planning the project structure is to clearly identify our goals and requirements. The primary objective is to build a Python-based application that can construct, analyze, and back-test butterfly spread strategies. To achieve this, we must break down the project into manageable components:

1. Data Acquisition and Preparation: Accessing reliable financial data, both historical and real-time, from sources such as APIs or data vendors.

2. Strategy Construction: Writing functions to construct butterfly spreads based on specified strike prices and market conditions.

3. Payoff Diagrams: Implementing visualization tools to generate and interpret payoff diagrams.

4. Profit and Loss Calculation: Developing functions to calculate potential profits, losses, and breakeven points.

5. Integration with Pricing Models: Incorporating options pricing models like Black-Scholes or Binomial to enhance strategy accuracy.

6. Market Simulation: Simulating various market scenarios to test the robustness of the butterfly spread strategy.

to understand risk and sensitivity.

8. Handling Implied Volatility: Factoring in implied volatility to refine strategy parameters.

9. Back-testing Framework: Creating a comprehensive back-testing framework to validate the strategy against historical data.

Designing the Project Architecture

With goals and requirements in place, the next step is to design the project architecture. This involves organizing the project into a well-defined structure that promotes modularity and reusability.

1. Directory Structure: Organize the project into directories that separate different components. A suggested structure

could be:

- data/: Scripts and tools for data acquisition and preparation.

- strategies/: Functions and classes for constructing butterfly spreads and other strategies.

- visualization/: Modules for generating and displaying payoff diagrams.

- analysis/: Tools for profit/loss calculations, Greeks analysis, and market simulation.

- tests/: Unit tests and back-testing frameworks.

- notebooks/: Jupyter notebooks for exploratory data analysis and documentation.

2. Modular Design: Each component should be designed as a module with a clear interface. For example, the `data` module will have functions to fetch data from APIs, clean and preprocess it, and return it in a usable format.

3. Configuration Management: Use configuration files (e.g., `.env` or `config.yaml`) to store parameters and settings. This makes it easier to manage and modify configurations without altering the codebase.

4. Version Control: Utilize version control systems like Git to track changes, collaborate with others, and maintain a history of the project. Setting up a remote repository on platforms like GitHub or GitLab is advisable for backup and collaboration purposes.

Setting Up the Development Environment

A standardized development environment ensures

consistency across different stages of the project. This includes:

1. Python Environment: Use virtual environments (e.g., `virtualenv` or `conda`) to create isolated Python environments. This avoids dependency conflicts and ensures reproducibility.

2. Required Libraries: Install essential libraries such as:
    - `pandas` for data manipulation
    - `numpy` for numerical operations
    - `matplotlib` and `seaborn` for data visualization
    - `scikit-learn` and `tensorflow` for machine learning tasks
    - `quantlib` for advanced options pricing models

3. IDE and Tools: Choose a robust integrated development environment (IDE) like PyCharm or VS Code. Additionally, Jupyter Notebooks can be invaluable for exploratory data analysis and documentation.

Creating a Project Roadmap

With the structure and environment in place, it's time to create a roadmap that outlines the development process. This roadmap will act as a guide, ensuring that the project stays on track and milestones are met.

1. Milestones and Deadlines: Define key milestones (e.g., data acquisition, strategy construction, back-testing) and set realistic deadlines for each. This helps in maintaining focus and achieving incremental progress.

2. Task Breakdown: Break down each milestone into smaller tasks. For instance, under the milestone "data acquisition," tasks could include identifying data sources, writing scripts to fetch data, and cleaning and preprocessing the data.

3. Documentation: Maintain comprehensive documentation throughout the project. This includes code comments, README files, and detailed explanations of each module and function. Good documentation is crucial for collaboration and future maintenance.

Effective Collaboration and Version Control

If working in a team, effective collaboration is vital. Use collaborative tools such as:

1. Version Control Platforms: GitHub or GitLab for version control and collaboration. Create branches for different features or modules, and use pull requests for code reviews.

2. Project Management Tools: Tools like Trello or Asana can help in tracking progress, assigning tasks, and managing workflows.

3. Communication: Regular communication through platforms like Slack or Microsoft Teams ensures that everyone is aligned and informed.

Meticulously planning the project structure, we set a solid foundation for developing a robust and scalable Python-based butterfly spread strategy application. This structured approach not only enhances efficiency and maintainability but also ensures that the project remains focused and aligned with its goals. As we move forward into the implementation phase, this well-laid groundwork will guide us in translating theoretical concepts into practical, executable code.

Writing a Function for Butterfly Spread Construction

Creating a function to construct a butterfly spread in Python is a crucial step in operationalizing our strategy. This function will serve as the backbone of our trading application, allowing us to build, analyze, and execute butterfly spreads with precision and efficiency. We'll walk through the process of writing this function, step-by-step, ensuring that it encompasses all necessary components and adheres to best practices.

Defining the Function's Purpose and Parameters

The primary purpose of this function is to construct a butterfly spread by selecting appropriate strike prices and option types (calls or puts). The function should be flexible enough to handle different market conditions and user inputs. Let's start by defining the necessary parameters for our function:

1. Underlying Price (`underlying_price`): The current price of the underlying asset.

2. Strike Prices (`strike_price1`, `strike_price2`, `strike_price3`): The strike prices for the butterfly spread. Typically, `strike_price2` is the at-the-money (ATM) strike, while `strike_price1` and `strike_price3` are the lower and higher strikes, respectively.

3. Option Type (`option_type`): Specifies whether we are

using call or put options ("call" or "put").

4. Expiration Date (`expiration_date`): The expiration date of the options.

5. Option Prices (`price1`, `price2`, `price3`): The market prices of the options at the specified strike prices.

6. Quantity (`quantity`): The number of contracts for each option.

Here is the definition of our function:

```python
def construct_butterfly_spread(underlying_price,
strike_price1, strike_price2, strike_price3,

                option_type, expiration_date, price1,
price2, price3, quantity=1):
    """

    Constructs a butterfly spread strategy.

    Parameters:
    underlying_price (float): Current price of the underlying
asset.
    strike_price1 (float): Strike price of the lower leg.
    strike_price2 (float): Strike price of the middle leg (ATM).
    strike_price3 (float): Strike price of the upper leg.
    option_type (str): Type of option ('call' or 'put').
    expiration_date (datetime): Expiration date of the options.
    price1 (float): Market price of the option at strike_price1.
    price2 (float): Market price of the option at strike_price2.
    price3 (float): Market price of the option at strike_price3.
```

quantity (int): Number of contracts for each option (default is 1).

Returns:

dict: A dictionary containing details of the butterfly spread.
"""

```
```

Constructing the Butterfly Spread

The butterfly spread typically consists of three legs: buying one lower strike option, selling two middle strike options, and buying one higher strike option. The function needs to handle both calls and puts, so we'll include conditional logic to accommodate both scenarios.

Let's expand our function to include the construction logic:

```python
def          construct_butterfly_spread(underlying_price,
strike_price1, strike_price2, strike_price3,

                    option_type, expiration_date, price1,
price2, price3, quantity=1):
    """

    Constructs a butterfly spread strategy.
```

Parameters:

underlying_price (float): Current price of the underlying asset.

strike_price1 (float): Strike price of the lower leg.

strike_price2 (float): Strike price of the middle leg (ATM).

strike_price3 (float): Strike price of the upper leg.

option_type (str): Type of option ('call' or 'put').

expiration_date (datetime): Expiration date of the options.

price1 (float): Market price of the option at strike_price1.

price2 (float): Market price of the option at strike_price2.

price3 (float): Market price of the option at strike_price3.

quantity (int): Number of contracts for each option (default is 1).

Returns:

dict: A dictionary containing details of the butterfly spread.
"""

```
# Validate option type
if option_type not in ['call', 'put']:
    raise ValueError("option_type must be 'call' or 'put'")

# Create the butterfly spread structure
butterfly_spread = {
    'underlying_price': underlying_price,
    'legs': []
}

# Add legs to the butterfly spread
if option_type == 'call':
    butterfly_spread['legs'].append({'type': 'long', 'option': 'call', 'strike': strike_price1, 'price': price1, 'quantity': quantity})
```

```python
    butterfly_spread['legs'].append({'type': 'short', 'option':
'call', 'strike': strike_price2, 'price': price2, 'quantity': 2 *
quantity})
    butterfly_spread['legs'].append({'type': 'long', 'option':
'call', 'strike': strike_price3, 'price': price3, 'quantity': quantity})
  elif option_type == 'put':
    butterfly_spread['legs'].append({'type': 'long', 'option':
'put', 'strike': strike_price1, 'price': price1, 'quantity': quantity})
    butterfly_spread['legs'].append({'type': 'short', 'option':
'put', 'strike': strike_price2, 'price': price2, 'quantity': 2 *
quantity})
    butterfly_spread['legs'].append({'type': 'long', 'option':
'put', 'strike': strike_price3, 'price': price3, 'quantity': quantity})


  return butterfly_spread
```

Calculating the Initial Cost and Maximum Profit/Loss

Next, we need to calculate the initial cost of the butterfly spread, as well as the potential maximum profit and loss. The initial cost is the net premium paid or received when establishing the position. The maximum profit and loss are determined by the spread between the strike prices and the premiums paid.

Let's extend our function to include these calculations:

```python
def                   construct_butterfly_spread(underlying_price,
strike_price1, strike_price2, strike_price3,
```

```
                        option_type,   expiration_date,   price1,
price2, price3, quantity=1):
    """
```

Constructs a butterfly spread strategy.

Parameters:

underlying_price (float): Current price of the underlying asset.

strike_price1 (float): Strike price of the lower leg.

strike_price2 (float): Strike price of the middle leg (ATM).

strike_price3 (float): Strike price of the upper leg.

option_type (str): Type of option ('call' or 'put').

expiration_date (datetime): Expiration date of the options.

price1 (float): Market price of the option at strike_price1.

price2 (float): Market price of the option at strike_price2.

price3 (float): Market price of the option at strike_price3.

quantity (int): Number of contracts for each option (default is 1).

Returns:

dict: A dictionary containing details of the butterfly spread.
```
    """
```

```
    # Validate option type
    if option_type not in ['call', 'put']:
        raise ValueError("option_type must be 'call' or 'put'")

    # Create the butterfly spread structure
    butterfly_spread = {
```

```python
    'underlying_price': underlying_price,
    'legs': [],
    'initial_cost': 0,
    'max_profit': 0,
    'max_loss': 0
}


# Add legs to the butterfly spread
if option_type == 'call':
    butterfly_spread['legs'].append({'type': 'long', 'option': 'call', 'strike': strike_price1, 'price': price1, 'quantity': quantity})
    butterfly_spread['legs'].append({'type': 'short', 'option': 'call', 'strike': strike_price2, 'price': price2, 'quantity': 2 * quantity})
    butterfly_spread['legs'].append({'type': 'long', 'option': 'call', 'strike': strike_price3, 'price': price3, 'quantity': quantity})
elif option_type == 'put':
    butterfly_spread['legs'].append({'type': 'long', 'option': 'put', 'strike': strike_price1, 'price': price1, 'quantity': quantity})
    butterfly_spread['legs'].append({'type': 'short', 'option': 'put', 'strike': strike_price2, 'price': price2, 'quantity': 2 * quantity})
    butterfly_spread['legs'].append({'type': 'long', 'option': 'put', 'strike': strike_price3, 'price': price3, 'quantity': quantity})


# Calculate initial cost
initial_cost = (price1 - 2 * price2 + price3) * quantity
butterfly_spread['initial_cost'] = initial_cost


# Calculate maximum profit and loss
```

```
    max_profit = (strike_price2 - strike_price1 - initial_cost) *
quantity
    max_loss = initial_cost * quantity
    butterfly_spread['max_profit'] = max_profit
    butterfly_spread['max_loss'] = max_loss

    return butterfly_spread
```

Testing the Function

To ensure our function works correctly, we should test it with various inputs. Here's an example test case:

```python
# Example test case
underlying_price = 100
strike_price1 = 95
strike_price2 = 100
strike_price3 = 105
option_type = 'call'
expiration_date = '2023-12-31'
price1 = 3
price2 = 1.5
price3 = 1
quantity = 1

butterfly_spread                                         =
construct_butterfly_spread(underlying_price,    strike_price1,
```

strike_price2, strike_price3,

option_type, expiration_date, price1, price2, price3, quantity)

print(butterfly_spread)
``` ` `

Output:
``` ` `python
```python
{
    'underlying_price': 100,
    'legs': [
        {'type': 'long', 'option': 'call', 'strike': 95, 'price': 3, 'quantity': 1},
        {'type': 'short', 'option': 'call', 'strike': 100, 'price': 1.5, 'quantity': 2},
        {'type': 'long', 'option': 'call', 'strike': 105, 'price': 1, 'quantity': 1}
    ],
    'initial_cost': 1.0,
    'max_profit': 4.0,
    'max_loss': 1.0
}
```
` ` `

Implementing Payoff Diagrams

Setting Up the Environment

Before diving into the code, ensure your Python environment is ready. You'll need to have `pandas`, `numpy`, and `matplotlib` installed. Use the following commands to install these libraries if you haven't already:

```bash
pip install pandas numpy matplotlib
```

Defining the Payoff Calculation Function

A critical aspect of creating payoff diagrams is computing the payoff of each option leg at various underlying prices. We'll start by defining a function to calculate the payoff for individual call and put options. Here is an example:

```python
import numpy as np

def option_payoff(underlying_prices, strike_price, premium, option_type):
    """
    Calculate the payoff of an individual option.

    Parameters:
    underlying_prices (array): Array of underlying asset prices at expiration.
    strike_price (float): Strike price of the option.
    premium (float): Initial premium paid for the option.
    option_type (str): Type of option ('call' or 'put').
```

Returns:

array: Payoff of the option at each underlying price.

"""

```python
    if option_type == 'call':
        return np.maximum(underlying_prices - strike_price, 0) - premium
    elif option_type == 'put':
        return np.maximum(strike_price - underlying_prices, 0) - premium
    else:
        raise ValueError("option_type must be 'call' or 'put'")

# Example usage
underlying_prices = np.linspace(80, 120, 100)
payoff = option_payoff(underlying_prices, strike_price=100, premium=2, option_type='call')
```

Constructing the Butterfly Spread Payoff

Next, we will use the previously defined `option_payoff` function to compute the payoff for each leg of the butterfly spread and then combine them. This involves buying one lower strike option, selling two at-the-money options, and buying one higher strike option. We'll encapsulate this logic in a function:

```python
def butterfly_spread_payoff(underlying_prices, strike_price1,
```

strike_price2, strike_price3,

                        price1, price2, price3, quantity=1):

    """

Calculate the payoff of a butterfly spread.

Parameters:

underlying_prices (array): Array of underlying asset prices at expiration.

strike_price1 (float): Strike price of the lower leg.

strike_price2 (float): Strike price of the middle leg (ATM).

strike_price3 (float): Strike price of the upper leg.

price1 (float): Market price of the option at strike_price1.

price2 (float): Market price of the option at strike_price2.

price3 (float): Market price of the option at strike_price3.

quantity (int): Number of contracts for each option (default is 1).

Returns:

array: Payoff of the butterfly spread at each underlying price.

    """

```python
payoff_lower_leg = quantity * option_payoff(underlying_prices, strike_price1, price1, 'call')
payoff_middle_leg = -2 * quantity * option_payoff(underlying_prices, strike_price2, price2, 'call')
payoff_upper_leg = quantity * option_payoff(underlying_prices, strike_price3, price3, 'call')

total_payoff = payoff_lower_leg + payoff_middle_leg +
```

payoff_upper_leg

```
    return total_payoff
```

```
# Example usage
payoff = butterfly_spread_payoff(underlying_prices, 95, 100, 105, 3, 1.5, 1)
```
` ` `

Visualizing the Payoff Diagram

With the payoff calculations in place, we turn to visualization. Here, we'll use `matplotlib` to plot the butterfly spread's payoff diagram. This graphical representation will help you intuitively understand the strategy's potential outcomes.

```python
import matplotlib.pyplot as plt

def plot_butterfly_spread_payoff(underlying_prices, payoff):
    """
    Plot the payoff diagram of a butterfly spread.

    Parameters:
    underlying_prices (array): Array of underlying asset prices at expiration.
    payoff (array): Payoff of the butterfly spread at each underlying price.
    """
    plt.figure(figsize=(10, 6))
    plt.plot(underlying_prices, payoff, label='Butterfly Spread
```

Payoff')

```
    plt.axhline(0, color='black', lw=2)
    plt.axvline(100, color='red', linestyle='--', label='ATM Strike')
    plt.title('Butterfly Spread Payoff Diagram')
    plt.xlabel('Underlying Asset Price at Expiration')
    plt.ylabel('Payoff')
    plt.legend()
    plt.grid(True)
    plt.show()

# Example usage
underlying_prices = np.linspace(80, 120, 100)
payoff = butterfly_spread_payoff(underlying_prices, 95, 100, 105, 3, 1.5, 1)
plot_butterfly_spread_payoff(underlying_prices, payoff)
``` `
```

This plot will show a symmetrical diagram, peaking at the middle strike price. The maximum profit is achieved when the underlying price equals the middle strike price at expiration, while the losses are capped at the initial cost.

Integrating with Real Data

To enhance the practical utility of our payoff diagrams, integrate real market data. This allows you to tailor the analysis to current market conditions and refine your decision-making. Here's an example of how you can fetch and use real data:
```

```python
import yfinance as yf

# Fetching historical data
ticker = 'AAPL'
data = yf.download(ticker, start='2023-01-01', end='2023-12-31')
underlying_price = data['Close'][-1]

# Example with real data
strike_price1 = 95
strike_price2 = 100
strike_price3 = 105
price1 = 3
price2 = 1.5
price3 = 1
quantity = 1

# Generate underlying prices around the current price
underlying_prices = np.linspace(underlying_price * 0.8, underlying_price * 1.2, 100)
payoff = butterfly_spread_payoff(underlying_prices, strike_price1, strike_price2, strike_price3, price1, price2, price3, quantity)
plot_butterfly_spread_payoff(underlying_prices, payoff)
```

Incorporating real-time data, you gain a more realistic and up-to-date perspective of the butterfly spread's potential performance, aiding in sound strategy formulation.

Optimizing the Visualization

For a more refined and informative diagram, consider adding features such as annotations, interactive elements, and comparison with other strategies. Libraries like `plotly` can provide interactive capabilities, enhancing user engagement and analysis depth.

Example with Plotly

Here's a brief example of how to use `plotly` for interactive plots:

```python
import plotly.graph_objects as go

def interactive_butterfly_payoff(underlying_prices, payoff):
    """
    Create an interactive payoff diagram using plotly.

    Parameters:
    underlying_prices (array): Array of underlying asset prices at expiration.
    payoff (array): Payoff of the butterfly spread at each underlying price.
    """
    fig = go.Figure()
    fig.add_trace(go.Scatter(x=underlying_prices, y=payoff, mode='lines', name='Butterfly Spread Payoff'))
```

```
fig.add_trace(go.Scatter(x=[strike_price2],
y=[np.max(payoff)], mode='markers', name='Max Profit Point',
marker=dict(size=10, color='red')))

    fig.update_layout(title='Interactive Butterfly Spread Payoff
Diagram',

                xaxis_title='Underlying    Asset    Price    at
Expiration',

                yaxis_title='Payoff',

                showlegend=True)
    fig.show()


# Example usage

interactive_butterfly_payoff(underlying_prices, payoff)
` ` `
```

This interactive plot allows you to hover over data points to see exact values, zoom in and out, and better understand the strategy's payoff structure.

Implementing payoff diagrams for butterfly spreads in Python bridges the gap between theoretical understanding and practical application. By leveraging Python's powerful libraries, you can create insightful visualizations that inform your trading decisions. These diagrams not only illustrate potential profits and losses but also help in identifying optimal strike prices and managing risks effectively. As you continue to refine and utilize these tools, your ability to navigate the complexities of options trading will be significantly enhanced.

Calculating P&L, Breakevens, and Risk-Reward

Setting Up the Python Environment

Before we begin, ensure that your Python environment is correctly configured. You should have `pandas`, `numpy`, and `matplotlib` installed. If they're not installed, you can do so using the following commands:

```bash
pip install pandas numpy matplotlib
```

Defining the P&L Calculation Function

The first step is to define a function that calculates the P&L for a butterfly spread. This involves computing the net profit or loss at various underlying asset prices, considering the premiums paid for the options.

```python
def butterfly_spread_pl(underlying_prices, strike_price1,
strike_price2, strike_price3,
            price1, price2, price3, quantity=1):
    """
```

Calculate the P&L of a butterfly spread.

Parameters:

underlying_prices (array): Array of underlying asset prices at expiration.

strike_price1 (float): Strike price of the lower leg.

strike_price2 (float): Strike price of the middle leg (ATM).

strike_price3 (float): Strike price of the upper leg.

price1 (float): Market price of the option at strike_price1.

price2 (float): Market price of the option at strike_price2.

price3 (float): Market price of the option at strike_price3.

quantity (int): Number of contracts for each option (default is 1).

Returns:

array: P&L of the butterfly spread at each underlying price.
"""

```
payoff    =    butterfly_spread_payoff(underlying_prices,
strike_price1, strike_price2, strike_price3,
                    price1, price2, price3, quantity)
total_premium = quantity * (price1 + 2 * price2 + price3)
pl = payoff - total_premium
return pl


# Example usage
underlying_prices = np.linspace(80, 120, 100)
pl = butterfly_spread_pl(underlying_prices, 95, 100, 105, 3, 1.5, 1)
```
```

Identifying Breakeven Points

Breakeven points are crucial in options trading as they indicate the underlying price levels at which the strategy neither makes a profit nor incurs a loss. For a butterfly spread, there are typically two breakeven points.

```python

```
def    find_breakeven_points(strike_price1,    strike_price2,
strike_price3, premium):
    """
```

Calculate the breakeven points of a butterfly spread.

Parameters:

strike_price1 (float): Strike price of the lower leg.

strike_price2 (float): Strike price of the middle leg (ATM).

strike_price3 (float): Strike price of the upper leg.

premium (float): Total premium paid for the butterfly spread.

Returns:

tuple: Lower and upper breakeven points.
```
    """

    lower_breakeven = strike_price2 - premium
    upper_breakeven = strike_price2 + premium
    return lower_breakeven, upper_breakeven

# Example usage
total_premium = 3 + 2 * 1.5 + 1
lower_breakeven,    upper_breakeven    =
find_breakeven_points(95, 100, 105, total_premium)
print(f"Lower    Breakeven:    {lower_breakeven},    Upper
Breakeven: {upper_breakeven}")
```
```

Evaluating the Risk-Reward Ratio
```

The risk-reward ratio is a fundamental metric in trading, helping you assess whether the potential reward justifies the risk taken. For a butterfly spread, this involves comparing the maximum potential profit with the maximum potential loss.

```python
def risk_reward_ratio(max_profit, max_loss):
    """

    Calculate the risk-reward ratio of a butterfly spread.

    Parameters:
    max_profit (float): Maximum profit of the butterfly spread.
    max_loss (float): Maximum loss of the butterfly spread.

    Returns:
    float: Risk-reward ratio.
    """

    ratio = max_profit / max_loss
    return ratio

# Example usage
max_profit = strike_price2 - strike_price1 - total_premium
max_loss = total_premium
ratio = risk_reward_ratio(max_profit, max_loss)
print(f"Risk-Reward Ratio: {ratio}")
```

Integrating with Visualizations

To make these calculations more intuitive, we can visualize the P&L, breakeven points, and risk-reward ratio using `matplotlib`.

```python
def    plot_butterfly_spread_pl(underlying_prices,    pl,
lower_breakeven, upper_breakeven):
    """
    Plot the P&L diagram of a butterfly spread, including breakeven points.

    Parameters:
    underlying_prices (array): Array of underlying asset prices at expiration.
    pl (array): P&L of the butterfly spread at each underlying price.
    lower_breakeven (float): Lower breakeven point.
    upper_breakeven (float): Upper breakeven point.
    """
    plt.figure(figsize=(10, 6))
    plt.plot(underlying_prices, pl, label='P&L')
    plt.axhline(0, color='black', lw=2)
    plt.axvline(lower_breakeven, color='green', linestyle='--', label='Lower Breakeven')
    plt.axvline(upper_breakeven, color='red', linestyle='--', label='Upper Breakeven')
    plt.title('Butterfly Spread P&L Diagram')
    plt.xlabel('Underlying Asset Price at Expiration')
    plt.ylabel('P&L')
```

```python
plt.legend()
plt.grid(True)
plt.show()
```

```python
# Example usage
plot_butterfly_spread_pl(underlying_prices,          pl,
lower_breakeven, upper_breakeven)
```
```
```

This plot provides a clear visual representation of how the butterfly spread performs across different underlying prices, highlighting the breakeven points and potential profits and losses.

Practical Example with Real Data

To make the analysis more relevant, let's integrate real market data for a practical example.

```python
import yfinance as yf

# Fetching historical data
ticker = 'AAPL'
data      =      yf.download(ticker,      start='2023-01-01',
end='2023-12-31')
underlying_price = data['Close'][-1]

# Example with real data
strike_price1 = 95
```

```
strike_price2 = 100
strike_price3 = 105
price1 = 3
price2 = 1.5
price3 = 1
quantity = 1

# Generate underlying prices around the current price
underlying_prices = np.linspace(underlying_price * 0.8,
underlying_price * 1.2, 100)
pl = butterfly_spread_pl(underlying_prices, strike_price1,
strike_price2, strike_price3, price1, price2, price3, quantity)
lower_breakeven,        upper_breakeven        =
find_breakeven_points(strike_price1,        strike_price2,
strike_price3, total_premium)
plot_butterfly_spread_pl(underlying_prices,        pl,
lower_breakeven, upper_breakeven)
```

Using real market data, you can evaluate the butterfly spread strategy's performance under actual market conditions, providing insights into its practical applicability.

Calculating P&L, identifying breakeven points, and evaluating the risk-reward ratio are fundamental components of options trading. By integrating these calculations into your Python scripts, you gain a comprehensive understanding of a butterfly spread's financial metrics. This empowers you to make informed trading decisions, optimizing your strategy for better performance. As you continue to refine your analytical tools and techniques, your proficiency in navigating the complexities of options trading will grow, enhancing your potential for success in the financial markets.

Integrating Options Pricing Models

Setting Up the Python Environment

Ensure that your Python environment is equipped with essential libraries. You'll need `pandas`, `numpy`, `scipy`, and `matplotlib`. If these libraries are not installed, use the following commands:

```bash
pip install pandas numpy scipy matplotlib
```

Additionally, for more advanced options pricing, the `QuantLib` library can be incredibly useful:

```bash
pip install QuantLib-Python
```

Black-Scholes Model Implementation

The Black-Scholes model is a cornerstone in options pricing. It helps determine the fair price of European call and put options. Let's start by implementing the Black-Scholes formula in Python.

```python
```

```
import numpy as np
from scipy.stats import norm

def black_scholes_call(S, K, T, r, sigma):
    """
    Calculate the Black-Scholes price for a European call option.

    Parameters:
    S (float): Current stock price.
    K (float): Option strike price.
    T (float): Time to maturity (in years).
    r (float): Risk-free interest rate (annualized).
    sigma (float): Volatility of the underlying asset (annualized).

    Returns:
    float: Black-Scholes price of the call option.
    """
    d1 = (np.log(S / K) + (r + 0.5 * sigma  2) * T) / (sigma * np.sqrt(T))
    d2 = d1 - sigma * np.sqrt(T)
    call_price = S * norm.cdf(d1) - K * np.exp(-r * T) * norm.cdf(d2)
    return call_price

def black_scholes_put(S, K, T, r, sigma):
    """
    Calculate the Black-Scholes price for a European put option.
```

Parameters:

S (float): Current stock price.

K (float): Option strike price.

T (float): Time to maturity (in years).

r (float): Risk-free interest rate (annualized).

sigma (float): Volatility of the underlying asset (annualized).

Returns:

float: Black-Scholes price of the put option.
"""

```python
d1 = (np.log(S / K) + (r + 0.5 * sigma  2) * T) / (sigma * np.sqrt(T))
d2 = d1 - sigma * np.sqrt(T)
put_price = K * np.exp(-r * T) * norm.cdf(-d2) - S * norm.cdf(-d1)
return put_price

# Example usage
S = 100 # Current stock price
K = 100 # Option strike price
T = 1   # Time to maturity (1 year)
r = 0.05 # Risk-free interest rate (5%)
sigma = 0.2 # Volatility (20%)

call_price = black_scholes_call(S, K, T, r, sigma)
put_price = black_scholes_put(S, K, T, r, sigma)
print(f"Call Price: {call_price}, Put Price: {put_price}")
```

```
` ` `
```

This implementation provides a fundamental understanding of how the Black-Scholes model can be used to price European options, which form the base components of our butterfly spread strategy.

Binomial Tree Model Implementation

The Binomial Tree model offers a versatile approach by discretizing time and simulating the possible paths of the underlying asset price. This model is particularly useful for American options, which can be exercised at any time before expiration.

```python
def binomial_tree_call(S, K, T, r, sigma, steps):
    """
```

Calculate the Binomial Tree price for a European call option.

Parameters:

S (float): Current stock price.

K (float): Option strike price.

T (float): Time to maturity (in years).

r (float): Risk-free interest rate (annualized).

sigma (float): Volatility of the underlying asset (annualized).

steps (int): Number of time steps.

Returns:

float: Binomial Tree price of the call option.
"""

```
dt = T / steps
u = np.exp(sigma * np.sqrt(dt))
d = 1 / u
p = (np.exp(r * dt) - d) / (u - d)

option_values = np.zeros((steps + 1, steps + 1))

for i in range(steps + 1):
    option_values[i, steps] = max(0, S * (u (steps - i)) * (d i) - K)

for j in range(steps - 1, -1, -1):
    for i in range(j + 1):
        option_values[i, j] = np.exp(-r * dt) * (p * option_values[i, j + 1] + (1 - p) * option_values[i + 1, j + 1])

return option_values[0, 0]

# Example usage
call_price_binomial = binomial_tree_call(S, K, T, r, sigma, 100)
print(f"Binomial Tree Call Price: {call_price_binomial}")
```
` ` `

The Binomial Tree model's flexibility allows for more granular control over the simulation of option prices, accommodating various exercise styles and complex payoffs.

Integrating Pricing Models into Butterfly Spread

With the pricing models ready, the next step is to integrate them into the butterfly spread strategy. This involves using these models to price the individual legs of the spread and then combining them to evaluate the overall strategy.

```python
def butterfly_spread_prices(S, K1, K2, K3, T, r, sigma, model='black-scholes'):
    """

    Calculate the prices of the options in a butterfly spread using specified pricing model.

    Parameters:
    S (float): Current stock price.
    K1 (float): Strike price of the lower leg.
    K2 (float): Strike price of the middle leg (ATM).
    K3 (float): Strike price of the upper leg.
    T (float): Time to maturity (in years).
    r (float): Risk-free interest rate (annualized).
    sigma (float): Volatility of the underlying asset (annualized).
    model (str): The pricing model to use ('black-scholes' or 'binomial').

    Returns:
    tuple: Prices of the options at K1, K2, and K3.
    """

    if model == 'black-scholes':
        price1 = black_scholes_call(S, K1, T, r, sigma)
```

```python
    price2 = black_scholes_call(S, K2, T, r, sigma)
    price3 = black_scholes_call(S, K3, T, r, sigma)
elif model == 'binomial':
    price1 = binomial_tree_call(S, K1, T, r, sigma, 100)
    price2 = binomial_tree_call(S, K2, T, r, sigma, 100)
    price3 = binomial_tree_call(S, K3, T, r, sigma, 100)
else:
    raise ValueError("Invalid pricing model. Choose 'black-scholes' or 'binomial'.")

    return price1, price2, price3


# Example usage
prices_bs = butterfly_spread_prices(S, 95, 100, 105, T, r, sigma, model='black-scholes')
prices_binomial = butterfly_spread_prices(S, 95, 100, 105, T, r, sigma, model='binomial')
print(f"Black-Scholes Prices: {prices_bs}")
print(f"Binomial Tree Prices: {prices_binomial}")
```

By providing a choice between different pricing models, this function enhances flexibility and accuracy in evaluating the butterfly spread strategy.

Visualizing the Butterfly Spread Strategy

Visual representation aids in comprehending the dynamics of the butterfly spread. Utilizing `matplotlib`, we can create a P&L diagram that integrates the calculated prices.

````python
def plot_butterfly_spread(S, K1, K2, K3, T, r, sigma, model='black-scholes'):
    """
````

Plot the P&L diagram of a butterfly spread using specified pricing model.

Parameters:

S (float): Current stock price.

K1 (float): Strike price of the lower leg.

K2 (float): Strike price of the middle leg (ATM).

K3 (float): Strike price of the upper leg.

T (float): Time to maturity (in years).

r (float): Risk-free interest rate (annualized).

sigma (float): Volatility of the underlying asset (annualized).

model (str): The pricing model to use ('black-scholes' or 'binomial').
```
    """
```

underlying_prices = np.linspace(S * 0.8, S * 1.2, 100)

prices = butterfly_spread_prices(S, K1, K2, K3, T, r, sigma, model)

pl = butterfly_spread_pl(underlying_prices, K1, K2, K3, *prices)

lower_breakeven, upper_breakeven = find_breakeven_points(K1, K2, K3, sum(prices))

plt.figure(figsize=(10, 6))

```python
plt.plot(underlying_prices, pl, label='P&L')

plt.axhline(0, color='black', lw=2)

plt.axvline(lower_breakeven, color='green', linestyle='--', label='Lower Breakeven')

plt.axvline(upper_breakeven, color='red', linestyle='--', label='Upper Breakeven')

plt.title('Butterfly Spread P&L Diagram')

plt.xlabel('Underlying Asset Price at Expiration')

plt.ylabel('P&L')

plt.legend()

plt.grid(True)

plt.show()


# Example usage
plot_butterfly_spread(S, 95, 100, 105, T, r, sigma, model='black-scholes')
```

This visualization helps traders to visually assess the strategy's performance and the impact of different pricing models.

Practical Example with Real Data

To solidify the concepts, let's utilize real market data for a practical example.

```python
import yfinance as yf
```

```
# Fetching historical data
ticker = 'AAPL'
data      =      yf.download(ticker,      start='2023-01-01',
end='2023-12-31')
underlying_price = data['Close'][-1]

# Example with real data
strike_price1 = 95
strike_price2 = 100
strike_price3 = 105
T = 0.5  # 6 months to expiration
r = 0.02  # 2% risk-free rate
sigma = 0.25  # 25% volatility

# Generate underlying prices around the current price
underlying_prices  =  np.linspace(underlying_price  *  0.8,
underlying_price * 1.2, 100)
prices       =       butterfly_spread_prices(underlying_price,
strike_price1,  strike_price2,  strike_price3,  T,  r,  sigma,
model='black-scholes')
pl  =  butterfly_spread_pl(underlying_prices,  strike_price1,
strike_price2, strike_price3, *prices)
lower_breakeven,            upper_breakeven            =
find_breakeven_points(strike_price1,            strike_price2,
strike_price3, sum(prices))
plot_butterfly_spread(underlying_price,            strike_price1,
strike_price2, strike_price3, T, r, sigma, model='black-scholes')
```

Applying real market data, traders can evaluate the butterfly spread strategy in a pragmatic context, honing their analytical skills and improving decision-making.

Integrating options pricing models into your butterfly spread strategy is fundamental for precise evaluation and execution. By implementing both the Black-Scholes and Binomial Tree models, traders can enhance their analytical toolkit, enabling better-informed trading decisions. The ability to visualize these strategies further aids in understanding and optimizing performance in real-world scenarios. This comprehensive approach ensures a robust and dynamic trading strategy, capable of adapting to the ever-changing financial markets.

Simulating Market Scenarios

Setting Up Your Simulation Environment

Before diving into the simulations, ensure you have the necessary Python libraries installed. We will primarily use `pandas`, `numpy`, `scipy`, and `matplotlib`. Additionally, we will introduce `yfinance` for fetching historical data and `statsmodels` for advanced statistical simulations.

```bash
pip install pandas numpy scipy matplotlib yfinance statsmodels
```

Historical Data and Basic Statistics

To simulate realistic market scenarios, we start by examining historical data. This data provides the foundation for understanding price movements and volatility, which are crucial for accurate simulations.

```python
import yfinance as yf
import pandas as pd

# Fetch historical data for a given ticker
ticker = 'AAPL'
data = yf.download(ticker, start='2020-01-01', end='2023-01-01')
data['Return'] = data['Adj Close'].pct_change()
data = data.dropna()

# Calculate basic statistics
mean_return = data['Return'].mean()
std_return = data['Return'].std()

print(f"Mean Return: {mean_return}, Standard Deviation: {std_return}")
```

The mean return and standard deviation of returns provide a baseline for simulating future prices. These statistics inform the parameters for our simulation models.

Monte Carlo Simulation

Monte Carlo simulations are a powerful tool for modeling the possible future prices of an underlying asset. By generating numerous random price paths, we can estimate the distribution of potential outcomes.

```python
import numpy as np

def monte_carlo_simulation(S, T, mu, sigma, num_simulations, num_steps):
    """
    Perform a Monte Carlo simulation for an underlying asset.

    Parameters:
    S (float): Current stock price.
    T (float): Time to maturity (in years).
    mu (float): Expected return (annualized).
    sigma (float): Volatility of the underlying asset (annualized).
    num_simulations (int): Number of simulation paths.
    num_steps (int): Number of time steps.

    Returns:
    np.ndarray: Simulated price paths.
    """
    dt = T / num_steps
    price_paths = np.zeros((num_steps + 1, num_simulations))
    price_paths[0] = S
```

```
    for t in range(1, num_steps + 1):
        z = np.random.standard_normal(num_simulations)
        price_paths[t] = price_paths[t - 1] * np.exp((mu - 0.5 *
sigma2) * dt + sigma * np.sqrt(dt) * z)

    return price_paths

# Example usage
S = data['Adj Close'].iloc[-1]
T = 1  # 1 year
mu = mean_return * 252  # annualized
sigma = std_return * 2520.5  # annualized
num_simulations = 1000
num_steps = 252

simulated_paths = monte_carlo_simulation(S, T, mu, sigma,
num_simulations, num_steps)

# Plotting the simulations
import matplotlib.pyplot as plt

plt.figure(figsize=(10, 6))
plt.plot(simulated_paths)
plt.title('Monte Carlo Simulation - Asset Price Paths')
plt.xlabel('Time Steps')
plt.ylabel('Simulated Prices')
plt.show()
```
```
```

This code generates 1000 simulated price paths for one year, providing a visual representation of the range of possible future prices.

Applying Simulations to Butterfly Spread Strategy

With the simulated price paths, we can now evaluate the butterfly spread strategy under various market conditions. This involves calculating the payoff for each simulated path and analyzing the distribution of outcomes.

```python
def butterfly_spread_payoff(S, K1, K2, K3):
    """

    Calculate the payoff of a butterfly spread at expiration.

    Parameters:
    S (np.ndarray): Simulated end prices.
    K1 (float): Strike price of the lower leg.
    K2 (float): Strike price of the middle leg (ATM).
    K3 (float): Strike price of the upper leg.

    Returns:
    np.ndarray: Payoff of the butterfly spread.
    """

    payoff = np.maximum(S - K1, 0) - 2 * np.maximum(S - K2, 0) + np.maximum(S - K3, 0)
    return payoff
```

```python
# Calculate payoff for each simulation
K1, K2, K3 = 95, 100, 105
payoffs = butterfly_spread_payoff(simulated_paths[-1], K1, K2, K3)

# Analyze the results
mean_payoff = np.mean(payoffs)
std_payoff = np.std(payoffs)

print(f"Mean Payoff: {mean_payoff}, Standard Deviation of Payoff: {std_payoff}")
```

By calculating the payoff for each simulated path, we obtain a distribution of potential outcomes. This analysis helps in understanding the risk-reward profile of the butterfly spread under different market conditions.

Scenario Analysis with Merton Jump-Diffusion Model

For more advanced simulations, the Merton Jump-Diffusion model incorporates sudden, significant changes in asset price, reflecting real-world market shocks.

```python
import statsmodels.api as sm

def merton_jump_diffusion(S, T, mu, sigma, lam, m, v, num_simulations, num_steps):
    """
```

Perform a Merton Jump-Diffusion simulation for an underlying asset.

Parameters:

S (float): Current stock price.

T (float): Time to maturity (in years).

mu (float): Expected return (annualized).

sigma (float): Volatility of the underlying asset (annualized).

lam (float): Average frequency of jumps per year.

m (float): Mean of jump size.

v (float): Standard deviation of jump size.

num_simulations (int): Number of simulation paths.

num_steps (int): Number of time steps.

Returns:

np.ndarray: Simulated price paths.

"""

```
dt = T / num_steps
price_paths = np.zeros((num_steps + 1, num_simulations))
price_paths[0] = S

for t in range(1, num_steps + 1):
    z = np.random.standard_normal(num_simulations)
    j = np.random.poisson(lam * dt, num_simulations)
    price_paths[t] = price_paths[t - 1] * np.exp((mu - 0.5
* sigma2) * dt + sigma * np.sqrt(dt) * z + j * (m + v *
np.random.standard_normal(num_simulations)))
```

```
    return price_paths

# Example usage
lam = 0.1  # 10% chance of jump per year
m = -0.02  # Mean jump size (2% drop)
v = 0.1    # Jump size volatility (10%)

simulated_paths_merton = merton_jump_diffusion(S, T, mu,
sigma, lam, m, v, num_simulations, num_steps)

# Plotting the Merton simulations
plt.figure(figsize=(10, 6))
plt.plot(simulated_paths_merton)
plt.title('Merton Jump-Diffusion Simulation - Asset Price
Paths')
plt.xlabel('Time Steps')
plt.ylabel('Simulated Prices')
plt.show()
```
` ` `

The Merton Jump-Diffusion model captures the impact of rare but significant price movements, providing a comprehensive view of potential market scenarios.

Stress Testing and Sensitivity Analysis

Stress testing involves evaluating the butterfly spread strategy under extreme market conditions. This helps identify vulnerabilities and improve resilience.

```python
def stress_test(payoffs, extreme_conditions):
    """

    Perform stress testing on the payoffs under extreme market
    conditions.

    Parameters:

    payoffs (np.ndarray): Payoffs from simulated scenarios.

    extreme_conditions (dict): Dictionary of extreme market
    conditions with their likelihood.

    Returns:

    dict: Expected payoffs under each extreme condition.
    """

    results = {}
    for condition, likelihood in extreme_conditions.items():
        condition_payoffs = payoffs * likelihood

        results[condition]    =    np.mean(condition_payoffs),
np.std(condition_payoffs)

    return results

# Example usage
extreme_conditions = {
    'Market Crash': 0.7,
    'Market Rally': 1.5,
    'High Volatility': 1.2
}
```

```
stress_test_results = stress_test(payoffs, extreme_conditions)
for condition, (mean_payoff, std_payoff) in
stress_test_results.items():
    print(f"{condition} - Mean Payoff: {mean_payoff}, Std Dev:
{std_payoff}")
` ` `
```

By applying stress testing, traders can evaluate the robustness of their strategies and make informed adjustments to mitigate risks.

Simulating market scenarios is a critical aspect of refining and validating the butterfly spread strategy. By leveraging historical data, Monte Carlo simulations, the Merton Jump-Diffusion model, and stress testing, traders can gain a comprehensive understanding of potential market dynamics. This approach not only enhances decision-making but also builds resilience, ensuring that strategies remain effective in the face of unpredictable market conditions. Through meticulous simulation and analysis, traders can navigate the complexities of options trading with greater confidence and precision.

Incorporating Greeks Analysis

Understanding the Greeks: A Primer

The Greeks are measures of sensitivity that describe how the price of an option changes in response to different variables. Each Greek provides insights into specific risk factors:

1. Delta (Δ): Measures the sensitivity of an option's price to changes in the price of the underlying asset.

2. Gamma (Γ): Measures the sensitivity of Delta to changes in the price of the underlying asset.

3. Theta (Θ): Measures the sensitivity of an option's price to the passage of time.

4. Vega (ν): Measures the sensitivity of an option's price to changes in the volatility of the underlying asset.

5. Rho (ρ): Measures the sensitivity of an option's price to changes in interest rates.

Calculating the Greeks in Python

We first need the necessary libraries and a method to calculate the Greeks. The `QuantLib` library in Python is particularly useful for this purpose.

```bash
pip install QuantLib-Python
```

Delta and Gamma Calculation

Delta and Gamma are critical for understanding the price sensitivity of the option and the rate of change of this sensitivity, respectively. Here's how to calculate them:

```python
import QuantLib as ql
```

```
def calculate_greeks(option_type, spot_price, strike_price,
maturity, risk_free_rate, volatility):
    """

    Calculate Delta and Gamma for a European option.

    Parameters:
    option_type (str): 'call' or 'put'
    spot_price (float): Current price of the underlying asset
    strike_price (float): Strike price of the option
    maturity (float): Time to expiration in years
    risk_free_rate (float): Risk-free interest rate
    volatility (float): Volatility of the underlying asset

    Returns:
    tuple: Delta and Gamma of the option
    """

    # Set up the QuantLib parameters
    spot_handle = ql.QuoteHandle(ql.SimpleQuote(spot_price))
    vol_handle                                             =
ql.BlackVolTermStructureHandle(ql.BlackConstantVol(0,
ql.NullCalendar(),
ql.QuoteHandle(ql.SimpleQuote(volatility)), ql.Actual360()))
    rate_handle                                            =
ql.YieldTermStructureHandle(ql.FlatForward(0,
ql.NullCalendar(),
ql.QuoteHandle(ql.SimpleQuote(risk_free_rate)),
ql.Actual360()))
    payoff = ql.PlainVanillaPayoff(ql.Option.Call if option_type
== 'call' else ql.Option.Put, strike_price)
```

```python
    exercise = ql.EuropeanExercise(ql.Date().todaysDate() +
ql.Period(int(maturity * 360), ql.Days))
    option = ql.EuropeanOption(payoff, exercise)

    # Set up the Black-Scholes process
    process = ql.BlackScholesMertonProcess(spot_handle,
rate_handle, rate_handle, vol_handle)

    # Calculate and return the Greeks
    option.setPricingEngine(ql.AnalyticEuropeanEngine(proc
ess))
    delta = option.delta()
    gamma = option.gamma()

    return delta, gamma

# Example usage
spot_price = 100
strike_price = 105
maturity = 1  # 1 year
risk_free_rate = 0.05
volatility = 0.2

delta, gamma = calculate_greeks('call', spot_price, strike_price,
maturity, risk_free_rate, volatility)
print(f"Delta: {delta}, Gamma: {gamma}")
```

Theta and Vega Calculation

Theta and Vega provide insights into time decay and volatility sensitivity, respectively. Here's the implementation:

```python
def calculate_theta_vega(option_type, spot_price, strike_price, maturity, risk_free_rate, volatility):
    """

    Calculate Theta and Vega for a European option.

    Parameters:
    option_type (str): 'call' or 'put'
    spot_price (float): Current price of the underlying asset
    strike_price (float): Strike price of the option
    maturity (float): Time to expiration in years
    risk_free_rate (float): Risk-free interest rate
    volatility (float): Volatility of the underlying asset

    Returns:
    tuple: Theta and Vega of the option
    """

    # Set up the QuantLib parameters
    spot_handle = ql.QuoteHandle(ql.SimpleQuote(spot_price))
    vol_handle                                                =
ql.BlackVolTermStructureHandle(ql.BlackConstantVol(0,
ql.NullCalendar(),
ql.QuoteHandle(ql.SimpleQuote(volatility)), ql.Actual360()))
    rate_handle                                               =
ql.YieldTermStructureHandle(ql.FlatForward(0,
ql.NullCalendar(),
```

```
ql.QuoteHandle(ql.SimpleQuote(risk_free_rate)),
ql.Actual360()))

    payoff = ql.PlainVanillaPayoff(ql.Option.Call if option_type
== 'call' else ql.Option.Put, strike_price)

    exercise = ql.EuropeanExercise(ql.Date().todaysDate() +
ql.Period(int(maturity * 360), ql.Days))

    option = ql.EuropeanOption(payoff, exercise)


    # Set up the Black-Scholes process

    process = ql.BlackScholesMertonProcess(spot_handle,
rate_handle, rate_handle, vol_handle)


    # Calculate and return the Greeks

    option.setPricingEngine(ql.AnalyticEuropeanEngine(proc
ess))

    theta = option.theta()

    vega = option.vega()


    return theta, vega


# Example usage

theta, vega = calculate_theta_vega('call', spot_price,
strike_price, maturity, risk_free_rate, volatility)

print(f"Theta: {theta}, Vega: {vega}")
```

Rho Calculation

Rho measures the sensitivity of the option's price to interest rate changes, which is also essential for a comprehensive analysis.

```python
def calculate_rho(option_type, spot_price, strike_price,
maturity, risk_free_rate, volatility):
    """

    Calculate Rho for a European option.

    Parameters:
    option_type (str): 'call' or 'put'
    spot_price (float): Current price of the underlying asset
    strike_price (float): Strike price of the option
    maturity (float): Time to expiration in years
    risk_free_rate (float): Risk-free interest rate
    volatility (float): Volatility of the underlying asset

    Returns:
    float: Rho of the option
    """

    # Set up the QuantLib parameters
    spot_handle = ql.QuoteHandle(ql.SimpleQuote(spot_price))
    vol_handle                                              =
ql.BlackVolTermStructureHandle(ql.BlackConstantVol(0,
ql.NullCalendar(),
ql.QuoteHandle(ql.SimpleQuote(volatility)), ql.Actual360()))
    rate_handle                                             =
ql.YieldTermStructureHandle(ql.FlatForward(0,
ql.NullCalendar(),
ql.QuoteHandle(ql.SimpleQuote(risk_free_rate)),
ql.Actual360()))
```

```python
    payoff = ql.PlainVanillaPayoff(ql.Option.Call if option_type
== 'call' else ql.Option.Put, strike_price)
    exercise = ql.EuropeanExercise(ql.Date().todaysDate() +
ql.Period(int(maturity * 360), ql.Days))
    option = ql.EuropeanOption(payoff, exercise)

    # Set up the Black-Scholes process
    process = ql.BlackScholesMertonProcess(spot_handle,
rate_handle, rate_handle, vol_handle)

    # Calculate and return the Greek
    option.setPricingEngine(ql.AnalyticEuropeanEngine(proc
ess))
    rho = option.rho()

    return rho

# Example usage
rho = calculate_rho('call', spot_price, strike_price, maturity,
risk_free_rate, volatility)
print(f"Rho: {rho}")
```

Integrating Greeks into Butterfly Spread Strategy

By calculating the Greeks for each leg of the butterfly spread,
we can gain a comprehensive understanding of the strategy's
risk profile. Here's how to integrate these calculations:

```python
```

```python
# Define the butterfly spread components
spot_price = 100
strike_prices = [95, 100, 105] # K1, K2, K3
maturity = 0.5  # 6 months
risk_free_rate = 0.03
volatility = 0.25

# Calculate Greeks for each leg
greeks = {}
for strike_price in strike_prices:
    greeks[strike_price] = {}
    greeks[strike_price]['Delta'], greeks[strike_price]['Gamma'] = calculate_greeks('call', spot_price, strike_price, maturity, risk_free_rate, volatility)
    greeks[strike_price]['Theta'], greeks[strike_price]['Vega'] = calculate_theta_vega('call', spot_price, strike_price, maturity, risk_free_rate, volatility)
    greeks[strike_price]['Rho'] = calculate_rho('call', spot_price, strike_price, maturity, risk_free_rate, volatility)

# Display the Greeks
for strike_price, greek_values in greeks.items():
    print(f"Strike Price: {strike_price}")
    for greek, value in greek_values.items():
        print(f"  {greek}: {value}")
```

Analyzing Combined Greeks

To fully appreciate the butterfly spread's risk dynamics, we need to analyze the combined Greeks of the entire strategy. This involves summing the Greeks for each leg, weighted by the respective position sizes (positive for long positions and negative for short positions).

```python
def combine_greeks(greeks, weights):
    """
    Combine Greeks for a multi-leg strategy.

    Parameters:
    greeks (dict): Dictionary of Greeks for each leg.
    weights (list): Weights of each leg (positive for long, negative for short).

    Returns:
    dict: Combined Greeks.
    """
    combined_greeks = {'Delta': 0, 'Gamma': 0, 'Theta': 0, 'Vega': 0, 'Rho': 0}

    for strike_price, weight in zip(greeks.keys(), weights):
        for greek, value in greeks[strike_price].items():
            combined_greeks[greek] += weight * value

    return combined_greeks

# Define weights for the butterfly spread legs
```

```
weights = [1, -2, 1]  # +1 K1, -2 K2, +1 K3

combined_greeks = combine_greeks(greeks, weights)

# Display the combined Greeks
print("Combined Greeks for the Butterfly Spread:")
for greek, value in combined_greeks.items():
    print(f" {greek}: {value}")
` ` `
```

Practical Applications of Greeks Analysis

Incorporating Greeks analysis into the butterfly spread strategy provides several practical benefits:

1. Risk Management: By understanding the sensitivities of the strategy to various factors, traders can make informed adjustments to manage risk effectively.

2. Optimization: Greeks analysis helps in optimizing the strike prices and expiration dates for the butterfly spread, maximizing the risk-reward ratio.

3. Scenario Analysis: Evaluating how the combined Greeks change under different market conditions allows traders to anticipate potential outcomes and adjust their strategies accordingly.

4. Automated Trading: Integrating Greeks into automated trading algorithms ensures that the strategies remain dynamic and adaptive to market changes.

Incorporating Greeks analysis into the butterfly spread

strategy is essential for a thorough understanding of its risk and reward dynamics. By calculating and combining the Greeks for each leg of the spread, traders can optimize their strategies, manage risks, and anticipate market movements with greater precision. This comprehensive approach to Greeks analysis not only enhances decision-making but also builds a resilient trading framework capable of navigating the complexities of the options market. Through meticulous analysis and application of the Greeks, traders can achieve a higher level of sophistication and success in their trading endeavors.

Handling Implied Volatility

Implied volatility (IV) is a cornerstone of options trading, reflecting the market's expectations of future price fluctuations in the underlying asset. It is not derived from historical price movements but is instead implied by the current market prices of options. Understanding and handling implied volatility is crucial for the butterfly spread strategy as it directly influences the pricing, risk, and potential profitability of the strategy.

The Significance of Implied Volatility

Implied volatility is an invaluable metric because it provides insight into market sentiment and potential future volatility. High implied volatility generally indicates that the market expects substantial price movements, while low implied volatility suggests more stable price expectations.

1. Impact on Option Pricing: Implied volatility is a key input in option pricing models such as Black-Scholes. As IV increases, the prices of options tend to rise, and conversely, they fall

when IV decreases.

2. Risk Management: Understanding IV helps traders assess the risk associated with their positions. For butterfly spreads, which involve multiple options with different strike prices, IV can significantly affect the strategy's profitability and risk profile.

Calculating Implied Volatility

Calculating implied volatility typically involves using an option pricing model to solve for the volatility figure that equates the theoretical price of an option to its market price. Python, with the help of libraries like `QuantLib`, offers robust tools for this purpose.

```bash
pip install QuantLib-Python
```

```python
import QuantLib as ql

def calculate_implied_volatility(option_type, market_price, spot_price, strike_price, maturity, risk_free_rate):
    """
    Calculate the implied volatility for a European option.

    Parameters:
    option_type (str): 'call' or 'put'
    market_price (float): Current market price of the option
    spot_price (float): Current price of the underlying asset
```

strike_price (float): Strike price of the option

maturity (float): Time to expiration in years

risk_free_rate (float): Risk-free interest rate

Returns:

float: Implied volatility of the option

"""

```python
# Set up the QuantLib parameters
spot_handle = ql.QuoteHandle(ql.SimpleQuote(spot_price))
rate_handle                                        =
ql.YieldTermStructureHandle(ql.FlatForward(0,
ql.NullCalendar(),
ql.QuoteHandle(ql.SimpleQuote(risk_free_rate)),
ql.Actual360()))
payoff = ql.PlainVanillaPayoff(ql.Option.Call if option_type
== 'call' else ql.Option.Put, strike_price)
exercise  =  ql.EuropeanExercise(ql.Date().todaysDate()  +
ql.Period(int(maturity * 360), ql.Days))
option = ql.EuropeanOption(payoff, exercise)

# Use Black-Scholes process without volatility
process    =    ql.BlackScholesMertonProcess(spot_handle,
rate_handle, rate_handle, None)
engine = ql.AnalyticEuropeanEngine(process)
option.setPricingEngine(engine)

# Solve for implied volatility
volatility = ql.ImpliedVolatilityHelper()
implied_vol                                        =
volatility.solveImpliedVolatility(market_price,        option,
```

```
rate_handle.discount(maturity),    spot_price,    strike_price,
maturity, risk_free_rate)

    return implied_vol

# Example usage
market_price = 10
spot_price = 100
strike_price = 105
maturity = 1  # 1 year
risk_free_rate = 0.03

implied_vol = calculate_implied_volatility('call', market_price,
spot_price, strike_price, maturity, risk_free_rate)
print(f"Implied Volatility: {implied_vol}")
```
` ` `

Incorporating Implied Volatility into Butterfly Spread Strategy

Implied volatility's influence on the butterfly spread strategy
can be profound. Here's how it integrates into different aspects
of the strategy:

1. Strike Price Selection: When implied volatility is high,
choosing strike prices that are closer together may be more
beneficial, as the wider price movements can cover a broader
range. Conversely, in low volatility environments, selecting
strike prices further apart might be a better approach.

2. Profit and Loss Profiles: The breakeven points and maximum
profit/loss scenarios of a butterfly spread depend significantly
on the level of implied volatility. A thorough analysis of IV can

help optimize these profiles.

Scenario Analysis with Varying Implied Volatility

Performing scenario analysis with varying levels of implied volatility helps understand the potential outcomes of the butterfly spread under different market conditions. This approach involves recalculating the Greeks, and potential profits or losses, as IV changes.

```python
def scenario_analysis(volatilities, spot_price, strike_prices, maturity, risk_free_rate):
    """

    Perform scenario analysis of butterfly spread under different volatilities.

    Parameters:
    volatilities (list): List of volatilities to analyze
    spot_price (float): Current price of the underlying asset
    strike_prices (list): Strike prices of the butterfly spread [K1, K2, K3]
    maturity (float): Time to expiration in years
    risk_free_rate (float): Risk-free interest rate

    Returns:
    dict: Analysis results for each volatility
    """

    results = {}
```

```
    for vol in volatilities:
        greeks = {}
        for strike_price in strike_prices:
            greeks[strike_price] = {}
            greeks[strike_price]['Delta'],        greeks[strike_price]
['Gamma'] = calculate_greeks('call', spot_price, strike_price,
maturity, risk_free_rate, vol)
            greeks[strike_price]['Theta'],        greeks[strike_price]
['Vega'] = calculate_theta_vega('call', spot_price, strike_price,
maturity, risk_free_rate, vol)
            greeks[strike_price]['Rho']     =     calculate_rho('call',
spot_price, strike_price, maturity, risk_free_rate, vol)

        combined_greeks = combine_greeks(greeks, weights=[1,
-2, 1])

        results[vol] = combined_greeks

    return results

# Example usage
volatilities = [0.2, 0.25, 0.3, 0.35]  # Different volatilities to
analyze
strike_prices = [95, 100, 105]
maturity = 0.5  # 6 months
risk_free_rate = 0.03

analysis_results = scenario_analysis(volatilities, spot_price,
strike_prices, maturity, risk_free_rate)
```

```python
# Display the analysis results
for vol, greeks in analysis_results.items():
    print(f"Volatility: {vol}")
    for greek, value in greeks.items():
        print(f" {greek}: {value}")
```

Practical Strategies for Handling Implied Volatility

1. Volatility Skew Analysis: Traders often analyze volatility skew, the pattern of IV across different strike prices, to identify mispriced options and potential trading opportunities. For butterfly spreads, understanding the skew helps in positioning the strikes optimally.

2. Volatility Surface Modeling: Constructing a 3D surface of implied volatilities can provide a comprehensive view of how IV changes over different strikes and maturities. This model helps in dynamically adjusting the butterfly spread to exploit volatility discrepancies.

3. Hedging Volatility Risk: To mitigate the risk arising from changes in implied volatility, traders can employ hedging strategies such as delta-hedging or using volatility derivatives like VIX options.

Implementing a Volatility Surface in Python

To create a volatility surface, we need to gather implied volatility data for various strike prices and maturities. We then visualize this data in a 3D plot.

```python
```

```python
import numpy as np
import matplotlib.pyplot as plt
from mpl_toolkits.mplot3d import Axes3D

# Sample data for volatility surface
strike_prices = np.linspace(80, 120, 10)
maturities = np.linspace(0.1, 1, 10)
implied_vols = np.random.uniform(0.2, 0.4, size=(10, 10))

# Create a meshgrid for the surface plot
X, Y = np.meshgrid(strike_prices, maturities)
Z = np.array(implied_vols)

# Plotting the volatility surface
fig = plt.figure()
ax = fig.add_subplot(111, projection='3d')
surface = ax.plot_surface(X, Y, Z, cmap='viridis')

ax.set_xlabel('Strike Price')
ax.set_ylabel('Maturity (Years)')
ax.set_zlabel('Implied Volatility')
plt.title('Volatility Surface')
plt.colorbar(surface)
plt.show()
```

Handling implied volatility is a multifaceted task that requires a deep understanding of how market expectations influence option pricing and risk. By calculating implied volatility using Python, integrating it into the butterfly spread strategy, and performing scenario analysis, traders can enhance their decision-making and optimize their strategies. The practical approaches to managing IV, such as analyzing volatility skew and constructing a volatility surface, provide a robust framework for navigating the complexities of the options market. These insights into implied volatility not only fortify the butterfly spread strategy but also empower traders to achieve greater precision and adaptability in their trading endeavors.

Backtesting the Strategy

Preparation and Setup

Before diving into the code, it is imperative to have a well-structured environment. Ensure you have Python installed along with essential libraries such as `pandas`, `numpy`, `matplotlib`, and `quantlib`. If not already done, install these libraries using `pip`:

```python
pip install pandas numpy matplotlib quantlib
```

Data Collection

The foundation of any robust backtest is quality data. For

our butterfly spread strategy, we need historical options data, including strike prices, expiration dates, and underlying asset prices. We can fetch this data from various sources, including financial APIs like Yahoo Finance or Quandl. Here's a sample code snippet to fetch data from Yahoo Finance:

```python
import pandas as pd
import yfinance as yf

# Fetching historical data for a given stock
ticker = 'AAPL'
data = yf.download(ticker, start='2020-01-01', end='2022-01-01')

# Display the data
print(data.head())
```

Data Preparation

Once we have the data, the next step is to clean and prepare it. This involves handling missing values, filtering out irrelevant data, and structuring the dataset for analysis. For instance, let's filter the data to focus on specific columns:

```python
# Selecting relevant columns
data = data[['Open', 'High', 'Low', 'Close', 'Adj Close', 'Volume']]

# Handling missing values
```

```
data.dropna(inplace=True)

# Display the cleaned data
print(data.head())
```
` ` `

Constructing the Butterfly Spread

The butterfly spread involves buying and selling options at different strike prices. Typically, this involves buying one option at a lower strike price, selling two options at a middle strike price, and buying one option at a higher strike price. Here's how we can construct it programmatically:

` ` `python
```
def construct_butterfly_spread(option_chain, strike_prices):
    """

    Constructs a butterfly spread given an option chain and
strike prices.
    """

    # Extracting options at the given strike prices
    lower_strike   =   option_chain[option_chain['strike']   ==
strike_prices[0]]

    middle_strike   =   option_chain[option_chain['strike']   ==
strike_prices[1]]

    upper_strike   =   option_chain[option_chain['strike']   ==
strike_prices[2]]

    # Constructing the butterfly spread
    butterfly_spread = {
```

```
        'Buy Lower Strike': lower_strike,
        'Sell Middle Strike': middle_strike,
        'Buy Upper Strike': upper_strike
    }

    return butterfly_spread

# Example usage
strike_prices = [100, 110, 120]
option_chain = pd.read_csv('option_chain.csv')  # Assuming a
CSV file with option data
butterfly    =    construct_butterfly_spread(option_chain,
strike_prices)
print(butterfly)
```
```

Backtesting Framework

A comprehensive backtesting framework involves iterating over historical data, simulating trades, and calculating the performance of the strategy. We will use a for loop to iterate over our data and a function to calculate the profit and loss (P&L) of the butterfly spread:

```python
def calculate_pnl(butterfly, underlying_price):
    """

    Calculates the profit and loss of the butterfly spread given the underlying price.

    """
```
```

```python
    lower_leg = max(0, underlying_price - butterfly['Buy Lower
Strike']['strike'])

    middle_leg = max(0, butterfly['Sell Middle Strike']['strike'] -
underlying_price) * 2

    upper_leg = max(0, underlying_price - butterfly['Buy Upper
Strike']['strike'])

    pnl = lower_leg - middle_leg + upper_leg
    return pnl

# Running the backtest
historical_prices = data['Close']
pnl_series = []

for price in historical_prices:
    pnl = calculate_pnl(butterfly, price)
    pnl_series.append(pnl)

# Display the P&L series
print(pnl_series)
```

Analyzing Results

Once the backtest is complete, it is crucial to analyze the results. We can visualize the P&L series using `matplotlib` to gain insights into the strategy's performance over time:

```python
import matplotlib.pyplot as plt
```

```python
plt.plot(historical_prices.index, pnl_series)
plt.title('Butterfly Spread Strategy P&L')
plt.xlabel('Date')
plt.ylabel('Profit and Loss')
plt.show()
```

Refining the Strategy

The initial backtest provides a foundational understanding of the strategy's performance. However, continuous refinement is key to success. Evaluate the results, identify patterns, and adjust parameters such as the selection of strike prices or the timing of trades. Incorporate more sophisticated techniques like Monte Carlo simulations or machine learning algorithms to enhance predictive accuracy.

Risk Management and Reporting

Finally, a comprehensive backtest includes robust risk management and reporting mechanisms. Calculate key metrics such as maximum drawdown, Sharpe ratio, and win/loss ratio to assess the strategy's risk-adjusted performance. Document these findings meticulously, as they inform future iterations and strategic decisions.

```python
# Example: Calculating Sharpe Ratio
import numpy as np
```

```
returns = np.diff(pnl_series) / pnl_series[:-1]

sharpe_ratio = np.mean(returns) / np.std(returns) * np.sqrt(252) # Assuming daily returns

print(f'Sharpe Ratio: {sharpe_ratio:.2f}')
```
` ` `

Following these steps, you transform theory into practice, validating the butterfly spread strategy through rigorous backtesting. This methodical approach not only bolsters confidence in the strategy's robustness but also equips you with the insights needed to navigate the dynamic landscape of options trading.

Case Study: Python Implementation

Setting the Scene

Let's consider a scenario where we want to implement a butterfly spread strategy on the stock of a well-known company, say Apple Inc. (AAPL). We will focus on constructing the strategy, backtesting it against historical data, and analyzing its performance. This case study will encompass data acquisition, strategy construction, backtesting framework, and performance evaluation.

Step 1: Data Acquisition

The first step is to gather the necessary data. We need historical price data for AAPL and options chain data for constructing the butterfly spread. We'll use the `yfinance` library for stock price data and a hypothetical CSV file for options data.

```python
import pandas as pd
import yfinance as yf

# Fetching historical stock price data for AAPL
ticker = 'AAPL'
stock_data = yf.download(ticker, start='2020-01-01', end='2022-01-01')

# Loading options chain data from a CSV file
option_chain = pd.read_csv('aapl_option_chain.csv')

# Displaying the first few rows of the data
print(stock_data.head())
print(option_chain.head())
```

Step 2: Data Preparation

Next, we clean and prepare the data. This involves handling missing values, filtering relevant columns, and structuring the dataset for analysis.

```python
# Selecting relevant columns from stock data
stock_data = stock_data[['Open', 'High', 'Low', 'Close', 'Adj Close', 'Volume']]
```

```
stock_data.dropna(inplace=True)

# Assuming the option chain has columns: 'strike', 'type',
'expiry', 'price'
option_chain.dropna(inplace=True)

# Displaying the cleaned data
print(stock_data.head())
print(option_chain.head())
```

Step 3: Constructing the Butterfly Spread

We construct the butterfly spread by selecting options at different strike prices. The strategy involves buying one option at a lower strike price, selling two options at a middle strike price, and buying one option at a higher strike price.

```python
def construct_butterfly_spread(option_chain, lower_strike,
middle_strike, upper_strike):
    """

    Constructs a butterfly spread given an option chain and
strike prices.
    """

    lower_option = option_chain[(option_chain['strike'] ==
lower_strike) & (option_chain['type'] == 'call')]
    middle_option = option_chain[(option_chain['strike'] ==
middle_strike) & (option_chain['type'] == 'call')]
    upper_option = option_chain[(option_chain['strike'] ==
```

```
upper_strike) & (option_chain['type'] == 'call')]

    butterfly_spread = {
        'Buy Lower Strike': lower_option,
        'Sell Middle Strike': middle_option,
        'Buy Upper Strike': upper_option
    }

    return butterfly_spread

# Example usage
lower_strike = 100
middle_strike = 110
upper_strike = 120
butterfly     =     construct_butterfly_spread(option_chain,
lower_strike, middle_strike, upper_strike)
print(butterfly)
```

Step 4: Backtesting Framework

To evaluate the strategy, we implement a backtesting framework. This involves iterating over historical stock prices, simulating trades, and calculating the strategy's profit and loss (P&L).

```python
def calculate_pnl(butterfly, underlying_price):
    """
```

Calculates the profit and loss of the butterfly spread given the underlying price.

```
    """

    lower_leg = max(0, underlying_price - butterfly['Buy Lower Strike']['strike'].iloc[0])
    middle_leg = max(0, butterfly['Sell Middle Strike']['strike'].iloc[0] - underlying_price) * 2
    upper_leg = max(0, underlying_price - butterfly['Buy Upper Strike']['strike'].iloc[0])

    pnl = lower_leg - middle_leg + upper_leg
    return pnl

# Running the backtest
historical_prices = stock_data['Close']
pnl_series = []

for price in historical_prices:
    pnl = calculate_pnl(butterfly, price)
    pnl_series.append(pnl)

# Displaying the P&L series
print(pnl_series)
```

Step 5: Performance Analysis

Analyzing the results is crucial for understanding the strategy's effectiveness. We visualize the P&L series and calculate key performance metrics.

```python
import matplotlib.pyplot as plt
import numpy as np

# Plotting the P&L series
plt.plot(historical_prices.index, pnl_series)
plt.title('Butterfly Spread Strategy P&L')
plt.xlabel('Date')
plt.ylabel('Profit and Loss')
plt.show()

# Calculating Sharpe Ratio
returns = np.diff(pnl_series) / pnl_series[:-1]
sharpe_ratio = np.mean(returns) / np.std(returns) * np.sqrt(252) # Assuming daily returns

print(f'Sharpe Ratio: {sharpe_ratio:.2f}')
```

Step 6: Refining the Strategy

Based on the analysis, we refine the strategy. This could involve adjusting the strike prices, exploring different expiration dates, or incorporating advanced techniques like machine learning for predictive modeling.

```python
# Example: Adjusting strike prices and re-running the backtest
lower_strike = 105
```

```python
middle_strike = 115
upper_strike = 125
butterfly      =      construct_butterfly_spread(option_chain,
lower_strike, middle_strike, upper_strike)

pnl_series = []

for price in historical_prices:
    pnl = calculate_pnl(butterfly, price)
    pnl_series.append(pnl)

# Plotting the refined P&L series
plt.plot(historical_prices.index, pnl_series)
plt.title('Refined Butterfly Spread Strategy P&L')
plt.xlabel('Date')
plt.ylabel('Profit and Loss')
plt.show()

# Re-calculating Sharpe Ratio
returns = np.diff(pnl_series) / pnl_series[:-1]
sharpe_ratio    =    np.mean(returns)    /    np.std(returns)    *
np.sqrt(252) # Assuming daily returns

print(f'Refined Sharpe Ratio: {sharpe_ratio:.2f}')
```
```

Meticulously walking through this case study, you gain a comprehensive understanding of implementing and refining the butterfly spread strategy using Python. This hands-
```

on approach not only solidifies your grasp on theoretical concepts but also equips you with practical skills to navigate the dynamic world of options trading. Through continuous iteration and analysis, you can enhance the strategy's robustness, paving the way for informed and strategic trading decisions.

CHAPTER 6: PRACTICAL APPLICATIONS AND REAL-TIME EXECUTION

B roker APIs provide a set of protocols and tools that allow traders to interact programmatically with a brokerage's trading platform. These APIs typically offer functionalities such as fetching market data, placing orders, managing accounts, and retrieving transaction histories. By leveraging these capabilities, traders can automate their trading strategies, reduce human error, and execute trades swiftly.

Choosing the Right Broker API

The first step is selecting a broker that offers a robust and reliable API. Key factors to consider include:

- API Documentation: Comprehensive and clear

documentation is essential for smooth integration.

- Latency: Low latency is critical for high-frequency trading strategies.

- Data Access: Ensure the API provides access to the necessary market data and historical data.

- Support and Community: Active support forums and community contributions can be invaluable.

- Cost: Be mindful of any fees associated with API usage.

Popular brokers with well-documented APIs include Interactive Brokers (IBKR), Alpaca, and TD Ameritrade.

Setting Up the Python Environment

Before interfacing with a broker API, ensure your Python environment is set up correctly. Install necessary libraries such as `requests` for handling HTTP requests, and `pandas` for data manipulation.

```python
# Install required libraries
!pip install requests pandas
```

Authentication and API Keys

Most broker APIs require authentication using API keys, which are unique identifiers provided by the broker. These keys must be kept secure. Follow the broker's documentation to generate your API keys.

```python
import requests

# Example API key (replace with your actual key)
API_KEY = 'your_api_key_here'

# Base URL for the broker's API
BASE_URL = 'https://api.broker.com/v1'
```

Fetching Market Data

One of the primary uses of broker APIs is to fetch real-time and historical market data. This data forms the backbone of data-driven trading strategies.

```python
# Function to fetch market data
def fetch_market_data(symbol, start_date, end_date):
    endpoint = f'{BASE_URL}/marketdata/{symbol}/history'
    params = {
        'apikey': API_KEY,
        'startdate': start_date,
        'enddate': end_date
    }
    response = requests.get(endpoint, params=params)
    data = response.json()
    return pd.DataFrame(data['prices'])
```

```python
# Example usage
symbol = 'AAPL'
start_date = '2021-01-01'
end_date = '2022-01-01'
market_data = fetch_market_data(symbol, start_date, end_date)
print(market_data.head())
```

Placing Orders

Automating order placement is a critical feature of broker APIs. By programmatically placing orders, traders can execute strategies with precision and speed.

```python
# Function to place an order
def place_order(symbol, qty, order_type, price=None):
    endpoint = f'{BASE_URL}/orders'
    order = {
        'symbol': symbol,
        'qty': qty,
        'type': order_type,
        'price': price,
        'apikey': API_KEY
    }
    response = requests.post(endpoint, json=order)
    return response.json()
```

```
# Example usage
response      =      place_order(symbol='AAPL',      qty=1,
order_type='market')
print(response)
```

Managing Open Positions

Monitoring and managing open positions in real-time is crucial for risk management and strategic adjustments.

```python
# Function to fetch open positions
def fetch_open_positions():
    endpoint = f'{BASE_URL}/positions'
    params = {'apikey': API_KEY}
    response = requests.get(endpoint, params=params)
    return pd.DataFrame(response.json()['positions'])

# Example usage
open_positions = fetch_open_positions()
print(open_positions)
```

Implementing a Trading Algorithm

With the ability to fetch data and place orders, you can now implement a trading algorithm. Below is a simple example of a moving average crossover strategy.

```python
def moving_average_strategy(symbol, short_window, long_window):
    # Fetch historical data
    market_data = fetch_market_data(symbol, '2021-01-01', '2022-01-01')

    # Calculate moving averages
    market_data['short_ma'] = market_data['close'].rolling(window=short_window).mean()
    market_data['long_ma'] = market_data['close'].rolling(window=long_window).mean()

    # Generate trading signals
    market_data['signal'] = 0
    market_data['signal'][short_window:] = np.where(
        market_data['short_ma'][short_window:] > market_data['long_ma'][short_window:], 1, 0
    )
    market_data['position'] = market_data['signal'].diff()

    # Execute trades based on signals
    for i in range(1, len(market_data)):
        if market_data['position'].iloc[i] == 1:
            place_order(symbol, 1, 'market')
        elif market_data['position'].iloc[i] == -1:
            place_order(symbol, -1, 'market')
```

```
    return market_data

# Example usage
strategy_data        =        moving_average_strategy('AAPL',
short_window=40, long_window=100)
print(strategy_data.tail())
```

Real-Time Monitoring and Execution

For real-time trading, you need to continuously monitor market conditions and execute trades promptly. This can be achieved by setting up a loop that fetches the latest data and makes trading decisions based on predefined conditions.

```python
import time

def real_time_trading(symbol, short_window, long_window,
interval=60):
    while True:
        strategy_data    =    moving_average_strategy(symbol,
short_window, long_window)
        print(f'Latest data: {strategy_data.tail(1)}')
        time.sleep(interval)

# Example usage
real_time_trading('AAPL',                    short_window=40,
long_window=100, interval=60)
```

` ` `

Interfacing with broker APIs opens a realm of possibilities for automated and algorithmic trading. By leveraging these APIs, you can fetch market data, place orders, manage positions, and implement sophisticated trading strategies with precision. The examples provided illustrate the fundamental steps in integrating and utilizing broker APIs using Python, offering you the tools to enhance your trading efficiency and effectiveness. Through continuous refinement and adaptation, you'll be well-equipped to navigate the dynamic world of options trading.

Importance of Live Market Data

Real-time market data provides the most current information about price movements, trading volumes, and order book dynamics. This data is essential for:

- Timely Decision-Making: Making informed trading decisions based on the latest market conditions.
- High-Frequency Trading: Executing trades within milliseconds to capitalize on fleeting opportunities.
- Dynamic Strategy Adjustment: Adapting strategies in real-time based on evolving market trends and conditions.

Selecting a Data Provider

Choosing a reliable data provider is pivotal. Key factors to consider include:

- Data Coverage: Ensure the provider offers comprehensive

coverage of the assets you are interested in.

- Latency: Lower latency ensures you receive data with minimal delay, which is crucial for high-frequency trading.

- API Access: The provider should offer robust and well-documented APIs for easy integration.

- Cost: Evaluate the cost of data feeds and ensure it aligns with your trading budget.

Popular data providers include Alpha Vantage, IEX Cloud, and Quandl.

Setting Up the Python Environment

To start integrating live market data, ensure your Python environment is equipped with necessary libraries such as `websocket-client` for handling WebSocket connections, and `pandas` for data manipulation.

```python
# Install required libraries
!pip install websocket-client pandas
```

Establishing a WebSocket Connection

WebSockets provide a continuous stream of real-time data. Here's how you can establish a WebSocket connection to receive live market data.

```python
import websocket
```

```python
import json

# URL for the WebSocket endpoint
WS_URL = 'wss://data-provider-websocket-url'

def on_message(ws, message):
    data = json.loads(message)
    print(data)

def on_error(ws, error):
    print(error)

def on_close(ws):
    print("Connection closed")

def on_open(ws):
    # Subscribe to the market data feed
    ws.send(json.dumps({
        "type": "subscribe",
        "symbol": "AAPL"
    }))

# Establish WebSocket connection
ws = websocket.WebSocketApp(
    WS_URL,
    on_message=on_message,
    on_error=on_error,
    on_close=on_close
```

```
)
ws.on_open = on_open
ws.run_forever()
```
` ` `

Handling Real-Time Data

Once the WebSocket connection is established, you need to process incoming data and store it in a structured format for analysis and trading decisions.

` ` `python

```python
import pandas as pd

# Data storage
market_data = pd.DataFrame(columns=['timestamp', 'price', 'volume'])

def on_message(ws, message):
    data = json.loads(message)
    new_data = {
        'timestamp': data['timestamp'],
        'price': data['price'],
        'volume': data['volume']
    }
    global market_data
    market_data = market_data.append(new_data, ignore_index=True)
    print(market_data.tail())
```

` ` `

Integrating Live Data with Trading Algorithms

With live data streaming in, you can now integrate this data into your trading algorithms. Below is an example of a simple moving average crossover strategy that uses live data.

```python
def moving_average_strategy(live_data, short_window, long_window):
    # Calculate moving averages
    live_data['short_ma'] = live_data['price'].rolling(window=short_window).mean()
    live_data['long_ma'] = live_data['price'].rolling(window=long_window).mean()

    # Generate trading signals
    live_data['signal'] = 0
    live_data['signal'][short_window:] = np.where(
        live_data['short_ma'][short_window:] > live_data['long_ma'][short_window:], 1, 0
    )
    live_data['position'] = live_data['signal'].diff()

    # Execute trades based on signals
    for i in range(1, len(live_data)):
        if live_data['position'].iloc[i] == 1:
            place_order(symbol='AAPL', qty=1, order_type='market')
```

```python
    elif live_data['position'].iloc[i] == -1:
        place_order(symbol='AAPL',                    qty=-1,
order_type='market')

    return live_data

# Example integration
live_strategy_data = moving_average_strategy(market_data,
short_window=40, long_window=100)
print(live_strategy_data.tail())
```

Managing Data Latency and Quality

Ensuring low latency and high-quality data is crucial for the effectiveness of your trading strategy. Here are some tips:

- Minimize Network Latency: Use servers located close to the data source.
- Efficient Data Processing: Optimize your code to handle and process data swiftly.
- Data Cleansing: Implement mechanisms to filter out erroneous data points.

Handling Disconnections

Handling WebSocket disconnections gracefully is important to maintain continuous data flow.

```python
def on_close(ws):
```

```
    print("Connection closed, attempting to reconnect...")
    ws.run_forever()

# Reconnect logic
while True:
    try:
        ws.run_forever()
    except Exception as e:
        print(f"Error: {e}, reconnecting...")
        time.sleep(5)
```

Real-Time Monitoring and Alerts

Setting up alerts based on predefined conditions can help in making timely decisions.

```python
def monitor_market_conditions(live_data):
    # Example condition: Price drop alert
    if live_data['price'].iloc[-1] < live_data['price'].iloc[-2] * 0.95:
        print("Alert: Significant price drop detected!")

# Integrate monitoring logic
while True:
    monitor_market_conditions(market_data)
    time.sleep(60)  # Check every minute
```

Integrating live market data into your trading strategy is a game-changer, offering the ability to make timely and informed decisions. By setting up WebSocket connections, handling real-time data efficiently, and integrating this data with your trading algorithms, you can enhance your trading precision and responsiveness. The provided examples illustrate the core steps in achieving live data integration using Python, equipping you with the tools to thrive in the fast-paced world of options trading.

Defining the Trading Strategy

The first step in designing a trading algorithm is to define the trading strategy. This involves selecting the type of strategy that aligns with your trading goals, risk tolerance, and market conditions. Common strategies include trend-following, mean reversion, arbitrage, and market-making.

1. Trend-Following Strategy: This strategy aims to capitalize on the momentum of market trends by buying when the price is rising and selling when it is falling. Indicators such as moving averages and the Relative Strength Index (RSI) are commonly used.

2. Mean Reversion Strategy: This strategy is based on the assumption that asset prices will revert to their mean over time. It involves buying when the price is below the mean and selling when it is above.

3. Arbitrage Strategy: This strategy exploits price discrepancies between different markets or instruments. It involves simultaneous buying and selling of correlated assets to lock in risk-free profits.

4. Market-Making Strategy: This strategy provides liquidity to

the market by placing both buy and sell orders around the current market price, profiting from the bid-ask spread.

Algorithm Design and Workflow

Once the strategy is defined, the next step is to design the algorithm's workflow. This includes outlining the key components and logical flow of the algorithm.

1. Data Collection: The algorithm must collect real-time and historical market data from reliable sources. This includes price data, trading volumes, and other relevant indicators.

2. Data Processing: Raw data is cleaned, filtered, and structured into a format suitable for analysis. This involves handling missing values, outliers, and ensuring data consistency.

3. Signal Generation: The core of the algorithm is the logic that generates trading signals based on the defined strategy. This involves calculating technical indicators, applying statistical models, and evaluating market conditions.

4. Risk Management: Implementing robust risk management rules is crucial to protect against significant losses. This includes setting stop-loss and take-profit levels, position sizing, and diversification.

5. Order Execution: The algorithm must interface with a broker's API to place and manage orders. This includes handling order types, execution speed, and monitoring the status of open positions.

6. Monitoring and Logging: Continuous monitoring and logging of algorithm performance, trades, and market conditions are essential for debugging and optimization.

Implementing the Algorithm in Python

Python is an excellent choice for implementing trading algorithms due to its extensive libraries and ease of use. Below, we outline the steps to implement a simple moving average crossover strategy.

1. Setting Up the Environment

Ensure you have the necessary Python libraries installed, such as `pandas`, `numpy`, and `ccxt` for connecting to exchanges.

```python
# Install required libraries
!pip install pandas numpy ccxt
```

2. Data Collection and Processing

Use the `ccxt` library to fetch real-time market data from an exchange.

```python
import ccxt
import pandas as pd

# Initialize exchange
exchange = ccxt.binance()

# Fetch historical data
symbol = 'BTC/USDT'
```

```python
timeframe = '1h'
bars = exchange.fetch_ohlcv(symbol, timeframe)

# Convert data to DataFrame
df = pd.DataFrame(bars, columns=['timestamp', 'open', 'high', 'low', 'close', 'volume'])
df['timestamp'] = pd.to_datetime(df['timestamp'], unit='ms')
```

3. Signal Generation

Calculate moving averages and generate trading signals.

```python
# Calculate moving averages
short_window = 40
long_window = 100
df['short_ma'] = df['close'].rolling(window=short_window).mean()
df['long_ma'] = df['close'].rolling(window=long_window).mean()

# Generate signals
df['signal'] = 0
df['signal'][short_window:] = np.where(df['short_ma'][short_window:] > df['long_ma'][short_window:], 1, 0)
df['position'] = df['signal'].diff()
```

4. Risk Management

Implement basic risk management by setting stop-loss and take-profit levels.

```python
def        set_risk_management(price,        stop_loss_pct, take_profit_pct):
    stop_loss = price * (1 - stop_loss_pct / 100)
    take_profit = price * (1 + take_profit_pct / 100)
    return stop_loss, take_profit

# Example usage
current_price = df['close'].iloc[-1]
stop_loss, take_profit = set_risk_management(current_price, stop_loss_pct=2, take_profit_pct=5)
print(f"Stop Loss: {stop_loss}, Take Profit: {take_profit}")
```

5. Order Execution

Use the exchange's API to place orders based on the generated signals.

```python
def place_order(symbol, order_type, side, amount):
    if order_type == 'market':
        order = exchange.create_market_order(symbol, side, amount)
```

```python
    elif order_type == 'limit':
        order = exchange.create_limit_order(symbol, side,
amount, price)
    return order

# Example order placement based on signals
for i in range(1, len(df)):
    if df['position'].iloc[i] == 1:
        place_order(symbol='BTC/USDT', order_type='market',
side='buy', amount=0.001)
    elif df['position'].iloc[i] == -1:
        place_order(symbol='BTC/USDT', order_type='market',
side='sell', amount=0.001)
```

6. Monitoring and Logging

Log trades and performance metrics for analysis and debugging.

```python
import logging

# Set up logging
logging.basicConfig(filename='trading_log.txt',
level=logging.INFO, format='%(asctime)s - %(message)s')

# Log trades
for i in range(1, len(df)):
    if df['position'].iloc[i] != 0:
```

```
    logging.info(f"Trade executed: {df['position'].iloc[i]} at
{df['close'].iloc[i]}")
```
` ` `

Optimization and Backtesting

Before deploying the algorithm in a live trading environment, it is crucial to optimize and backtest it using historical data. This allows for fine-tuning of parameters, validation of the strategy's robustness, and identification of potential weaknesses.

1. Parameter Optimization

Use grid search or other optimization techniques to find the best parameters for your strategy.

` ` `python
from sklearn.model_selection import ParameterGrid

# Define parameter grid
param_grid = {'short_window': [20, 40, 60], 'long_window': [80, 100, 120]}
grid = ParameterGrid(param_grid)

# Optimize parameters
best_params = None
best_performance = -float('inf')

for params in grid:
    df['short_ma']   =

```python
df['close'].rolling(window=params['short_window']).mean()
    df['long_ma']                                            =
df['close'].rolling(window=params['long_window']).mean()
    df['signal'] = 0
    df['signal'][params['short_window']:]                    =
np.where(df['short_ma'][params['short_window']:]             >
df['long_ma'][params['short_window']:], 1, 0)
    df['position'] = df['signal'].diff()
    performance = df['position'].sum()  # Example performance
metric

    if performance > best_performance:
        best_performance = performance
        best_params = params

print(f"Best Parameters: {best_params}, Best Performance:
{best_performance}")
```

2. Backtesting

Backtest the algorithm using historical data to evaluate its performance.

```python
def backtest_strategy(df, short_window, long_window):
    df['short_ma']                                           =
df['close'].rolling(window=short_window).mean()
    df['long_ma']                                            =
df['close'].rolling(window=long_window).mean()
```

```
df['signal'] = 0

df['signal'][short_window:]    =    np.where(df['short_ma']
[short_window:] > df['long_ma'][short_window:], 1, 0)

df['position'] = df['signal'].diff()

df['returns'] = df['close'].pct_change()

df['strategy_returns'] = df['returns'] * df['position'].shift(1)

return df['strategy_returns'].cumsum()


# Example backtest

strategy_performance    =    backtest_strategy(df,
short_window=40, long_window=100)

print(strategy_performance)
` ` `
```

Designing a trading algorithm involves a meticulous process of strategy definition, algorithm design, implementation, optimization, and backtesting. By leveraging Python and its robust libraries, you can create sophisticated trading algorithms that operate autonomously, making informed decisions based on real-time market data. The key to success lies in continuous refinement and adaptation to evolving market conditions, ensuring that your algorithm remains effective and profitable in the dynamic world of trading.

Real-time Monitoring of Positions

Importance of Real-time Monitoring

Real-time monitoring is essential for several reasons:

1. Risk Management: By continuously tracking your positions, you can quickly identify and react to adverse market movements, reducing the risk of significant losses.

2. Performance Optimization: Monitoring real-time data allows you to assess the effectiveness of your strategies and make necessary adjustments to enhance performance.

3. Compliance: Ensuring adherence to regulatory requirements and internal trading rules is facilitated by real-time tracking, helping to maintain compliance.

4. Decision Making: Access to up-to-date information enables informed decision-making, allowing you to capitalize on market opportunities and avoid pitfalls.

Setting Up Real-time Monitoring

To establish a robust real-time monitoring system, follow these steps:

1. Data Acquisition

2. Data Processing and Visualization

3. Alerting and Notifications

4. Performance Metrics Tracking

Data Acquisition

The first step is to acquire real-time market data and track your open positions. This can be achieved by interfacing with broker APIs or using market data providers. Below is an example of how to fetch real-time data using the `ccxt` library and track open positions.

```python
import ccxt
import pandas as pd

# Initialize exchange
exchange = ccxt.binance()

# Function to fetch real-time data
def fetch_real_time_data(symbol, timeframe='1m'):
    bars = exchange.fetch_ohlcv(symbol, timeframe)
    df = pd.DataFrame(bars, columns=['timestamp', 'open', 'high', 'low', 'close', 'volume'])
    df['timestamp'] = pd.to_datetime(df['timestamp'], unit='ms')
    return df

# Fetch real-time data for BTC/USDT
real_time_data = fetch_real_time_data('BTC/USDT')
print(real_time_data.tail())
```

Data Processing and Visualization

Processing and visualizing the data in real-time is crucial for effective monitoring. You can use libraries such as `pandas`, `matplotlib`, and `plotly` to process and visualize data.

```python
```

```python
import matplotlib.pyplot as plt

# Function to plot real-time data
def plot_real_time_data(df):
    plt.figure(figsize=(10, 6))
    plt.plot(df['timestamp'], df['close'], label='Close Price')
    plt.xlabel('Timestamp')
    plt.ylabel('Price')
    plt.title('Real-time BTC/USDT Price')
    plt.legend()
    plt.show()

# Plot the real-time data
plot_real_time_data(real_time_data)
```

For more interactive visualizations, `plotly` can be used.

```python
import plotly.graph_objs as go

# Plotly interactive plot
def plot_interactive_real_time_data(df):
    fig = go.Figure(data=[go.Candlestick(x=df['timestamp'],
                    open=df['open'],
                    high=df['high'],
                    low=df['low'],
                    close=df['close'])])
```

```python
fig.update_layout(title='Real-time BTC/USDT Price',
            xaxis_title='Timestamp',
            yaxis_title='Price')
fig.show()

# Interactive plot
plot_interactive_real_time_data(real_time_data)
```

Alerting and Notifications

Setting up alerts and notifications ensures you don't miss critical events. You can use libraries like `smtplib` for email alerts or integrate with messaging platforms like Slack.

```python
import smtplib
from email.mime.text import MIMEText

# Function to send email alert
def send_email_alert(subject, body, to_email):
    msg = MIMEText(body)
    msg['Subject'] = subject
    msg['From'] = 'your_email@example.com'
    msg['To'] = to_email

    with smtplib.SMTP('smtp.example.com', 587) as server:
        server.starttls()
        server.login('your_email@example.com',
```

HAYDEN VAN DER POST

'your_password')

    server.send_message(msg)

Example usage

send_email_alert('BTC/USDT Price Alert', 'BTC/USDT price dropped below threshold.', 'recipient@example.com')
` ` `

Performance Metrics Tracking

Tracking performance metrics in real-time allows you to evaluate the effectiveness of your trading strategies and make timely adjustments. Key metrics include:

1. Profit and Loss (P&L): Tracks the profitability of your positions in real-time.

2. Drawdown: Measures the peak-to-trough decline in your portfolio value.

3. Sharpe Ratio: Evaluates risk-adjusted returns.

```python
# Function to calculate real-time P&L
def calculate_real_time_pnl(open_positions, current_prices):
    pnl = 0
    for position in open_positions:
        symbol = position['symbol']
        entry_price = position['entry_price']
        current_price = current_prices[symbol]
        pnl += (current_price - entry_price) * position['quantity']
```

```
    return pnl
```

\# Example usage

```
open_positions = [{'symbol': 'BTC/USDT', 'entry_price': 45000,
'quantity': 0.1}]
current_prices = {'BTC/USDT': 47000}
pnl = calculate_real_time_pnl(open_positions, current_prices)
print(f"Real-time P&L: ${pnl}")
```
` ` `

Continuous Improvement

Real-time monitoring is not a set-it-and-forget-it task. Continuous improvement is vital for maintaining the efficacy of your monitoring system. This involves:

1. Regularly Updating Algorithms: Ensure your algorithms are up-to-date with the latest market conditions and technological advancements.

2. Feedback Loops: Implement feedback loops to learn from past trades and refine your strategies.

3. Scalability: Design your monitoring system to handle increasing data volumes and complexity as you scale your trading operations.

Automating trade execution offers numerous benefits:

1. Speed and Efficiency: Automated systems can execute trades in milliseconds, far faster than any human can react.

2. Consistency: Automation ensures that trading strategies are executed consistently without the influence of emotions or

fatigue.

3. Scalability: An automated system can handle multiple trades and complex strategies simultaneously, making it scalable.

4. Risk Management: Automated systems can include risk management rules to limit losses and protect profits.

Setting Up the Environment

Before diving into the automation of trade execution, it's essential to set up the necessary environment. This includes installing relevant Python libraries and configuring your broker's API.

Installing Required Libraries

To begin with, install the essential libraries for data handling, API interaction, and scheduling.

```bash
pip install ccxt pandas schedule
```

Configuring Broker API

Next, configure your broker's API to enable trade execution. For this example, we'll use the `ccxt` library to interface with the Binance exchange.

```python
import ccxt
```

```
# Initialize the exchange with API credentials
exchange = ccxt.binance({
    'apiKey': 'YOUR_API_KEY',
    'secret': 'YOUR_API_SECRET',
})

# Test the connection by fetching the account balance
balance = exchange.fetch_balance()
print(balance)
```

Building the Automation Framework

With the environment set up, the next step is to build the framework for automating trade execution. This involves creating functions to place orders, monitor positions, and handle errors.

Placing Orders

The core functionality of an automated trading system is placing orders. Below is an example function to place a market order.

```python
def place_market_order(symbol, side, amount):
    try:
        order = exchange.create_market_order(symbol, side, amount)
```

```python
        print(f"Order placed: {order}")
    except Exception as e:
        print(f"Error placing order: {e}")

# Example usage
place_market_order('BTC/USDT', 'buy', 0.01)
```

Monitoring Orders and Positions

Monitoring open orders and positions is crucial for managing your trades and making timely adjustments.

```python
def check_open_orders(symbol):
    try:
        open_orders = exchange.fetch_open_orders(symbol)
        return open_orders
    except Exception as e:
        print(f"Error fetching open orders: {e}")
        return []

# Example usage
open_orders = check_open_orders('BTC/USDT')
print(open_orders)
```

Handling Errors

Error handling ensures that the system remains robust and can recover from unexpected issues.

```python
def safe_execute(function, *args):
    try:
        result = function(*args)
        return result
    except Exception as e:
        print(f"Error during execution: {e}")
        return None

# Example usage
result = safe_execute(place_market_order, 'BTC/USDT', 'buy', 0.01)
```

Scheduling and Execution

To automate the execution of trades based on predefined criteria, use the `schedule` library to create a scheduler that runs your trading functions at specified intervals.

Setting Up the Scheduler

Define a function that encapsulates your trading logic and schedule it to run at regular intervals.

```python
```

```
import schedule
import time

def trading_strategy():
    # Example trading logic
    symbol = 'BTC/USDT'
    side = 'buy'
    amount = 0.01
    place_market_order(symbol, side, amount)

# Schedule the trading strategy to run every minute
schedule.every(1).minutes.do(trading_strategy)

# Keep the script running
while True:
    schedule.run_pending()
    time.sleep(1)
```

```
```

Risk Management and Safeguards

Incorporating risk management rules into your automated system is essential for protecting your capital and ensuring long-term profitability.

Setting Stop-Loss and Take-Profit Levels

Define functions to place stop-loss and take-profit orders to limit potential losses and secure profits.

```python
def place_stop_loss_order(symbol, amount, stop_price):
    try:
        order = exchange.create_order(symbol, 'STOP_MARKET', 'sell', amount, {'stopPrice': stop_price})
        print(f"Stop-loss order placed: {order}")
    except Exception as e:
        print(f"Error placing stop-loss order: {e}")

# Example usage
place_stop_loss_order('BTC/USDT', 0.01, 45000)
```

Implementing Position Sizing Rules

Position sizing rules help manage risk by determining the appropriate amount to trade based on account size and risk tolerance.

```python
def calculate_position_size(account_balance, risk_per_trade, entry_price, stop_price):
    risk_amount = account_balance * risk_per_trade
    position_size = risk_amount / (entry_price - stop_price)
    return position_size

# Example usage
account_balance = 10000
```

```python
risk_per_trade = 0.01
entry_price = 47000
stop_price = 45000
position_size = calculate_position_size(account_balance, risk_per_trade, entry_price, stop_price)
print(f"Calculated position size: {position_size}")
```

Continuous Improvement and Testing

Continuous testing and refinement of your automated trading system are crucial for adapting to changing market conditions and improving performance.

Backtesting

Backtesting involves testing your trading strategy on historical data to evaluate its performance.

```python
def backtest_strategy(symbol, start_date, end_date):
    # Fetch historical data
    historical_data = exchange.fetch_ohlcv(symbol, '1d', since=start_date, limit=end_date)
    # Implement your backtesting logic here
    # ...

# Example usage
start_date = exchange.parse8601('2021-01-01T00:00:00Z')
end_date = exchange.parse8601('2021-12-31T23:59:59Z')
```

```
backtest_strategy('BTC/USDT', start_date, end_date)
```
` ` `

Paper Trading

Paper trading allows you to test your automated system in real-time without risking actual capital.

` ` `python
```python
def place_paper_trade(symbol, side, amount, price):
    print(f"Paper trade - Symbol: {symbol}, Side: {side}, Amount: {amount}, Price: {price}")

# Example usage
place_paper_trade('BTC/USDT', 'buy', 0.01, 47000)
```
` ` `

Monitoring Open Positions

The first step in managing open positions is real-time monitoring. Keeping a close watch on your trades allows you to react swiftly to market movements. Tools like broker APIs and trading platforms provide the necessary data for monitoring.

Real-time Data Integration

Integrate real-time data feeds from your broker to monitor the status of your positions. Here's a Python snippet using the `ccxt` library to fetch real-time data.

```python
import ccxt

# Initialize exchange with API credentials
exchange = ccxt.binance({
    'apiKey': 'YOUR_API_KEY',
    'secret': 'YOUR_API_SECRET',
})

def get_real_time_data(symbol):
    try:
        ticker = exchange.fetch_ticker(symbol)
        return ticker
    except Exception as e:
        print(f"Error fetching real-time data: {e}")
        return None

# Example usage
real_time_data = get_real_time_data('BTC/USDT')
print(real_time_data)
```

Adjusting Positions

Adjusting positions involves modifying your trades based on market conditions to optimize profitability or mitigate losses. Adjustments are critical when the market deviates from your initial expectations.

Rolling Options

Rolling involves closing an existing position and opening a new one with different strike prices or expiration dates. This technique helps in managing risk and maximizing potential returns.

```python
def roll_option(symbol, old_strike, new_strike, old_expiry, new_expiry, amount):
    try:
        # Close the existing position
        exchange.create_market_order(symbol, 'sell', amount, {'strike': old_strike, 'expiry': old_expiry})
        # Open a new position with adjusted parameters
        exchange.create_market_order(symbol, 'buy', amount, {'strike': new_strike, 'expiry': new_expiry})
        print(f"Rolled option from {old_strike} to {new_strike}")
    except Exception as e:
        print(f"Error rolling option: {e}")

# Example usage
roll_option('BTC/USDT', 47000, 48000, '2021-10-01', '2021-11-01', 1)
```

Delta Hedging

Delta hedging involves adjusting the position to maintain a

neutral delta, reducing the impact of price movements in the underlying asset.

```python
def delta_hedge(symbol, target_delta):
    try:
        # Fetch the current delta of the position
        current_delta = fetch_position_delta(symbol)
        hedge_amount = target_delta - current_delta
        # Adjust the position to achieve the target delta
        if hedge_amount > 0:
            exchange.create_market_order(symbol,        'buy',
hedge_amount)
        else:
            exchange.create_market_order(symbol,        'sell',
abs(hedge_amount))
        print(f"Delta hedged to target: {target_delta}")
    except Exception as e:
        print(f"Error delta hedging: {e}")

# Example usage
delta_hedge('BTC/USDT', 0)
```

Exiting Positions

Exiting a position is as important as entering one. The goal is to maximize profits or limit losses by closing positions at the optimal time.

Profit-taking

Setting profit targets and exiting positions when these targets are met is a common strategy. This ensures that gains are secured before the market reverses.

```python
def take_profit(symbol, target_price, amount):
    try:
        current_price = get_real_time_data(symbol)['last']
        if current_price >= target_price:
            exchange.create_market_order(symbol, 'sell', amount)
            print(f"Profit taken at {current_price}")
        else:
            print(f"Target price not reached. Current price: {current_price}")
    except Exception as e:
        print(f"Error taking profit: {e}")

# Example usage
take_profit('BTC/USDT', 50000, 0.01)
```

Stop-loss

Implementing stop-loss orders helps in limiting potential losses by automatically closing positions when the market moves against you.

```python
def place_stop_loss(symbol, stop_price, amount):
    try:
        exchange.create_order(symbol, 'STOP_MARKET', 'sell', amount, {'stopPrice': stop_price})
        print(f"Stop-loss order placed at {stop_price}")
    except Exception as e:
        print(f"Error placing stop-loss: {e}")

# Example usage
place_stop_loss('BTC/USDT', 45000, 0.01)
```

Continuous Monitoring and Adjustment

Effective management of open positions requires continuous monitoring and adjustments based on real-time data and market conditions. Utilize automated scripts to regularly check and adjust your positions.

```python
import schedule
import time

def manage_positions():
    # Example logic for managing positions
    check_open_orders('BTC/USDT')
    delta_hedge('BTC/USDT', 0)
```

```
take_profit('BTC/USDT', 50000, 0.01)

place_stop_loss('BTC/USDT', 45000, 0.01)


# Schedule the position management function to run every 5
minutes

schedule.every(5).minutes.do(manage_positions)


# Keep the script running

while True:

    schedule.run_pending()

    time.sleep(1)

` ` `
```

Case Study: Real-world Position Management

Consider an example where a trader uses a butterfly spread on the S&P 500 index options. The trader sets up the initial spread with the expectation that the index will remain range-bound. However, due to unexpected market volatility, the index starts trending. The trader decides to roll the position by adjusting the strike prices and expiration dates to better align with the new market outlook. Additionally, the trader employs delta hedging to maintain a neutral delta and protect against further adverse movements.

Managing open positions through adjustments and exits is a sophisticated process that combines real-time data analysis, strategic decision-making, and automated execution. By implementing these techniques, traders can optimize their butterfly spread strategies and enhance their overall trading performance.

Risk Management Techniques

In the intricate and volatile world of options trading, risk management is paramount. The butterfly spread strategy, while offering a balanced risk-reward profile, still necessitates a robust risk management framework. Without such a framework, even the most promising strategies can falter. Let's explore a comprehensive array of risk management techniques, focusing on their practical applications within the context of the butterfly spread strategy.

Understanding Risk in Butterfly Spreads

The butterfly spread strategy inherently limits both potential gains and losses. However, its success largely hinges on the trader's ability to manage and mitigate various forms of risk. These include market risk, volatility risk, and liquidity risk, among others. By understanding these risks, traders can take preemptive measures to safeguard their positions.

Diversification

Diversification is a cornerstone of risk management in any trading strategy. For butterfly spreads, diversifying across different stocks, sectors, or even different types of options strategies can help mitigate risk. By not putting all your capital into a single butterfly spread, you reduce the impact of adverse price movements in one particular asset.

Consider an example: Suppose you have allocated $10,000 to butterfly spreads. Instead of placing all $10,000 into a single spread on one stock, you could allocate $2,000 to spreads on five different stocks. This way, if one stock performs poorly, it doesn't devastate your entire portfolio.

Position Sizing

Another crucial technique is position sizing, which involves determining the optimal amount of capital to allocate to each trade. This technique is particularly important in limiting losses. A common rule of thumb is to risk only a small percentage of your capital, such as 1-2%, on any single trade.

For instance, if you have a trading account with $50,000, risking 2% per trade means you would not allocate more than $1,000 to any butterfly spread. This approach ensures that even if one trade goes awry, your overall capital remains relatively intact.

Setting Stop-Loss Orders

Stop-loss orders are automated instructions to sell a position when it reaches a certain price. This tool is indispensable for controlling losses and protecting your capital. When applied to butterfly spreads, stop-loss orders can help you exit a position before losses become too significant.

Imagine you have entered a butterfly spread with a total cost of $500. You might set a stop-loss order to exit the trade if the spread's value drops to $300. This way, you cap your maximum loss at $200, preserving the majority of your initial investment.

Hedging Strategies

Hedging involves taking positions that offset potential losses in your primary trades. In the context of butterfly spreads, you could use other options strategies as hedges. For example, if you have a long butterfly spread, you might also take a small position in a bear put spread to protect against a significant downward move in the stock price.

Monitoring and Adjustments

Active monitoring of positions is critical in options trading. Market conditions can change rapidly, and what may have been a sound trade initially might require adjustments. Regularly reviewing your positions and being prepared to make adjustments is essential.

For instance, if the underlying stock price moves significantly away from the middle strike price of your butterfly spread, you might consider adjusting the strikes or transitioning to a different strategy that better matches the new market conditions.

Using Technical Analysis

Technical analysis can provide valuable insights into market trends and potential price movements. By examining charts, identifying patterns, and utilizing various technical indicators, you can make more informed decisions about entering and exiting trades.

For butterfly spreads, key technical indicators might include moving averages, Bollinger Bands, and Relative Strength Index (RSI). These tools can help you identify optimal entry and exit points, enhancing your overall risk management.

Risk Metrics and Analytics

provide a deeper understanding of the potential risks and rewards associated with your trades.

For example, calculating the Delta of your butterfly spread can help you understand how much your position's value will change with a change in the underlying stock price. Similarly, monitoring Vega can inform you about the impact of volatility changes on your spread.

Psychological Discipline

Finally, psychological discipline is an often-overlooked but vital aspect of risk management. Emotions can cloud judgment and lead to impulsive decisions that deviate from your trading plan. Establishing and adhering to a disciplined approach, with well-defined rules and guidelines, helps maintain objectivity and consistency.

Integrating these risk management techniques into your butterfly spread strategy, you enhance your ability to navigate the complex terrain of options trading. These methods, when applied diligently, can safeguard your capital, optimize your trades, and ultimately contribute to your long-term success in the markets.

Options Portfolio Management

Strategic allocation is the foundational pillar of portfolio management. This involves determining the optimal distribution of capital across various options strategies, asset classes, and time horizons. By aligning your portfolio with your risk tolerance, investment goals, and market outlook, you create a robust framework for sustainable growth.

Consider an example: if your portfolio is worth $100,000, you might allocate 30% to traditional equities, 20% to bonds, and the remaining 50% to options strategies. Within the options allocation, you could further diversify by allocating 20% to butterfly spreads, 15% to iron condors, and 15% to vertical spreads. This structured approach helps in balancing potential returns with associated risks.

Diversification

Diversification is a time-tested technique for mitigating risk. By spreading investments across various underlying assets, sectors, and strategies, you reduce the impact of adverse movements in any single entity. In the context of options trading, diversification extends beyond simply choosing different stocks—it encompasses the use of different option types and strategies.

Imagine diversifying your butterfly spreads across different market sectors such as technology, healthcare, and finance. Additionally, incorporating a mix of call and put options, along with spreads of different expirations, further enhances your portfolio's resilience against market volatility.

Dynamic Adjustments

Active portfolio management requires continuous monitoring and the ability to make dynamic adjustments. Market conditions are in constant flux, and a static portfolio can quickly become misaligned with your investment objectives.

Regularly reviewing your positions, assessing market trends, and adjusting your allocations are crucial.

For instance, if you notice an upward trend in the technology sector, you might decide to increase your allocation to tech-related options strategies. Conversely, if market volatility spikes, you might reduce exposure to high-risk trades and increase positions in hedging strategies.

Risk Assessment and Metrics

provides a comprehensive understanding of your portfolio's risk profile. These metrics help in identifying potential vulnerabilities and making data-driven adjustments.

For example, calculating VaR allows you to estimate the potential loss in your portfolio over a specific time frame with a given confidence level. Monitoring the Greeks, on the other hand, helps you understand the sensitivity of your portfolio to changes in the underlying asset prices, volatility, and time decay.

Hedging and Protective Strategies

Incorporating hedging strategies within your portfolio is a prudent approach to safeguarding against adverse market movements. While butterfly spreads inherently limit risks, other options strategies can serve as effective hedges. Protective puts, covered calls, and collars are common hedging techniques that provide an added layer of security.

Suppose you have a significant position in a long butterfly spread on a tech stock. To hedge against a potential downturn in the tech sector, you could purchase a protective put on a tech index ETF. This way, any losses in your butterfly spread might be offset by gains in the protective put, thereby stabilizing your overall portfolio.

Portfolio Rebalancing

Regularly rebalancing your portfolio ensures that it remains aligned with your strategic allocation and risk tolerance. Market movements can skew your portfolio's composition, necessitating periodic adjustments. Rebalancing involves selling overperforming assets and buying underperforming ones to maintain your desired allocation.

For example, if your butterfly spreads in the technology sector have significantly appreciated, you might sell a portion of those positions and allocate the proceeds to underperforming sectors such as healthcare or finance. This disciplined approach helps in locking in profits and capitalizing on potential opportunities across different market segments.

Performance Evaluation

Assessing the performance of your portfolio is vital for continuous improvement. This involves analyzing your returns relative to benchmarks, understanding the drivers of performance, and identifying areas for enhancement. Performance evaluation should be an ongoing process, incorporating both quantitative metrics and qualitative insights.

Consider using metrics such as the Sharpe ratio, which measures risk-adjusted returns, and the Sortino ratio, which focuses on downside risk. Additionally, conducting a postmortem analysis of trades—examining what worked, what didn't, and why—provides valuable lessons that inform future strategies.

Leveraging Technology

In the modern trading landscape, technology plays a pivotal role in portfolio management. Utilizing advanced software platforms, algorithmic trading systems, and data analytics tools enhances your ability to manage an options portfolio effectively. These technologies facilitate real-time monitoring, automated adjustments, and sophisticated analytics.

For instance, using a trading platform that integrates with broker APIs allows for seamless execution and monitoring of trades. Employing data analytics tools can uncover patterns and insights that inform strategic decisions. Machine learning algorithms can predict market trends and optimize portfolio allocations dynamically.

Ethical Considerations

Ethical considerations are paramount in portfolio management. Ensuring transparency, integrity, and accountability in your trading practices fosters trust and sustainability. Ethical trading involves adhering to regulatory standards, avoiding conflicts of interest, and prioritizing the long-term well-being of your stakeholders.

Adopting a principled approach to trading, you not only comply with legal requirements but also contribute to the broader goal of promoting fairness and stability in financial markets.

Managing an options portfolio is a multifaceted endeavor that requires strategic planning, continuous monitoring, and dynamic adjustments. By integrating techniques such as strategic allocation, diversification, hedging, and performance evaluation, you create a resilient portfolio capable of navigating the complexities of the options market. Leveraging technology and adhering to ethical standards further enhances your ability to achieve sustainable success.

As you apply these principles to your butterfly spread strategies and beyond, you equip yourself with the tools and insights necessary to excel in the ever-evolving landscape of options trading.

Understanding Sentiment Analysis

Sentiment analysis involves evaluating text data to determine the sentiment expressed—whether it is positive, negative, or neutral. In the context of financial markets, sentiment analysis can be applied to news articles, social media posts, analyst reports, and other textual data sources to gauge the prevailing mood and expectations of market participants.

For example, a surge in positive sentiment surrounding a particular stock might indicate bullish market expectations, potentially leading to an increase in its price. Conversely, a wave of negative sentiment could signal bearish outlooks and a potential decline in value.

Tools and Libraries for Sentiment Analysis

Python offers a plethora of libraries that facilitate sentiment analysis. Some of the most popular ones include:

1. NLTK (Natural Language Toolkit):

NLTK is a powerful library for working with human language data. It provides tools for text processing, tokenization, classification, and more, making it a great choice for building sentiment analysis models.

2. TextBlob:

TextBlob is a simple library built on top of NLTK and provides an intuitive API for common NLP tasks, including sentiment analysis.

3. VADER (Valence Aware Dictionary and sEntiment Reasoner):

VADER is specifically designed for sentiment analysis in social media texts and provides a pre-trained model that is effective for assessing sentiment in text data.

4. spaCy:

spaCy is an advanced library for NLP with high performance and ease of use. It offers pre-trained models for various NLP tasks, including sentiment analysis.

5. Hugging Face Transformers:

This library provides access to state-of-the-art NLP models like BERT, GPT-3, and more. These models can be fine-tuned for specific sentiment analysis tasks.

Implementing Sentiment Analysis in Python

To illustrate the application of sentiment analysis, let's walk through a practical example using Python.

Step 1: Setting Up the Environment

First, ensure you have the necessary libraries installed. You can install them using pip:

```bash
pip install nltk textblob vaderSentiment spacy transformers
```

Step 2: Data Collection

For this example, let's assume we are analyzing tweets about a tech stock to gauge market sentiment. We use the `tweepy` library to collect tweets.

```python
import tweepy

# Twitter API credentials
consumer_key = 'your_consumer_key'
consumer_secret = 'your_consumer_secret'
access_token = 'your_access_token'
access_token_secret = 'your_access_token_secret'

# Set up the API
auth = tweepy.OAuth1UserHandler(consumer_key, consumer_secret, access_token, access_token_secret)
api = tweepy.API(auth)
```

```
# Collect tweets
tweets = api.search_tweets(q='TechStock', count=100, lang='en')
tweets_text = [tweet.text for tweet in tweets]
```

Step 3: Preprocessing the Data

Text data often requires preprocessing to remove noise and prepare it for analysis.

```python
import re

def preprocess_text(text):
    text = re.sub(r'http\S+', '', text) # Remove URLs
    text = re.sub(r'@\w+', '', text) # Remove mentions
    text = re.sub(r'#', '', text) # Remove hashtags
    text = re.sub(r'\W+', ' ', text.lower())  # Remove special characters and convert to lowercase
    return text

cleaned_tweets = [preprocess_text(tweet) for tweet in tweets_text]
```

Step 4: Performing Sentiment Analysis

We can use TextBlob and VADER for sentiment analysis:

```python
from textblob import TextBlob
from vaderSentiment.vaderSentiment import SentimentIntensityAnalyzer

# TextBlob Sentiment Analysis
textblob_sentiments = [TextBlob(tweet).sentiment.polarity for tweet in cleaned_tweets]

# VADER Sentiment Analysis
analyzer = SentimentIntensityAnalyzer()
vader_sentiments = [analyzer.polarity_scores(tweet)['compound'] for tweet in cleaned_tweets]

# Averaging the sentiments
average_textblob_sentiment = sum(textblob_sentiments) / len(textblob_sentiments)
average_vader_sentiment = sum(vader_sentiments) / len(vader_sentiments)

print(f"Average TextBlob Sentiment: {average_textblob_sentiment}")
print(f"Average VADER Sentiment: {average_vader_sentiment}")
```

Step 5: Integrating Sentiment Analysis with Options Trading Strategies

The sentiment scores can be used to inform trading decisions.

For instance, if the average sentiment is significantly positive, you might consider bullish strategies like long call options or bull call spreads. Conversely, negative sentiment might prompt bearish strategies such as long put options or bear put spreads.

Advanced Techniques and Applications

While basic sentiment analysis provides a starting point, more advanced techniques can offer deeper insights. Machine learning models, such as those available through the Hugging Face Transformers library, can be fine-tuned for more accurate sentiment predictions. Additionally, combining sentiment analysis with other data sources and quantitative models can enhance the robustness of trading strategies.

For example, you could use a sentiment-weighted moving average to adjust your trading signals based on sentiment trends. Alternatively, integrating sentiment analysis with technical indicators and options pricing models can create a comprehensive trading framework.

It's important to consider ethical implications when utilizing sentiment analysis. Ensuring data privacy, avoiding manipulation, and maintaining transparency in how sentiment data is used are crucial. Additionally, challenges such as handling sarcasm, contextual nuances, and language variations require careful consideration and advanced modeling techniques.

Sentiment analysis with NLP provides a powerful tool for gauging market sentiment and informing options trading strategies. By leveraging Python libraries and advanced models, traders can gain valuable insights into public sentiment and incorporate these insights into their trading decisions. As you integrate sentiment analysis into your options trading framework, you enhance your ability to navigate the complexities of financial markets and make informed, data-driven decisions.

Case Study: Real-time Implementation

Setting Up the Trading Environment

To begin, we need to establish a robust trading environment. This involves setting up a connection with a broker API, enabling real-time data acquisition, and ensuring secure and reliable trade execution. For this case study, we will use the `alpaca-trade-api` to interact with Alpaca's brokerage services.

Step 1: Installing and Configuring Alpaca API

First, ensure you have the Alpaca API installed:

```bash
pip install alpaca-trade-api
```

Next, configure the API keys and set up the connection:

```python
import alpaca_trade_api as tradeapi

# API credentials
API_KEY = 'your_api_key'
```

```python
API_SECRET = 'your_api_secret'
BASE_URL = 'https://paper-api.alpaca.markets'   # Paper trading URL

# Initialize the API connection
api = tradeapi.REST(API_KEY, API_SECRET, BASE_URL, api_version='v2')
```

Real-time Data Acquisition

Acquiring real-time data is crucial for making informed trading decisions. We will use Alpaca's streaming API to monitor the market and obtain real-time quotes for the underlying asset and its options.

```python
import asyncio

async def stream_data():
    conn = tradeapi.stream2.StreamConn(API_KEY, API_SECRET, BASE_URL)

    @conn.on(r'^AM$') # Listen to minute-level bars
    async def on_minute_bar(conn, channel, data):
        print(f'Minute Bar: {data}')

    @conn.on(r'^T$') # Listen to trades
    async def on_trade(conn, channel, data):
        print(f'Trade: {data}')
```

```python
@conn.on(r'^Q$')  # Listen to quotes
async def on_quote(conn, channel, data):
    print(f'Quote: {data}')

# Subscribe to the desired symbols
conn.run(['AM.SPY', 'T.SPY', 'Q.SPY'])

# Run the streaming function
loop = asyncio.get_event_loop()
loop.run_until_complete(stream_data())
```

Constructing the Butterfly Spread

For this case study, let's construct a butterfly spread on SPY (SPDR S&P 500 ETF) with the following strike prices:
- Buy 1 SPY 400 Call
- Sell 2 SPY 410 Calls
- Buy 1 SPY 420 Call

Step 2: Placing Orders

We will place the orders using Alpaca's API, ensuring that we execute them in a single transaction to avoid partial fills.

```python
def place_butterfly_spread():
    orders = [
```

```python
{
    'symbol': 'SPY',
    'qty': 1,
    'side': 'buy',
    'type': 'limit',
    'time_in_force': 'gtc',
    'order_class': 'bracket',
    'limit_price': 5.00,  # Example price
    'stop_loss': {
        'stop_price': 4.50,
        'limit_price': 4.40
    },
    'take_profit': {
        'limit_price': 5.50
    }
},
{
    'symbol': 'SPY',
    'qty': 2,
    'side': 'sell',
    'type': 'limit',
    'time_in_force': 'gtc',
    'limit_price': 2.50,  # Example price
},
{
    'symbol': 'SPY',
    'qty': 1,
```

```
            'side': 'buy',
            'type': 'limit',
            'time_in_force': 'gtc',
            'limit_price': 1.20,  # Example price
        }
    ]

    for order in orders:
        try:
            api.submit_order(
                symbol=order['symbol'],
                qty=order['qty'],
                side=order['side'],
                type=order['type'],
                time_in_force=order['time_in_force'],
                limit_price=order.get('limit_price', None),
                order_class=order.get('order_class', None),
                stop_loss=order.get('stop_loss', None),
                take_profit=order.get('take_profit', None),
            )
            print(f"Order     for      {order['symbol']}      placed
successfully.")
        except Exception as e:
            print(f"Error placing order: {e}")

# Place the butterfly spread orders
place_butterfly_spread()
```
```
```

Monitoring and Adjusting Positions

Real-time monitoring is essential to ensure that the strategy performs as expected. We need to track the positions, account for market fluctuations, and make necessary adjustments.

Step 3: Real-time Monitoring

Using Alpaca's streaming API, we can monitor the current market prices and our position status.

```python
def monitor_positions():
    positions = api.list_positions()
    for position in positions:
        print(f"Symbol: {position.symbol}, Qty: {position.qty}, Current Price: {position.current_price}")

# Monitor positions periodically
import time

while True:
    monitor_positions()
    time.sleep(60)  # Check every minute
```

Step 4: Adjusting the Strategy

Adjustments might be required based on market movements

or changes in volatility. For instance, if the underlying asset moves significantly, rolling the strikes or closing the positions might be necessary to mitigate losses or lock in profits.

```python
def adjust_positions():
    # Example of closing a position
    try:
        api.close_position('SPY')
        print("Position closed successfully.")
    except Exception as e:
        print(f"Error closing position: {e}")

# Adjust positions based on certain criteria
adjust_positions()
```

Evaluating Performance and Outcomes

After executing and monitoring the butterfly spread in real-time, it's essential to evaluate the performance. This involves analyzing the profit and loss (P&L) of the trades, assessing the effectiveness of the strategy, and identifying any areas for improvement.

Step 5: Analyzing P&L

Retrieve and analyze the account's P&L to understand the performance of the implemented strategy.

```python
def analyze_performance():
    account = api.get_account()
    print(f"Equity: {account.equity}")
    print(f"Profit/Loss: {account.pnl}")

# Analyze performance after a trading period
analyze_performance()
```

This case study demonstrates the practical implementation of a butterfly spread strategy using Python and real-time data. By setting up a secure trading environment, acquiring and processing real-time data, placing orders, monitoring positions, and making necessary adjustments, we bridge the gap between theoretical knowledge and real-world application.

CHAPTER 7:
ADVANCED TOPICS

The iron condor is a cousin to the butterfly spread, designed to benefit from low volatility by selling both a lower strike put spread and a higher strike call spread. By combining it with a butterfly spread, you can create a hybrid strategy that profits from a broader range of market conditions.

Rationale:

The iron condor provides a wider profit range but with limited gains. Integrating a butterfly spread can enhance profitability in the event of a significant move within a specific range.

Construction:

1. Iron Condor:

    - Sell one out-of-the-money (OTM) put.

    - Buy one further out-of-the-money (FOTM) put.

    - Sell one OTM call.

    - Buy one FOTM call.

2. Butterfly Spread:

- Place a butterfly spread at a strike price that is expected to be the center of the trading range.

- Buy one lower strike call.

- Sell two mid-strike calls.

- Buy one higher strike call.

Example:

Suppose SPY is trading at $400. You believe it will remain between $390 and $410, but you see potential for a significant move within this range.

Iron Condor:

- Sell 1 SPY 390 Put at $4.00.

- Buy 1 SPY 380 Put at $2.00.

- Sell 1 SPY 410 Call at $3.00.

- Buy 1 SPY 420 Call at $1.50.

Butterfly Spread:

- Buy 1 SPY 395 Call at $7.00.

- Sell 2 SPY 400 Calls at $5.00 each.

- Buy 1 SPY 405 Call at $3.00.

This hybrid strategy helps capture profits from SPY staying within the $390-$410 range while maximizing gains if it centers around $400.

Enhancing with Calendar Spreads

Calendar spreads involve buying and selling options with the same strike price but different expiration dates. Integrating calendar spreads with butterfly spreads can provide a balanced exposure to both time decay and volatility.

Rationale:

Calendar spreads capitalize on time decay and differences in implied volatility between near-term and long-term options. This can smooth out the profit curve and reduce risk.

Construction:

1. Butterfly Spread:

   - Create a standard butterfly spread centered at a target strike price.

2. Calendar Spread:

   - Buy a long-term option at the same strike price as one leg of the butterfly spread.

   - Sell a short-term option at the same strike price.

Example:

Assuming SPY is at $400 and you expect slight volatility but believe that in the long term, it will stay around $400.

Butterfly Spread:

- Buy 1 SPY 395 Call expiring in one month.

- Sell 2 SPY 400 Calls expiring in one month.

- Buy 1 SPY 405 Call expiring in one month.

Calendar Spread:

- Buy 1 SPY 400 Call expiring in three months.

- Sell 1 SPY 400 Call expiring in one month.

This setup takes advantage of the time decay of the short-term options while maintaining a longer-term outlook.

Integrating with Ratio Spreads

A ratio spread involves buying a certain number of options and selling a higher number of options of the same class with a different strike price. Combining ratio spreads with butterfly spreads can enhance potential returns while maintaining a defined risk.

Rationale:

Ratio spreads can profit from directional moves and volatility expansion. Integrating them with butterfly spreads can provide a balanced approach to market movements.

Construction:

1. Butterfly Spread:

   - Construct a standard butterfly spread.

2. Ratio Spread:

   - Create a ratio spread by buying and selling options with an imbalanced ratio.

Example:

SPY is at $400, and you expect a slight upward move but want to hedge against a significant swing.

Butterfly Spread:

- Buy 1 SPY 395 Call.

- Sell 2 SPY 400 Calls.
- Buy 1 SPY 405 Call.

Ratio Spread:
- Buy 1 SPY 400 Call.
- Sell 2 SPY 405 Calls.

This combination allows you to profit from SPY moving slightly above $400 while hedging against larger fluctuations.

Dynamic Adjustments with Straddles and Strangles

Straddles and strangles are strategies used to profit from significant moves in either direction. By layering these with butterfly spreads, you can create a dynamic approach that adjusts to underlying volatility and market changes.

Rationale:
Straddles and strangles benefit from large price movements. When combined with butterfly spreads, they offer a hedge against unexpected volatility spikes.

Construction:
1. Butterfly Spread:
    - Set up a standard butterfly spread.

2. Straddle/Strangle:
    - Place a straddle or strangle around key strike prices.

Example:

SPY at $400, anticipating a significant move but uncertain of the direction.

Butterfly Spread:
- Buy 1 SPY 395 Call.
- Sell 2 SPY 400 Calls.
- Buy 1 SPY 405 Call.

Straddle:
- Buy 1 SPY 400 Call.
- Buy 1 SPY 400 Put.

Strangle:
- Buy 1 SPY 395 Put.
- Buy 1 SPY 405 Call.

These combinations allow you to capture significant movements while maintaining a balanced risk profile.

Practical Considerations and Execution

While combining strategies can enhance the butterfly spread's effectiveness, it is essential to consider practical aspects such as margin requirements, transaction costs, and trade execution. Ensure that your brokerage supports multi-leg strategies and provides real-time data and analytics for effective monitoring.

Margin and Transaction Costs:
- Be aware of the increased margin requirements when combining multiple strategies.

- Factor in transaction costs, as multi-leg strategies can incur higher fees.

Real-time Monitoring:

- Use advanced trading platforms or custom Python scripts to monitor positions in real-time.

- Adjust strategies dynamically based on market conditions and performance.

Risk Management:

- Employ robust risk management techniques, including stop-loss orders and position sizing.

By integrating butterfly spreads with other strategies, you achieve a more nuanced and adaptable trading approach, capable of navigating various market conditions. This synthesis not only enhances your ability to profit but also provides a comprehensive framework for advanced options trading.

This detailed guide on enhancing butterfly spreads with other strategies provides a practical, hands-on approach to advanced options trading. By following these examples and considerations, you can leverage Python and real-time data to implement sophisticated trading strategies that maximize your potential for success.

Understanding the Need for Adjustments

Before diving into specific techniques, it is essential to

understand why adjustments are necessary. Market conditions can change rapidly, rendering an initially profitable strategy less effective. Adjustments help in managing risk, locking in profits, and enhancing the probability of success. They are not only reactive measures but can also be proactive, anticipating market movements.

Delta Neutral Adjustments

One of the primary goals when adjusting a butterfly spread is to maintain a delta-neutral position, thereby minimizing directional risk. Delta measures the sensitivity of an option's price to changes in the price of the underlying asset. By making delta-neutral adjustments, traders can hedge against adverse price movements.

Technique: Rolling the Spread

- Rolling Up/Down: If the underlying asset moves significantly and the position becomes delta-positive or delta-negative, you can roll the spread up or down. This involves closing the current butterfly spread and opening a new one at a higher or lower strike price.

Example:

Suppose you hold a SPY butterfly spread centered at $400, and SPY rises to $410.

- Close the current butterfly spread (buy back 395/400/405).

- Open a new butterfly spread centered at $410 (buy 405, sell 410 twice, buy 415).

This adjustment re-centers the position around the new price level, maintaining a neutral delta.

Vega Adjustments

Vega measures an option's sensitivity to changes in implied volatility. The butterfly spread's profitability can be affected by volatility shifts, making vega adjustments crucial.

Technique: Adding Calendar Spreads

- Calendar Spreads: Incorporating calendar spreads can adjust the vega exposure of a butterfly spread. By adding a calendar spread, you can offset potential losses due to volatility changes.

Example:

If you have a SPY butterfly spread and expect an increase in volatility:

- Add a calendar spread by buying a longer-term SPY 400 call and selling a shorter-term SPY 400 call.

This adjustment increases the position's vega, making it more profitable if volatility rises.

Gamma Scalping

Gamma is a measure of the rate of change in delta with respect to changes in the underlying asset's price. Gamma scalping involves dynamically adjusting positions to capitalize on fluctuations in the underlying asset's price, enhancing the overall profitability of the butterfly spread.

Technique: Dynamic Hedging

- Hedging with Short Options: To scalp gamma, you can

dynamically hedge with short options at varying price levels. This involves selling short options when the underlying asset's price approaches the wings of the butterfly spread.

Example:

If SPY is trading at $400 with a butterfly spread at 395/400/405:

- When SPY approaches $405, sell a SPY 405 call option short.

- When SPY drops towards $395, sell a SPY 395 put option short.

This technique captures profit from price movements, leveraging the position's gamma.

Adjusting for Time Decay (Theta)

Theta represents the rate of change in an option's price due to the passage of time. Butterfly spreads tend to benefit from time decay, but adjustments might be necessary to optimize this aspect.

Technique: Adding Short Straddles

- Short Straddles: Selling short straddles can enhance theta, increasing the position's sensitivity to time decay. This involves selling both a call and a put at the central strike price of the butterfly spread.

Example:

With a SPY butterfly spread centered at $400:

- Sell a SPY 400 call.

- Sell a SPY 400 put.

This adjustment boosts theta, accelerating the rate at which the position gains value as expiration approaches.

Ratio Spreads for Adjustments

Ratio spreads involve buying a certain number of options and selling a higher number of options of the same class. They can be used to adjust butterfly spreads by altering the risk-reward profile.

Technique: Implementing Ratio Spreads

- Ratio Adjustment: Adding a ratio spread can adjust the position's exposure to large price movements, providing a balanced approach to market volatility.

Example:

If SPY is at $400 with a butterfly spread at 395/400/405:

- Buy 2 SPY 405 calls.

- Sell 3 SPY 410 calls.

This adjustment modifies the risk-reward profile, allowing for potential profits from significant price movements while maintaining controlled risk.

Real-Time Monitoring and Automation

Effective adjustments require real-time monitoring and sometimes automation to react swiftly to market changes. Using Python scripts and trading algorithms can ensure timely and accurate adjustments.

Technique: Python for Adjustments

- Automated Scripts: Develop Python scripts to monitor delta, vega, gamma, and theta. Automatically execute trades to adjust the butterfly spread based on predefined criteria.

Example:

Python script to monitor SPY position:

```python
import yfinance as yf

# Fetching SPY data
spy = yf.Ticker("SPY")
data = spy.history(period="1d", interval="1m")

# Define adjustment criteria
delta_threshold = 0.05
vega_threshold = 0.02
gamma_threshold = 0.01

# Monitoring function
def monitor_position():
    current_delta = calculate_delta(data)
    current_vega = calculate_vega(data)
    current_gamma = calculate_gamma(data)

> delta_threshold:
        adjust_delta()
> vega_threshold:
```

```
        adjust_vega()
> gamma_threshold:
        scalp_gamma()

# Implement adjustment functions
def adjust_delta():
    # Logic to roll the spread
    pass

def adjust_vega():
    # Logic to add calendar spreads
    pass

def scalp_gamma():
    # Logic to dynamically hedge
    pass

# Run the monitoring function
monitor_position()
```
` ` `

This automated approach ensures that adjustments are timely and precise, enhancing the overall effectiveness of the strategy.

Practical Considerations and Risks

While advanced adjustment techniques can significantly enhance the performance of a butterfly spread, they also come with risks. Increased complexity can lead to higher transaction costs, potential execution delays, and margin requirements. Therefore, it is crucial to weigh these factors and implement robust risk management practices.

Risk Management:

- Position Sizing: Ensure that position sizes are manageable and within risk tolerance.

- Stop-Loss Orders: Use stop-loss orders to limit potential losses.

- Diversification: Diversify strategies and assets to spread risk.

Integrating these advanced adjustment techniques, you can adapt the butterfly spread to a wide range of market conditions, improving its resilience and profitability. These methods, combined with real-time monitoring and automation, provide a comprehensive framework for advanced options trading, ensuring you stay ahead in dynamic markets.

Machine Learning in Options Trading

Machine learning is a subset of artificial intelligence (AI) that focuses on developing algorithms that enable computers to learn from and make decisions based on data. Unlike traditional programming, where rules are explicitly defined, ML algorithms identify patterns and relationships within data, learning to make predictions or decisions without explicit instructions.

Categories of Machine Learning:

1. Supervised Learning: Algorithms learn from labeled data, making predictions based on known outcomes.

2. Unsupervised Learning: Algorithms identify patterns and relationships in data without pre-existing labels.

3. Reinforcement Learning: Algorithms learn by interacting with an environment, receiving feedback in the form of rewards or penalties.

Data Acquisition and Preparation

The cornerstone of successful machine learning applications in options trading is high-quality data. This involves obtaining historical and real-time market data, ensuring it is clean, structured, and relevant for analysis.

Data Sources:

- Financial APIs: Platforms like Yahoo Finance, Alpha Vantage, and Quandl provide extensive historical and real-time market data.

- Broker APIs: Many brokers offer APIs for accessing live market data and executing trades.

- Web Scraping: Techniques to extract data from websites such as financial news and sentiment analysis.

Data Cleaning and Transformation:

- Handling Missing Values: Impute or remove missing data points to ensure dataset integrity.

- Normalization: Scale features to a standard range, improving algorithm performance.

- Feature Engineering: Create new features that capture relevant information, such as moving averages, volatility indices, and sentiment scores.

Example: Data Preparation with Python:

```python
import pandas as pd
import numpy as np
import yfinance as yf

# Fetching historical options data
ticker = 'AAPL'
data = yf.download(ticker, start='2020-01-01', end='2021-01-01')

# Handling missing values
data.fillna(method='ffill', inplace=True)

# Normalization
data['Close'] = (data['Close'] - data['Close'].mean()) / data['Close'].std()

# Feature Engineering
data['50_MA'] = data['Close'].rolling(window=50).mean()
data['200_MA'] = data['Close'].rolling(window=200).mean()

# Display prepared data
print(data.head())
```

Supervised Learning for Predictive Modeling

Supervised learning algorithms are particularly useful in predicting option prices and determining entry and exit points for trades. Key algorithms include linear regression, decision trees, and more complex neural networks.

Linear Regression for Option Pricing:

- Modeling: Use historical price data to predict future option prices.

- Features: Include underlying asset price, strike price, time to maturity, volatility, and interest rates.

Example: Linear Regression with Scikit-Learn:
```python
from sklearn.model_selection import train_test_split
from sklearn.linear_model import LinearRegression

# Preparing dataset
X = data[['Close', '50_MA', '200_MA']]
y = data['Close'].shift(-1) # Predicting next day's close price

# Splitting data
X_train, X_test, y_train, y_test = train_test_split(X[:-1], y[:-1],
test_size=0.2, random_state=42)

# Training model
model = LinearRegression()
model.fit(X_train, y_train)

# Predicting and evaluating
predictions = model.predict(X_test)
print(f"Predictions: {predictions[:5]}")
```

Unsupervised Learning for Pattern Recognition

Unsupervised learning algorithms, such as clustering and principal component analysis (PCA), can identify hidden patterns and correlations in options data, aiding in strategy development and anomaly detection.

Clustering for Market Segmentation:

- K-Means Clustering: Group options with similar characteristics, such as moneyness and implied volatility.

- Applications: Identify market segments and tailor strategies to specific clusters.

Example: K-Means Clustering with Scikit-Learn:

```python
from sklearn.cluster import KMeans

# Selecting features
features = data[['Close', '50_MA', '200_MA']].dropna()

# Applying K-Means
kmeans = KMeans(n_clusters=3)
data['Cluster'] = kmeans.fit_predict(features)

# Display clustered data
print(data[['Close', 'Cluster']].head())
```

Reinforcement Learning for Strategy Optimization

Reinforcement learning (RL) algorithms are suitable for developing adaptive trading strategies that evolve based on market feedback. These algorithms learn optimal actions by maximizing cumulative rewards through trial and error.

Deep Q-Learning for Strategy Development:

- Environment: Define the trading environment, including state representation (e.g., option prices, Greeks) and actions (e.g., buy, sell, hold).

- Reward Function: Design a reward function that incentivizes profitable trades and penalizes losses.

Example: RL Environment Setup with OpenAI Gym:

```python
import gym
import numpy as np

# Defining custom trading environment
class TradingEnv(gym.Env):
    def __init__(self, data):
        self.data = data
        self.current_step = 0
        self.done = False

    def reset(self):
        self.current_step = 0
        self.done = False
        return self._next_observation()
```

```
    def _next_observation(self):
        return self.data.iloc[self.current_step].values

    def step(self, action):
        self.current_step += 1
- 1:
            self.done = True
        reward = self._calculate_reward(action)
        return self._next_observation(), reward, self.done, {}

    def _calculate_reward(self, action):
        # Define reward calculation
        return np.random.rand()  # Placeholder

env = TradingEnv(data)
obs = env.reset()
print(f"Initial Observation: {obs}")
```

Combining Machine Learning with Traditional Techniques

While machine learning offers powerful tools, combining it with traditional options trading techniques can yield robust strategies. This involves integrating ML predictions with fundamental and technical analysis.

Hybrid Strategies:

- ML-Enhanced Greeks Analysis: Use ML to predict changes in Greeks, informing adjustments to your butterfly spreads.

- Sentiment Analysis: Incorporate textual data from financial news and social media to gauge market sentiment, refining entry and exit points.

Example: Sentiment Analysis with Natural Language Processing (NLP):

```python
from vaderSentiment.vaderSentiment import SentimentIntensityAnalyzer

# Sample text data
texts = ["The market is bullish on AAPL.", "Bearish sentiment due to economic slowdown."]

# Analyzing sentiment
analyzer = SentimentIntensityAnalyzer()
for text in texts:
    sentiment = analyzer.polarity_scores(text)
    print(f"Text: {text}, Sentiment: {sentiment}")
```

Practical Considerations and Risks

Implementing machine learning in options trading comes with its challenges and risks. Ensuring data quality, avoiding overfitting, handling non-stationary data, and addressing interpretability are crucial for successful deployment.

Risk Management:

- Validation and Testing: Use cross-validation and back-testing to ensure model robustness.

- Model Interpretability: Prioritize transparent models to understand and trust predictions.

- Continuous Monitoring: Regularly update and monitor models to adapt to changing market conditions.

Applying machine learning techniques to options trading, traders can unlock new dimensions of analysis and strategy optimization. These advanced methods, when combined with traditional trading knowledge, pave the way for innovative and resilient approaches to navigating the financial markets. This integration of technology and finance marks a significant step forward, offering a competitive edge in the ever-evolving landscape of options trading.

Quantitative Methods for Strategy Improvement

Quantitative methods hinge on the bedrock of data. The first step in refining any strategy is the meticulous acquisition, cleaning, and analysis of vast datasets. Leveraging historical market data and real-time feeds, we can discern patterns, validate hypotheses, and predict outcomes with a higher degree of confidence.

Data Acquisition and Cleaning

Begin by sourcing data from reliable providers such as Bloomberg, Quandl, or Interactive Brokers. Historical price data, option chains, and volatility indices form the core datasets. Employ Python libraries like `pandas` for data manipulation and `numpy` for numerical operations to clean and structure this data. For example:

```python
```

```python
import pandas as pd
import numpy as np

# Load data
data = pd.read_csv('market_data.csv')

# Clean data
data.dropna(inplace=True)
data['Date'] = pd.to_datetime(data['Date'])
data.set_index('Date', inplace=True)
```

Statistical Analysis and Modeling

Harnessing statistical tools to analyze this data is paramount. Techniques such as regression analysis, time-series forecasting, and Monte Carlo simulations enable a deeper understanding of market behaviors and the efficacy of the butterfly spread under various conditions.

Regression Analysis

Regression models help identify the relationship between variables such as the underlying asset's price and the option's implied volatility. By applying linear regression, we can predict price movements and implied volatility, which are crucial for setting strike prices in a butterfly spread.

```python
from sklearn.linear_model import LinearRegression
```

```python
# Prepare data
X = data[['Underlying_Price', 'Implied_Volatility']]
y = data['Option_Price']

# Train model
model = LinearRegression()
model.fit(X, y)

# Predict
predictions = model.predict(X)
```

Optimizing Strategy Parameters

Fine-tuning the parameters of a butterfly spread—such as the selection of strike prices and the timing of trades —can significantly enhance its performance. Optimization techniques such as genetic algorithms and Bayesian optimization provide robust frameworks for this purpose.

Genetic Algorithms

Genetic algorithms mimic natural selection to optimize parameters iteratively. They are particularly useful for navigating complex, multi-dimensional spaces where traditional optimization methods falter.

```python
from geneticalgorithm import geneticalgorithm as ga
```

```python
# Define fitness function
def fitness_function(params):
    strike1, strike2, strike3 = params
    return -calculate_profit(strike1, strike2, strike3)

# Set parameter bounds
varbound = np.array([[50, 150], [55, 145], [60, 140]])

# Run genetic algorithm
model = ga(function=fitness_function, dimension=3,
variable_type='real', variable_boundaries=varbound)
model.run()
```

Risk Management Through Quantitative Analysis

Quantitative methods also offer advanced risk management techniques. Value-at-Risk (VaR), Conditional Value-at-Risk (CVaR), and stress testing are pivotal in assessing the risk exposures and potential losses associated with a butterfly spread.

Value-at-Risk (VaR)

VaR quantifies the maximum potential loss over a specified period with a given confidence level. Using historical simulation, we can estimate VaR for the butterfly spread.

```python
import scipy.stats as stats
```

```python
# Calculate returns
returns = data['Option_Price'].pct_change().dropna()

# Calculate VaR
confidence_level = 0.95
VaR = np.percentile(returns, (1-confidence_level) * 100)
```

Machine Learning for Predictive Modeling

Machine learning algorithms such as Random Forests, Support Vector Machines (SVM), and Neural Networks provide powerful tools for predictive modeling. These models can enhance the accuracy of predictions regarding price movements, volatility, and optimal trade execution times.

Random Forest

Random Forests combine multiple decision trees to improve predictive accuracy and control over-fitting. They are particularly effective in capturing non-linear relationships in the data.

```python
from sklearn.ensemble import RandomForestRegressor

# Train model
model = RandomForestRegressor(n_estimators=100)
model.fit(X, y)
```

```python
# Predict
predictions = model.predict(X)
```

Neural Networks

Neural Networks, especially deep learning models, can capture intricate patterns in vast datasets, making them suitable for high-dimensional financial data. Using libraries like TensorFlow or PyTorch, we can build, train, and deploy sophisticated neural networks.

```python
import tensorflow as tf
from tensorflow.keras.models import Sequential
from tensorflow.keras.layers import Dense

# Build model
model = Sequential()
model.add(Dense(64, input_dim=X.shape[1], activation='relu'))
model.add(Dense(32, activation='relu'))
model.add(Dense(1, activation='linear'))

# Compile model
model.compile(optimizer='adam', loss='mean_squared_error')

# Train model
model.fit(X, y, epochs=50, batch_size=10)
```

```
```
```

## Real-Time Adjustments and Automation

Quantitative methods extend beyond strategy formulation to real-time implementation. Algorithmic trading systems, driven by quantitative models, can make instantaneous adjustments to open positions based on market conditions.

## Algorithmic Execution

Algorithmic execution involves deploying trading algorithms that execute trades based on pre-defined rules and real-time data. This automation reduces latency and human error, ensuring timely and accurate execution of trades.

```python
# Example using Alpaca API for trade execution
import alpaca_trade_api as tradeapi

# Initialize API
api = tradeapi.REST('APCA-API-KEY-ID', 'APCA-API-SECRET-KEY', base_url='https://paper-api.alpaca.markets')

# Place order
api.submit_order(
    symbol='AAPL',
    qty=1,
    side='buy',
    type='market',
```
```

```
    time_in_force='gtc'
)
```
``` ``` ```

The amalgamation of quantitative methods with the butterfly spread strategy transforms a fundamental approach into a sophisticated trading tool. By leveraging data analysis, statistical modeling, optimization techniques, risk management, and machine learning, traders can refine their strategies to achieve superior performance. These methods, grounded in rigorous quantitative analysis, empower traders to navigate the complexities of the options market with increased precision and confidence.

Understanding the Role of AI in Predictive Modeling

Artificial intelligence encompasses various algorithms and techniques designed to mimic human intelligence. In the context of options trading, AI can be employed to analyze historical data, predict price movements, and optimize trading strategies. The primary tools in this arsenal include machine learning (ML), deep learning, and natural language processing (NLP).

Machine Learning (ML)

Machine learning algorithms learn from historical data to make predictions about future events. These algorithms can be classified into supervised learning, unsupervised learning, and reinforcement learning. Supervised learning, which involves training a model on labeled data, is particularly useful for predicting price movements and implied volatility.
```

Deep Learning

Deep learning, a subset of machine learning, utilizes neural networks with multiple layers to capture intricate patterns in data. These models are especially effective in handling large, high-dimensional datasets and can be used for tasks such as predicting option prices and the timing of market movements.

Natural Language Processing (NLP)

NLP techniques analyze textual data to extract sentiment and relevant information from news articles, earnings reports, and social media. This information can be used to gauge market sentiment and predict price volatility, aiding in the timing and execution of trades.

Data Preparation for AI Models

AI models require vast amounts of high-quality data to function effectively. The initial step involves acquiring and preparing this data, including historical price data, option chains, and volatility indices. The data must be cleaned, normalized, and transformed into a format suitable for AI algorithms.

Data Cleaning and Normalization

Data cleaning involves removing missing values, duplicates, and outliers. Normalization scales the data to a standard range, ensuring that no single feature dominates the model's learning process.

```python
import pandas as pd
import numpy as np
from sklearn.preprocessing import MinMaxScaler

# Load data
data = pd.read_csv('market_data.csv')

# Clean data
data.dropna(inplace=True)

# Normalize data
scaler = MinMaxScaler()
normalized_data                                    = scaler.fit_transform(data[['Underlying_Price', 'Implied_Volatility', 'Option_Price']])
```

Building Predictive Models with AI

Once the data is prepared, we can build predictive models using AI techniques. We'll explore several AI models, including Random Forests, Support Vector Machines (SVM), and Deep Neural Networks, and demonstrate their application in predicting price movements and optimizing the butterfly spread strategy.

Random Forests

Random Forests are an ensemble learning method that

combines multiple decision trees to improve predictive accuracy and control over-fitting. They are particularly effective in capturing non-linear relationships in the data.

```python
from sklearn.ensemble import RandomForestRegressor

# Prepare data
X = data[['Underlying_Price', 'Implied_Volatility']]
y = data['Option_Price']

# Train model
model = RandomForestRegressor(n_estimators=100)
model.fit(X, y)

# Predict
predictions = model.predict(X)
```

Support Vector Machines (SVM)

SVM models are effective for classification and regression tasks. They work by finding the optimal hyperplane that separates data points into different classes or predicts continuous values.

```python
from sklearn.svm import SVR

# Train model
```

```python
model = SVR(kernel='rbf')
model.fit(X, y)

# Predict
predictions = model.predict(X)
```

Deep Neural Networks

Deep Neural Networks (DNN) consist of multiple layers of neurons, each layer transforming the input data into more abstract representations. These models are powerful tools for capturing complex patterns in large datasets.

```python
import tensorflow as tf
from tensorflow.keras.models import Sequential
from tensorflow.keras.layers import Dense

# Build model
model = Sequential()
model.add(Dense(64, input_dim=X.shape[1], activation='relu'))
model.add(Dense(32, activation='relu'))
model.add(Dense(1, activation='linear'))

# Compile model
model.compile(optimizer='adam', loss='mean_squared_error')

# Train model
```

```
model.fit(X, y, epochs=50, batch_size=10)
```
` ` `

Enhancing Predictive Accuracy with Ensemble Methods

Ensemble methods combine multiple AI models to improve predictive accuracy. Techniques such as bagging, boosting, and stacking ensure that the strengths of individual models are leveraged while mitigating their weaknesses.

Bagging

Bagging, or Bootstrap Aggregating, involves training multiple models on different subsets of the dataset and averaging their predictions. This reduces variance and helps prevent overfitting.

` ` `python
```
from sklearn.ensemble import BaggingRegressor

# Train model
model = BaggingRegressor(base_estimator=RandomForestRegressor(), n_estimators=10)
model.fit(X, y)

# Predict
predictions = model.predict(X)
```
` ` `

Boosting

Boosting sequentially trains models, each new model focusing on the errors of the previous ones. This iterative process improves accuracy by correcting the mistakes of earlier models.

```python
from sklearn.ensemble import GradientBoostingRegressor

# Train model
model = GradientBoostingRegressor(n_estimators=100)
model.fit(X, y)

# Predict
predictions = model.predict(X)
```

Stacking

Stacking combines the predictions of multiple models using a meta-model. The base models generate predictions, which serve as inputs for the meta-model, resulting in enhanced predictive performance.

```python
from sklearn.linear_model import LinearRegression
from sklearn.ensemble import StackingRegressor

# Define base models
base_models = [
```

```
    ('rf', RandomForestRegressor(n_estimators=50)),
    ('svm', SVR(kernel='rbf'))
]

# Define meta-model
meta_model = LinearRegression()

# Train stacking model
stacking_model                                        =
StackingRegressor(estimators=base_models,
final_estimator=meta_model)
stacking_model.fit(X, y)

# Predict
predictions = stacking_model.predict(X)
```

Real-Time Implementation and Automation

The true power of AI in options trading lies in its real-time implementation. By integrating AI models with trading platforms and broker APIs, we can automate trade execution, making instantaneous adjustments based on real-time data.

Algorithmic Trading Execution

Algorithmic trading systems, driven by AI models, can execute trades with precision and speed. These systems continuously monitor market conditions, making real-time decisions to open, adjust, or close positions.

```python
# Example using Alpaca API for trade execution
import alpaca_trade_api as tradeapi

# Initialize API
api = tradeapi.REST('APCA-API-KEY-ID', 'APCA-API-SECRET-KEY', base_url='https://paper-api.alpaca.markets')

# Define trading strategy
def trading_strategy():
    if predictions[-1] > threshold:
        api.submit_order(
            symbol='AAPL',
            qty=1,
            side='buy',
            type='market',
            time_in_force='gtc'
        )
    else:
        api.submit_order(
            symbol='AAPL',
            qty=1,
            side='sell',
            type='market',
            time_in_force='gtc'
        )
```

```
# Execute strategy
trading_strategy()
```
` ` `

Artificial intelligence brings transformative potential to options trading, offering sophisticated tools for predictive modeling and strategy optimization. By leveraging AI techniques such as machine learning, deep learning, and natural language processing, traders can enhance the precision and profitability of the butterfly spread strategy. Integrating these models with real-time data feeds and algorithmic trading systems ensures timely and effective execution, positioning traders to navigate the complexities of the financial markets with unparalleled expertise and confidence.

The Need for Stochastic Volatility Models

To understand the necessity of stochastic volatility models, we first need to appreciate the limitations of constant volatility assumptions. Real-world markets exhibit volatility that changes over time due to economic events, market sentiment, and other unforeseen factors. This variability impacts option prices and necessitates a more flexible model. Stochastic volatility models address this by allowing volatility to evolve according to a stochastic process, offering a more accurate and realistic framework for pricing options.

The Heston Model

One of the most renowned stochastic volatility models is

the Heston model, introduced by Steven Heston in 1993. The Heston model extends the Black-Scholes framework by assuming that volatility follows its own stochastic process, usually modeled as a mean-reverting square-root process.

The Heston model is characterized by the following system of stochastic differential equations:

1. The underlying asset price S_t follows:

$$
dS_t = \mu S_t \, dt + \sqrt{V_t} S_t \, dW_t^1
$$

2. The variance V_t follows:

$$
dV_t = \kappa (\theta - V_t) \, dt + \sigma \sqrt{V_t} \, dW_t^2
$$

Here, V_t represents the instantaneous variance, μ is the drift rate of the asset price, κ is the rate at which variance reverts to its long-term mean θ, σ is the volatility of volatility, and W_t^1 and W_t^2 are two Wiener processes with a correlation parameter ρ.

Key Features of the Heston Model

- Mean Reversion: The variance reverts to a long-term mean θ, capturing the observed tendency of volatility to fluctuate around a historical average.

- Stochastic Process for Volatility: Unlike constant volatility models, the Heston model assumes volatility itself follows a stochastic process, providing a dynamic, realistic representation.

- Correlation between Price and Volatility: The correlation parameter ρ allows for the modeling of the relationship between asset price changes and volatility changes, reflecting market phenomena such as the leverage effect.

Implementing the Heston Model in Python

Transitioning from theory to practice, we now explore how to implement the Heston model using Python. This involves setting up the stochastic differential equations and solving them using numerical methods. The following example demonstrates the implementation:

Setting Up the Environment

First, ensure that you have the necessary libraries installed. The `numpy`, `scipy`, and `matplotlib` libraries will be essential for numerical computation and visualization.

```bash
pip install numpy scipy matplotlib
```

Simulating the Heston Model

We'll start by simulating the paths of the underlying asset price and its variance using the Heston model equations.

```python
import numpy as np
import matplotlib.pyplot as plt

# Parameters
S0 = 100     # Initial stock price
V0 = 0.04     # Initial variance
kappa = 2.0   # Mean reversion rate
theta = 0.04   # Long-term variance
sigma = 0.3    # Volatility of variance
rho = -0.7    # Correlation between asset and variance
r = 0.01      # Risk-free rate
T = 1.0      # Time to maturity
dt = 0.01     # Time step
N = int(T / dt) # Number of time steps

# Wiener processes
W1 = np.random.normal(0, np.sqrt(dt), size=N)
W2 = rho * W1 + np.sqrt(1 - rho2) * np.random.normal(0,
np.sqrt(dt), size=N)

# Initialize arrays
S = np.zeros(N)
V = np.zeros(N)
S[0] = S0
V[0] = V0
```

```python
# Simulate paths
for t in range(1, N):
    V[t] = np.abs(V[t-1] + kappa * (theta - V[t-1]) * dt + sigma * np.sqrt(V[t-1]) * W2[t])
    S[t] = S[t-1] + r * S[t-1] * dt + np.sqrt(V[t-1]) * S[t-1] * W1[t]

# Plot the simulated paths
plt.plot(S)
plt.title("Simulated Asset Price Path using Heston Model")
plt.xlabel("Time Steps")
plt.ylabel("Asset Price")
plt.show()
```

In this simulation, we generate paths for both the asset price and variance using the Heston model's stochastic differential equations. The result is a dynamic, fluctuating asset price path that more accurately reflects real market behaviour.

Pricing Options with the Heston Model

Once we have the simulated paths, we can proceed to price options using the Heston model. This involves calculating the expected payoff of the option under the risk-neutral measure and discounting it to present value.

```python
from scipy.integrate import quad
```

```python
def heston_call_price(S0, K, T, r, kappa, theta, sigma, rho, V0):
    def integrand(phi):
        i = complex(0, 1)
        u = complex(0.5, -phi)
        b = kappa + rho * sigma * i * phi
        a = kappa * theta
        d = np.sqrt((rho * sigma * i * phi - b)2 - (sigma2) * (2 * u * i * phi - phi2))
        g1 = (b - d) / (b + d)
        C = (r * i * phi * T) + (a / sigma2) * ((b - d) * T - 2 * np.log((1 - g1 * np.exp(-d * T)) / (1 - g1)))
        D = ((b - d) / sigma2) * ((1 - np.exp(-d * T)) / (1 - g1 * np.exp(-d * T)))
        return np.real(np.exp(C + D * V0 + i * phi * np.log(S0 / K)) / (i * phi))

    integral_value, error = quad(integrand, 0, np.inf)
    return np.exp(-r * T) * (S0 * (0.5 + integral_value / np.pi) - K * (0.5 + integral_value / np.pi))


# Example usage
K = 100  # Strike price
option_price = heston_call_price(S0, K, T, r, kappa, theta, sigma, rho, V0)
print(f"The Heston model call option price is: {option_price:.2f}")
```

This example calculates the price of a European call option

using the Heston model. The approach involves integrating the characteristic function of the log asset price and applying numerical integration to obtain the option price.

Advantages and Applications

Stochastic volatility models, particularly the Heston model, offer numerous advantages in options pricing:

1. Realistic Volatility Dynamics: These models capture the fluctuating nature of market volatility, providing more accurate pricing and risk assessment.

2. Flexibility: The inclusion of mean reversion, correlation, and stochastic processes allows for a flexible framework adaptable to various market conditions.

3. Risk Management: By accurately modeling volatility, traders can better manage risks associated with options portfolios, enhancing hedging strategies and decision-making.

The adoption of stochastic volatility models such as the Heston model represents a significant advancement in options pricing. By accounting for the dynamic nature of market volatility, these models offer a more nuanced and realistic approach, aligning theoretical constructs with practical market behaviour. Integrating these models into Python provides traders and analysts with powerful tools to enhance their pricing accuracy, risk management, and overall trading strategies. As you continue to explore the applications of stochastic volatility models, you'll uncover deeper insights and more sophisticated techniques to navigate the complexities of the options market with confidence and precision.

Python Libraries for Advanced Financial Analysis

Pandas: The Backbone of Financial Data Manipulation

Pandas is an essential library for data manipulation and analysis. Its powerful data structures, namely DataFrames and Series, facilitate the handling of large datasets with ease. Pandas excels in transforming, cleaning, and aggregating data, making it indispensable for any quantitative analysis task.

To illustrate, consider a scenario where you need to analyze historical option prices. With Pandas, you can effortlessly import data from various sources, clean it, and perform complex transformations in a few lines of code.

```python
import pandas as pd

# Load historical option prices
data = pd.read_csv('historical_option_prices.csv')

# Display first few rows of the dataset
print(data.head())

# Data cleaning: Fill missing values
data.fillna(method='ffill', inplace=True)

# Data transformation: Calculate rolling volatility
data['Rolling_Volatility'] = data['Close'].rolling(window=20).std()
```

```python
# Display modified dataset
print(data.tail())
```

In this example, Pandas efficiently handles data loading, cleaning, and transformation, providing a streamlined workflow for financial data analysis.

NumPy: Numerical Computing Powerhouse

NumPy forms the foundation of numerical computing in Python. Its support for multi-dimensional arrays and mathematical functions makes it ideal for implementing complex financial models and performing high-speed numerical computations.

For instance, when simulating asset price paths for option pricing under the Black-Scholes model, NumPy's efficient array operations come into play.

```python
import numpy as np

# Parameters
S0 = 100    # Initial stock price
mu = 0.05    # Expected return
sigma = 0.2  # Volatility
T = 1.0     # Time to maturity
dt = 0.01    # Time step
N = int(T / dt) # Number of time steps
```

```
# Simulate random asset price paths using Geometric
Brownian Motion
np.random.seed(42)
W = np.random.standard_normal(size=N)
S = np.zeros(N)
S[0] = S0

for t in range(1, N):
    S[t] = S[t-1] * np.exp((mu - 0.5 * sigma2) * dt + sigma *
np.sqrt(dt) * W[t])

# Plot the simulated path
import matplotlib.pyplot as plt
plt.plot(S)
plt.title("Simulated Asset Price Path using Geometric
Brownian Motion")
plt.xlabel("Time Steps")
plt.ylabel("Asset Price")
plt.show()
```

NumPy's ability to handle large arrays and perform vectorized operations ensures that financial simulations and computations are both fast and reliable.

Matplotlib and Seaborn: Visualization Tools

Visual representation of data is crucial for insightful analysis and decision-making. Matplotlib and Seaborn are two libraries that excel in creating detailed and informative visualizations.

Matplotlib is highly customizable and capable of producing static, animated, and interactive plots. Seaborn, built on top of Matplotlib, provides a high-level interface for drawing attractive statistical graphics.

```python
import matplotlib.pyplot as plt
import seaborn as sns

# Plot historical option prices
plt.figure(figsize=(10, 6))
sns.lineplot(data=data, x='Date', y='Close', label='Closing Prices')
plt.title('Historical Option Prices')
plt.xlabel('Date')
plt.ylabel('Price')
plt.legend()
plt.show()

# Plot rolling volatility
plt.figure(figsize=(10, 6))
sns.lineplot(data=data, x='Date', y='Rolling_Volatility', label='Rolling Volatility')
plt.title('Rolling Volatility over Time')
plt.xlabel('Date')
plt.ylabel('Volatility')
plt.legend()
```

plt.show()

` ` `

These libraries enable the creation of clear and visually appealing charts, which are essential for presenting data trends and patterns effectively.

SciPy: Advanced Statistical and Numerical Methods

SciPy builds on NumPy to provide additional functionality for scientific and technical computing. It includes modules for optimization, integration, interpolation, eigenvalue problems, and other advanced mathematical functions.

If you need to solve optimization problems or perform statistical tests, SciPy offers robust solutions. For instance, calibrating a financial model to market data often requires optimization techniques provided by SciPy.

```python
import scipy.optimize as opt

# Define objective function for model calibration
def objective(params, data):
    model_prices = model_function(params, data['Strike'], data['Time'])
    return np.sum((model_prices - data['Market_Price'])2)

# Initial parameter guesses
initial_params = [0.2, 0.5, 0.3]
```

```python
# Perform optimization
result = opt.minimize(objective, initial_params, args=(data,))
optimal_params = result.x

print(f"Optimal Parameters: {optimal_params}")
```

SciPy's optimization functions are key to refining models for better alignment with observed market data.

QuantLib: Comprehensive Library for Quantitative Finance

QuantLib is a library specifically designed for quantitative finance. It provides tools for pricing options, bonds, and other financial instruments, as well as for managing risk and performing numerical analysis.

A practical example of QuantLib's usage is in pricing options using advanced models such as the Heston model.

```python
import QuantLib as ql

# Market data and model parameters
spot_price = 100
strike_price = 100
maturity_date = ql.Date(15, 1, 2022)
risk_free_rate = 0.01
dividend_yield = 0.02
```

```
volatility = 0.2

# Construct the Heston model
day_count = ql.Actual365Fixed()
calendar = ql.NullCalendar()
settlement_date = ql.Date.todaysDate()
ql.Settings.instance().evaluationDate = settlement_date

spot_handle = ql.QuoteHandle(ql.SimpleQuote(spot_price))
yield_handle                                            =
ql.YieldTermStructureHandle(ql.FlatForward(settlement_dat
e, risk_free_rate, day_count))
dividend_handle                                         =
ql.YieldTermStructureHandle(ql.FlatForward(settlement_dat
e, dividend_yield, day_count))
vol_handle                                              =
ql.BlackVolTermStructureHandle(ql.BlackConstantVol(settle
ment_date, calendar, volatility, day_count))

heston_process        =        ql.HestonProcess(yield_handle,
dividend_handle, spot_handle, volatility2, 1.0, volatility2,
volatility, -0.75)
heston_model = ql.HestonModel(heston_process)
engine = ql.AnalyticHestonEngine(heston_model)

# Option contract
option = ql.VanillaOption(ql.PlainVanillaPayoff(ql.Option.Call,
strike_price), ql.EuropeanExercise(maturity_date))
option.setPricingEngine(engine)
```

```python
# Calculate option price
heston_price = option.NPV()
print(f"The Heston model option price is: {heston_price:.2f}")
```

QuantLib's comprehensive suite of tools facilitates the implementation of complex financial models, making it a crucial library for advanced financial analysis.

Scikit-Learn: Machine Learning for Financial Predictions

Scikit-Learn is an invaluable library for implementing machine learning models. Its extensive range of algorithms and ease of use make it ideal for predictive modeling in finance.

For example, predicting future volatility or asset prices can be achieved using Scikit-Learn's regression models.

```python
from sklearn.model_selection import train_test_split
from sklearn.linear_model import LinearRegression

# Feature engineering: Prepare data for modeling
features = data[['Open', 'High', 'Low', 'Volume']]
target = data['Close']
X_train, X_test, y_train, y_test = train_test_split(features, target, test_size=0.2, random_state=42)

# Train a linear regression model
```

```python
model = LinearRegression()
model.fit(X_train, y_train)

# Predict and evaluate the model
predictions = model.predict(X_test)
print(f"Model R^2 Score: {model.score(X_test, y_test):.2f}")
```

Scikit-Learn's machine learning capabilities enable traders to build predictive models that can inform trading strategies and improve decision-making.

TensorFlow and PyTorch: Deep Learning for Advanced Analysis

TensorFlow and PyTorch are leading libraries for deep learning and neural networks. They allow for the construction and training of sophisticated models that can capture complex patterns in financial data.

For instance, using a neural network to predict option prices based on historical data can be implemented with TensorFlow.

```python
import tensorflow as tf
from tensorflow.keras.models import Sequential
from tensorflow.keras.layers import Dense

# Prepare data
X_train = np.array(features)
```

```python
y_train = np.array(target)

# Build neural network
model = Sequential([
    Dense(64,                                    activation='relu',
input_shape=(X_train.shape[1],)),
    Dense(64, activation='relu'),
    Dense(1) # Output layer for regression
])

# Compile and train the model
model.compile(optimizer='adam', loss='mse')
model.fit(X_train, y_train, epochs=50, batch_size=32)

# Predict option prices
predictions = model.predict(X_train)
print(f"Predicted Option Prices: {predictions[:5]}")
```

The deep learning capabilities of TensorFlow and PyTorch provide powerful tools for uncovering intricate relationships within financial data, offering a significant advantage in algorithmic trading and strategy development.

Python's extensive library ecosystem provides a comprehensive toolkit for advanced financial analysis. From data manipulation and visualization to implementing complex financial models and machine learning algorithms, these libraries empower traders and analysts to perform sophisticated analyses, develop robust trading strategies, and gain deeper insights into market behaviour. By mastering these tools, you can enhance your analytical capabilities and make more informed trading decisions in the ever-evolving world of finance.

www.ingramcontent.com/pod-product-compliance
Lightning Source LLC
LaVergne TN
LVHW051220050326
832903LV00028B/2175